Studies in the Continental Background of Renaissance English Literature: Essays Presented to John L. Lievsay

Studies in the Continental Background of Renaissance English Literature: Essays Presented to John L. Lievsay · *Edited by Dale B. J. Randall and George Walton Williams*

Duke University Press · Durham, N.C. · 1977

© 1977, Duke University Press

L.C.C. card no. 77–78523

I.S.B.N. 0–8223–0388–4

Printed in the United States
of America

Mas val onra que tesoro,
segúnd dizen los antigos. . . .

El poema de Alfonso XI, 1117

Contents

Prefatory Note

Though promising has sometimes been styled the pitfall of fools, the editors of this volume have sought to present a spectrum of essays that suggest the broad and yet ultimately unified interests of its dedicatee, a man who is a renaissance scholar in more than one sense of the term. To achieve our end, we have incurred many debts, large and small, and wish to thank here the various contributors of the essays, as well as Dr. Louis B. Wright for his *Foreword* and Professors Francis Newton and Marcel Tetel, both of Duke University, who have cheerfully aided by reading some of the essays and giving their advice. Further thanks are due to the staff of the Duke University Press for their care and friendly cooperation.

Since there are few who cannot glimpse some truth in Don Quixote's contention that "cada uno es hijo de sus obras," we would like to point out also that after the final essay we have placed a list of our dedicatee's publications. At the same time, concerning the present publication, we echo softly *El Libro de los Enxiemplos*:

> En la largueza fecha con bondad
> Mas quel fecho vale la voluntad.

D.B.J.R.
G.W.W.

Foreword: Jack Lievsay—Scholar for All Seasons

John L. Lievsay, known to all his friends in the academic profession as Jack, was born in Whitesboro, Texas, on 20 February 1906. But no one can accuse him of being a stereotyped Texan. So far as anyone knows, he has never been seen in a white Stetson hat or high-heeled boots. If he has ever burst into song boasting of his origins "Deep in the Heart of Texas," no one has heard the refrain. For Jack Lievsay is a modest man, one of the most unassuming but distinguished scholars in the land. He is widely recognized on two continents as an eminent authority on the literature of the Italian Renaissance.

Perhaps Jack left his native habitat too early to become a characteristic Texan. When I first knew him, he had long since migrated to the far Northwest, where he had taken his academic degrees—B.A., M.A., and Ph.D.—at the University of Washington. Having acquired the doctorate in 1937, he immediately became an instructor in English at Stanford University. He made the conventional progress through the ranks: Assistant Professor at Stanford, 1943–47; Associate Professor at the University of Tennessee, 1947–52; Professor, University of Tennessee, 1952–62; Professor, Duke University, 1962–70; and James B. Duke Professor, Duke University, from 1970 until his retirement in 1975.

During this progression through the normal academic grades, Jack established an enviable reputation for an interest in his students, while at the same time applying himself with enthusiasm to Renaissance research. His obvious competence as a scholar won for him a long list of fellowships. Beginning as a Research Fellow at the Huntington Library in 1943–44, he went on to become a Research Fellow at the Folger Shakespeare Library in 1946–47 and at the Newberry Library in 1952, a Fulbright Fellow in Italy in 1953–54, a Special Consultant in Italian at the Folger in 1959–60, a Guggenheim Fellow, 1968–69, and again, at frequent intervals, a consultant in Italian studies at the Folger. In 1969 he delivered the Rosenbach Lectures in Bibliography at the University of Pennsylvania. Meanwhile, in the early 1960s, he was one of the founders of the Southeastern Institute of Medieval and Renaissance Studies, which he served as chairman in 1966 and 1968.

Since Jack's complete bibliography appears elsewhere in this volume, it is unnecessary here to name his publications. But I cannot refrain from mentioning some of his most significant contributions. He will perhaps be remembered longest for his fine book entitled *Venetian Phoenix: Paolo Sarpi*, published in 1973. I suspect that Jack found in Sarpi a kindred spirit because of that iconoclastic Venetian's persistent opposition to authoritarianism. In any case, this book illuminates aspects of the Council of Trent that for too long have been forgotten or neglected. Influential as Sarpi was, scholars have overlooked many aspects of his cultural impact. The *Venetian Phoenix* explains the nature of that impact upon England in the seventeenth century, and, indeed, upon western Europe.

A succinct statement by Professor Zera S. Fink about the *Venetian Phoenix* deserves quotation:

A better book on Sarpi than this one is not likely ever to be written. It is intellectual history of a high order on a subject that has cried for such treatment for a long time, and that has several times been attempted and given up by other scholars. Lievsay has cleared up in a convincing manner several snarls in seventeenth century intellectual history and bibliography. The bibliography is the best in existence on this subject and extremely valuable in itself. No one interested in the religious controversies of the seventeenth century will be able to do without this book in the future.

Jack's Rosenbach lectures, published as *The Englishman's Italian Books, 1550–1700*, are an enlightening description of the influence of Italy upon England during a critical century and a half. His pamphlet entitled *The Elizabethan Image of Italy*, one of the Folger Booklets on Tudor and Stuart Civilization, is a succinct and readable account of the Renaissance Englishman's concept of Italy. His *Stefano Guazzo and the English Renaissance* is an extremely valuable contribution to the study of Italian courtesy books. One easily might continue with laudatory comments on Jack's bibliography, but the titles speak for themselves.

What may not be generally known about Jack is that he never let his scholarship extinguish his creative impulses. During his many periods at the Folger Library, for example, like a true Renaissance sonneteer, he showered the feminine members of the staff with almost daily evidence of his lyrical skill. Many of these recipients must have tucked away a little bundle of poetic tributes. Also like his Italian precursors, Jack frequently managed to work some timely comment into the traditional forms of his verse. A specimen of these sonnets will illustrate his whimsical touch:

Calculation

No one should look to me for sound advice
on love or workings of the female heart,
though I could whip out answers in a trice
upon some much less complicated art.
I do not rightly know how to extract
the square- or cube-root of a lover's pain;
so, if one wants an answer that's exact
from me, let him be told he seeks in vain.
But when the wind is southerly, I know
enough to tell the false love from the true—
enough, dear ones, to let the rest all go
to Watergate and trust my heart to you.
It will not matter much a thousand years
from now that you were *all* my Folger dears.

One might go on extolling the excellent qualities of this fine scholar with embarrassing iteration, but the extraordinary quantity and quality of his contributions to humanistic learning tell their own story. One personal quality, however, needs emphasis. Jack Lievsay has never been too busy to remember his friends—under any and all circumstances. As all who know him are aware, he has a host of friends, both within the academic profession and beyond, who regard him with affection and pride.

Louis B. Wright
Director Emeritus
Folger Shakespeare Library

Studies in the Continental Background of Renaissance
English Literature: Essays Presented to John L. Lievsay

I. Scripture for the Ploughboy and Some Others

Craig R. Thompson · *Professor of English, University of Pennsylvania*

According to a familiar anecdote in Foxe, William Tyndale, while still in England, was on one occasion (probably in 1522 or 1523) "in the companie of a learned man, and in communing and disputing with him, drove him to that issue that the learned manne sayde, we were better be without Gods lawe then the Popes: Maister Tyndall hearing that, answered hym, I defie the Pope and all his lawes, and sayde, if God spare my lyfe, ere many yeares I wyl cause a boye that dryveth the plough, shall knowe more of the scripture then thou doest."[1]

Scrutamini scripturas: search the Scriptures. "These two words have undone the world," wrote Selden in his *Table-Talk*. "Because Christ spake it to his disciples, therefore we must all, men, women, and children, read and interpret the Scriptures."[2] Searching the Scriptures meant, to Tyndale and his successors, implicit acceptance of two seeming paradoxes that, however difficult for reason to cope with, guided their successful efforts to translate and print the Bible in English. The first paradox was that divinely inspired words could be translated into other languages at all. The second was that despite obscurities and multiple meanings, the translated Bible ought to be printed and made available to everyone, man or woman, merchant or peasant, educated or uneducated.

Whether for better or worse, both paradoxes triumphed: the Bible was finally printed in English and became accessible to those who could read or would hear it. Before Tyndale died in 1536, his translations of the New Testament and portions of the Old had laid the sure founda-

---

1. This is the version in the first edition in English of Foxe's *Acts and Monuments* (1563), p. 514. It is slightly embellished in the next edition (1570): "M. Tyndall happened to be in the companye of a certayne Divine recounted for a learned man, and in commoning and disputing with hym, hee drove hym to that issue, that the sayd great Doctour burst out into these blasphemous wordes, and sayd: we were better to be without Gods law then the Popes. M. Tyndall hearyng this, full of godly zeale and not bearyng that blasphemous saying, replyed agayne and sayd: I defie the Pope and all hys lawes: and further added that if God spared hym life, ere many yeares he would cause a boy that driveth the plough to know more of the Scripture, then he did" (II, 1225). In the enlarged editions of 1576 (II, 1049) and 1583 (II, 1076) the text agrees with that of 1570.

2. *Table-Talk of John Selden* (London, 1689), p. 3.

tions of the English printed Bible, and Coverdale, building on what Tyndale and others had done, had finished an English version of the entire Bible (1535). Not until Edward VI's reign, however, were all restrictions against reading the English Bible lifted,[3] and not until Elizabeth's reign did the English people have a version, the Geneva Bible, that could be regarded as truly "popular."[4]

The appearance of Tyndale's, Coverdale's, and subsequent versions must have seemed to Elizabethan Protestants an assured, foreordained blessing; and with reason. Our own judgments of the controversies about the vernacular Bible may be (like Selden's) less clear-cut and simplified. For however highly we may value Luther's or Tyndale's achievements as translators of Scripture and therefore as contributors to enlightenment, we have to keep in mind that the debate over the vernacular Bible was more than a contention between heroic reformers and blind conservatives. We must in all fairness concede the sincerity of the academic and prelatical opponents of vernacular translations. They were honest men hostile to something they believed to be wrong. Hindsight may give us illusory notions about the irrefutable force of Erasmus' arguments for the vernacular Bible. The fact is that his critics never gave up. The proof texts long quoted against vernacular versions, for example Matthew 7:6, were used just as confidently against him as against other and earlier offenders. When, before the sixteenth century, the fourfold (and sometimes more than fourfold) interpretation of Scripture was normative, when the literate were only a distinct minority, when the clergy alone were the source of interpretation, any serious proposal to put the Bible into vulgar tongues and to give the laity free access to it must have seemed to many or most right-thinking

3. The royal injunctions of 1538 ordered the clergy to exhort everyone to read the Great Bible of 1539–40 (sometimes called "Cranmer's Bible") when it would be set up in churches, but by an act of 1543 this permission was limited to the upper classes. Others, such as laborers, apprentices, husbandmen, housewives, and the like, were forbidden to read it publicly or privately. How strictly this prohibition was enforced is hard to say, but in any event it was abolished, along with others, early in Edward VI's reign by an article in the *Act for Repeal of Certain Statutes Concerning Treasons and Felonies*, I Edw. VI. c. 12 (text in *The Statutes at Large*, V, ed. Danby Pickering [Cambridge, 1763], pp. 260–261).

4. In the earlier part of the Elizabethan reign Englishmen read the Bible, or heard it read, in reprints of the Great Bible of 1539–40; after 1568 in the Bishops' Bible. So long as Archbishop Parker lived, the Bishops' Bible was strongly favored, the one designated for pulpit use. After his death (1575) the Geneva Bible (1557, 1560) soon became the favorite and remained so until supplanted by the Authorized Version of 1611.

people a quite unnecessary as well as thoroughly impractical idea. Erasmus' adversaries reacted with indignation to his proposals for vernacular translations, even when those proposals had conditions attached to them. That they lost the argument, that the vernacular Bible became available in England as it had been (though unauthorized) in France and Germany, then authorized, then established, appeared to John Foxe and other earnest Protestants as the inevitable, ordained victory of piety and reason—and printing—over obscurantism.[5] Yet we cannot appraise the work of Erasmus or Tyndale or Luther as Biblical scholars and translators unless we are at least aware of the arguments they rejected.

Although it would be hazardous to conjecture how many of the ploughboys in Tyndale's England were wholly, partially, or (in the ominous phrase now common) "functionally" illiterate, we must surely assume that by "ploughboy" Tyndale meant, in the context of the passage quoted, a rustic who could read very little or not at all. We must also assume that Tyndale translated Scripture for those who could read well enough to grasp the basic meaning of the New Testament, Psalms, and narrative portions of the Pentateuch. Those unable to read, whether ploughboys or others, would or should hear the sacred books read in their own language, by pastors or neighbors. "Readers" in that or any other era were of various degrees of literacy. This fact is plain enough in the remarks of Erasmus and other early advocates of vernacular translations. They did not argue that forthwith everyone would *read* the Scriptures, whatever their hopes that someday peasants, weavers, ploughboys, and other mean characters would be able to understand (or, failing that, memorize) some of the cardinal passages. As translators driven by the urgency of their task, they addressed themselves to those who could already read, confident that if these people had copies of the Bible or easy access to copies, the Gospel message would thereby

---

5. "The science of Printyng beyng found, immediatly folowed the grace of God, whiche styred up good wittes aptely to conceave the light of knowledge and of judgement" (Foxe [1570], II, 967). An attractive oversimplification, to be sure, but Foxe was completely convinced that printing was a divine blessing conferred for the purpose of advancing true religion: "The reason wherof is this: for that hereby tongues are knowen, knowledge groweth, judgement increaseth, bookes are dispersed, the Scripture is sene, the doctours be red, stories be opened, times compared, truth decerned, falsehode detected, & with finger poynted, and all (as I sayd) through the benefite of printyng" ([1570], I, 837). The section on "The Benefit and Invention of Printing" in the 1570 edition (I, 837–838) is an expansion of a brief passage in the 1563 edition (p. 362).

become more available to the uneducated also. They were confident of the power of print.

In this essay our main concern will be the meanings and implications of certain passages in which Erasmus expresses his opinions and hopes on the question of the vernacular Bible. One of these passages, in *Paraclesis* (1516), is often quoted. Another, in one of the two prefatory letters to his Paraphrase of Matthew (1522), is probably less familiar to most readers of Erasmus. Third, there are his later comments and replies to critics concerning the 1516 and 1522 passages. Except in brief and scattered quotations, these apologies, too, are hard to find in English, yet worth knowing if we are to understand Erasmus' position on the vernacular Bible.

When his opponents exclaimed at proposals for a vernacular Bible, Erasmus liked to remind them that the Bible was read by the laity in ancient times. In the Middle Ages many vernacular versions of parts of Scripture were made, but private ownership and private reading of the entire Bible must have been rare indeed. The layman heard the Bible read and quoted in school and at divine service, may have memorized snatches of it, saw paintings and drawings of Biblical scenes (as in the *Biblia Pauperum*), and may have used or owned a service book—but hardly the whole Bible or many portions of it. Interpretation was the prerogative of the clergy, and depended on the Latin text.[6]

The whole Bible was printed in German at least ten times between 1466 and 1485, despite the hostility of ecclesiastics. Printed translations in French first appeared in the 1470s.[7] In England, as readers of More's writings against Tyndale will recall, unauthorized translation and reading, public or private, of any portion of the Bible in English were explicitly forbidden by a constitution adopted—as a reaction

---

6. As for priests in the first part of the sixteenth century, evidence of familiarity with Scripture apart from service books is limited and not altogether reassuring. In 869 wills of parish clergy proved in the consistory court of Norwich between 1500 and 1550, books are mentioned in 158, Bibles in only 17 (Peter Heath, *The English Parish Clergy on the Eve of the Reformation* [London, 1969], pp. 87, 88, 91).

7. British Museum: *General Catalogue of Printed Books*; W. J. Kooiman, *Luther and the Bible*, trans. John Schmidt (Philadelphia, 1961), pp. 85–87. For French versions, W. J. Van Eys, *Bibliographie des Bibles et des Nouveaux Testaments en Langue française des XVme et XVIme siècles* (Geneva, 1900–1), I, 1–12; II, 1–4. Van Eys lists three editions of the whole Bible, four of portions of the Old Testament, and two of the New Testament between ca. 1472 and 1496.

Erasmus says the Scriptures were read in French and German when he was young (*Erasmi Epistolae*, ed. P. S. Allen *et al.* [Oxford, 1906–58], VI, 105.735–736; VI, 85.156–160; hereinafter cited as *EE* with volume, page, and line). If he refers to his own neighborhood, *Germanice* could mean Dutch, but he seems to refer to time ("me puero").

against Lollardy and the Wyclifite Bible—by the Provincial Council of Oxford, 1407 (ratified in 1408 by the Provincial Council meeting at St. Paul's, London).[8] There is no convincing evidence that any translation of the Bible into English was authorized in the fourteenth century or the fifteenth, and certainly none had been printed in England by the time More was engaged in his controversy with Tyndale (1528–32).

In its English form the topos of the ploughboy and the Scriptures must owe its diffusion to Foxe's story about Tyndale, but for the first memorable appearance of it in a sixteenth-century setting we must go back to Erasmus' *Paraclesis*, a document known to divines of all parties because it was part of the prefatory material in the first edition of Erasmus' text of the Greek New Testament (1516). Tyndale was to use Erasmus' Greek text some years later when making his English translation.[9] After 1516 *Paraclesis* was sometimes printed separately, sometimes with Erasmus' *Ratio Verae Theologiae*.

Paraclesis (in the New Testament the word means both "exhortation" and "consolation") is rightly considered a *locus classicus* in the history of sixteenth-century religious literature.[10] With characteristic Erasmian eloquence it enunciates the distinctive *philosophia Christi* that Erasmus consistently preached: the practice of piety rather than of disputation; the return *ad fontes* in Christian life and learning; the humble acceptance of Gospels, Creed, *mysteria*; the spirit of Pauline liberty instead of the bondage of "Judaism" in laws or ceremonies. In Erasmian usage the "philosophy" of Christ is not philosophy at all as

8. Text in *Concilia Magnae Britanniae et Hiberniae*, ed. David Wilkins (London, 1737), III, 317.

9. Tyndale and Erasmus never met, so far as we know, and the Englishman's name appears only once in Erasmus' correspondence, in the last recorded letter from More (*EE*, X, 259.22–27), who calls him "haereticus nostras." See also *EE*, X, 328–329; and on this R. H. Bainton, *Erasmus of Christendom* (New York, 1969), p. 257. Tyndale valued Erasmus' scholarship, and used it, but disliked his flattery of patrons (see preface to his translation of the Pentateuch, 1530). Tyndale's authorship of the English version of Erasmus's *Enchiridion* (published 1533 but made a decade earlier) has been urged cogently but perhaps not decisively by J. A. Gee, *PMLA*, 49 (1934), 460–471. L. J. Trinterud finds that Tyndale was not a Lutheran "in the strict theological sense of the word" but only in the "contemporary loose sense of the word. From the beginning he was an Erasmian-biblical humanist who became interested in translating the Bible into English in order that it might do for Englishmen that which Erasmus, in his celebrated preface to the New Testament of 1516, had urged" (*Church History*, 31 [1962], 41–42 and *passim*).

10. Text in *Erasmi Opera Omnia*, ed. J. Clericus—i.e., Jean LeClerc—(Leiden, 1703–06), VI, *3–4v (cited hereinafter as LB); and *Erasmus, Ausgewählte Werke*, ed. Hajo and Annemarie Holborn (Munich, 1933), pp. 137–149 (cited hereinafter as Holborn). For a convenient translation, see John C. Olin, ed., *Christian Humanism and the Reformation* (New York, 1965), pp. 92–106; and for a good brief analysis, Margaret Mann Phillips, *Erasmus and the Northern Renaissance* (London, 1949), pp. 77–85.

that term was used by doctors in the schools; that is, not metaphysics but moral wisdom, based on Scripture and culminating in one's sincere endeavor to practice the precepts of the Gospels. That, at least, was the ideal. "What I call philosophy is not a method of analyzing first principles, matter, time, motion, infinity, but that wisdom which Solomon deemed more precious than all riches and on that account prayed that God would grant to him above all else."[11] This sentence of 1531 is wholly consonant with what we find in the *Paraclesis* of 1516.

Fundamental to one's commitment to follow the Christian "philosophy" in Erasmus' sense of that term is first-hand knowledge of the Bible. "Ignorance of the Bible is ignorance of Christ," as Jerome says.[12] The reading, hearing, or memorizing of Scripture is a recall to devotion, a safeguard against temptation and the weariness of secular distractions, an unfailing refreshment of spirit. Therefore, writes Erasmus in the passage of special interest to us,

I disagree emphatically with those who do not want the Scriptures to be read by simple people in vernacular translation, as if Christ taught such complicated doctrines that they could scarcely be understood by a handful of theologians, or as if the defense of the Christian religion rested on our ignorance of it. To conceal the mysteries of kings is perhaps expedient, but Christ wants his mysteries to be circulated as widely as possible. I would have all housewives[13] read the Gospels and Paul's letters. And would that these were translated into the tongues of all peoples, that they might be read and understood not only by Scots or Irish but by Turks and Saracens as well. Surely the first step is to gain understanding as best we can. Yes, many may ridicule, but some may be attracted. Would that the farmer at his plough recited something from Scripture, the weaver hummed something from it at his shuttle, the traveler lightened the tedium of his journey with talk of this kind. May all conversations of all Christians come from these Scriptures! For as a rule our daily conversations show us as we are.[14]

In this and in later pronouncements by Erasmus on the vernacular Bible for the laity, women, weavers, and farmers or ploughboys are named as examples of persons who, however decent or pious, cannot be

---

11. *EE*, IX, 339.109–113.

12. *Com. in Isaiam*; J. P. Migne, ed., *Patrologia Latina* (Paris, 1844–66), Vol. XXIV, col. 17 (cited hereinafter as Migne, *PL*).

13. "Mulierculae," literally "little women." A common word in Erasmus' writings, *muliercula* can mean "mere woman," "housewife," or "servant-girl." It denotes a woman of minor social standing and of little or no education; sometimes, but not always, it is a disparaging term.

14. LB, VI, *3ᵥ; Holborn, 142.10–25. The first edition (*Novum Instrumentum* [1516], aaa4ᵥ) has "Christi mysterium" instead of "Christus sua mysteria."

expected to be very literate but who may, for all that, be intelligent. Or they may be literate enough to make some sense of the most essential parts of the Gospels. Erasmus' farmer (*agricola*) in *Paraclesis* seems a less extreme example of sheer rustic ignorance than Tyndale's ploughboy, yet he is obviously a man who, even if he reads, reads little. Give him a New Testament in his own language and encourage him to read it, however, and it may do wonders for him. *Agricola* has perhaps more dignity if rendered "farmer" or "countryman" than simply "peasant"; more dignity at any rate than *arator*, "ploughman," and definitely more than *bubulcus*, "herdsman." From antiquity to the nineteenth century, or beyond, the herdsman, ploughman, countryman—whatever he was called—was usually considered a boor, a symbol of unlettered ignorance.[15] To someone asserting that any person who tried sincerely could understand the doctrines of the Church of England, Locke retorted: "If ever you were acquainted with a country parish, you must needs have a strange opinion of them, if you think all the plowmen and milkmaids at church understood all the propositions in Athanasius's Creed: 'tis more, truly, than I should be apt to think of any one of them."[16] Such ploughmen and milkmaids are the *agricolae*, *aratores*, *mulierculae* Erasmus and Tyndale have in mind. They are wholly unbookish, strangers to philosophy, without the slightest notion of theological subtleties. Still, like many characters in the Gospels, they may be men and women of goodwill, honesty, simple virtue; and that is why they keep turning up in parables, exempla, apologues, and sermons. A Dominican inquisitor, ca. 1246, speaks of having seen *iuvenem bubulcum* who, as a result of living for a year in the home of a Waldensian, learned by heart the four Gospels, which he had heard recited in his own language.[17] Salimbene's *Chronicle* relates that because of his devoutness a ploughman heard the famous Franciscan Berthold of Ratisbon preach thirty miles away.[18] Everyone remembers

15. Had Tyndale, like Erasmus, named more than one example of laborers who should have the Bible in their own language, he too might have included weavers as well as ploughmen. Weavers and other clothmakers were often identified with Lollards, who, whether literate or not, had special devotion to Scripture. Falstaff's "I would I were a weaver; I could sing psalms or anything" (*I Henry IV*, II.iv.146–147; cf. *Twelfth Night*, II.iii.60–61) testifies to the reputation of weavers for piety. It does no more than hint at their reputation for unorthodoxy, but that reputation had long existed.

16. *A Third Letter for Toleration* (1692), ix (*The Works of John Locke*, new ed., corrected [London, 1714], II, 412).

17. H. J. Chaytor, *From Script to Print* (Cambridge, 1945), pp. 116–117.

18. G. G. Coulton, *From St. Francis to Dante* (2nd ed., 1907; rpt. New York, 1968), pp. 33–34. The preface to the English New Testament printed at Rheims in 1582, which argues—obviously

Piers Ploughman and the pious ploughman in the Prologue to the *Canterbury Tales*, a worthy brother of the parson: "lyvynge in pees and parfit charitee." An idealized portrait, to be sure, but not a unique one. Evidently there are two literary traditions, not one, concerning the ploughman: he is a type of rustic ignorance, yet in Christian literature he may be also a type of simple piety, however unlettered. These types seem to blend in the passages cited from Erasmus and Tyndale. In Bishop Latimer's famous sermon *Of the Plough* (1548), parson and plough-man become one: "For preachyng of the Gospel is one of Goddes plough workes, and the preacher is one of Goddes plough men."

Paraclesis appeared in an English translation, thought to have been made by Tyndale's former amanuensis, William Roye, in 1529 (STC 10493), and purportedly printed by "Hans Luft" of Marburg but more probably by Johannes Hoochstraten in Antwerp.[19] In the same small volume is an English translation of a tractate by Luther on I Corinthi-ans 7.[20] Roye's version, *An Exhortation to the Diligent Study of Scripture*, is a spirited and sometimes amplified[21] presentation of Erasmus' message in *Paraclesis*, and gave to English readers ignorant of Latin their first acquaintance with the work. The passage on vernacular translation reads thus:

And trulye I do greatly dissent from those men / whiche wold not that the scripture of Christ shuld be translated in to all tonges / that it might be reade diligently of the private and seculare men and women / Other as though Christ had taught soch darke and insensible thinges / that they could scante be understonde of a few divines. Or els as though the pithe and substance of the christen religion consisted chefly in this / that it be not knowne. Paraventure it

---

with Erasmus, Tyndale, and other translators in mind—that people were better when the vernacu-lar Bible was *not* in everyone's hands, tells us that in earlier times "the poore ploughman could then in labouring the ground sing the hymnes and psalmes either in knowen or unknowen languages, as they heard them in the holy Church, though they could neither reade nor know the sense, meaning, and mysteries of the same" (a3r–a3v).

19. Reproduced in facsimile by Theatrum Orbis Terrarum (Amsterdam and New York, 1973) as No. 510 in The English Experience series. See also More's *Confutation of Tyndale's Answer*, ed. Louis A. Schuster, Richard C. Marius, James P. Lusardi, Richard J. Schoeck (New Haven and London, 1973), pp. 1072–73, 1192–94.

20. William A. Clebsch, *England's Earliest Protestants 1520–1535* (New Haven and London, 1964), pp. 234–235, points out that the Biblical citations in the English version of this tractate came from Tyndale's New Testament. He believes Roye was the translator. See his article in *Harvard Theological Review*, 56 (1963), 75–86.

21. For instance, "Primus certe gradus est, utcunque cognoscere" becomes: "Truly it is one degre to good livinge / yee the first (I had almoste sayde the cheffe) to have a litle sight in the scripture / though it be but a grosse knowledge / and not yet consummatte."

were moste expedient that the councels of kinges shuld be kept secret / but Christ wold that his councelles and misteries shuld be sprede abrode as moch as is possible. I wold desire that all women shuld reade the gospell and Paules epistles / and I wold to god they were translated in to the tonges of all men / So that they might not only be read / and knowne / of the scotes and yrishmen / But also of the Turkes and saracenes / Truly it is one degre to good livinge / yee the first (I had almoste sayde the cheffe) to have a litle sight in the scripture / though it be but a grosse knowledge / and not yet consummatte. Be it in case that some wold laugh at it / yee and that some shuld erre and be deceaved) I wold to god / the plowman wold singe a texte of the scripture at his plowbeme / And that the wever at his lowme / with this wold drive away the tediousnes of tyme. I wold the wayfaringe man with this pastyme / wold expelle the wearynes of his jorney. And to be shorte I wold that all the communication of the christen shuld be of the scripture / for in a maner soch are we oure selves / as oure daylye tales are ($\pi 5_v$–$\pi 6_r$).

The plea in *Paraclesis* for vernacular translations of Scripture was not the only one from Erasmus' pen. The 1516 passage was revised and expanded in a letter *pio lectori* printed as one of the two prefaces in the first edition of his Paraphrase of Matthew (1522), where it follows the formal dedication of the volume to the emperor Charles V. This letter was in the true sense an occasional piece, the occasion being a request by the printer for additional copy to fill a blank sheet.[22] The letter was omitted from subsequent editions of the Paraphrase.[23] It was omitted also in at least some of the issues or editions of the collected Paraphrases published in English translation in 1548–49. (I have checked four copies of *STC* 2854.) But it did appear in an anonymous English version (perhaps by Roye?) as *An Exhortation to the Study of the Gospel*, which follows (d3$_r$–i7$_r$) Roye's translation of *Paraclesis* in a volume printed by R. Wyer (*STC* 10494).[24] Like the earlier translation it is a vigorous, intelligible rendering that, despite its adventitious character as

22. LB, VII, **4$_v$; IX, 551E, 871F; *EE*, V, 46.20–22.

23. LB, IX, 551E, 871F. A German translation, possibly by Erasmus' friend Botzheim, was printed twice in 1522 (*EE*, V, 66.38n.).

24. The *STC* entry 10494 names only Roye's *Exhortation to the Diligent Study of Scripture*, without indicating whether the volume contains anything else. See further E. J. Devereux, *A Checklist of English Translations of Erasmus to 1700* (Oxford Bibliographical Society, Occasional Publications, No. 3, 1968), p. 22. Devereux thinks the date of *STC* 10494 was ca. 1533–34. His entries C65.1 and C65.3 record two other editions not in *STC*.

The letter *pio lectori* is quoted (V, 4–5) but not reprinted in *EE*. On prefaces to the Paraphrases see Joseph Coppens, *Les Idées Réformistes d'Érasme dans les Préfaces aux Paraphrases du Nouveau Testament* (Analecta Lovaniensia Biblica et Orientalia, ser. III, fasc. 27, 1961), pp. 344–371.

a last-minute composition, and despite Erasmus' polite depreciation of it in a letter, can easily stand comparison with *Paraclesis*.

The parts of this letter most relevant to our present inquiry may be translated or summarized here.[25]

"I strongly disagree with those who think that laity and unlettered folk ought to be wholly banished from reading the sacred books, that none should be admitted to these sanctuaries except a few men who have worn themselves out by many years' study of Aristotelian philosophy and Scholastic divinity." He has no quarrel with academic scholars provided they be pure in heart and search for God in the Scriptures with sincerity, untainted by worldly passions ($a3_r$–3_v; in LB, VII, **2_v). "But I do not see why untutored laymen should be kept from the Gospels particularly, or worldly men from sacred letters, which were produced for learned and unlearned alike, for Greeks and Scythians equally, slaves as well as free men, women and men both, commons as well as kings. What they teach applies equally to all people; what they promise applies to all. And they were proclaimed in such fashion that they are understood more readily by a godly, humble layman than by an arrogant philosopher. The Jews, who dwelt in the shadows, were wont to conceal their mysteries; the light of the Gospel cannot be hid. Of old a single priest entered the Holy of Holies. But when the veil of the Temple was rent in twain at the death of the Lord, everyone was granted access even to Christ himself, the true Holy of Holies and sanctifier of all, for he desires the salvation of all men. They[26] cry 'Outrage!' if a housewife or tanner talks about holy writ. As for me, I would rather listen to certain girls talking about Christ than some who are commonly reputed learned scholars" ($a3_v$; in LB, VII, **2_v).

Knowledge puffs up, ignorance no less; arrogance in sacred things is reprehensible whether in a learned or an unlearned man. Erasmus would allow anyone who is sensible and devout to search the Scriptures, especially those portions which contribute to better living. "Let us consider the hearers Christ himself had. Were they not the common multitude, and among them the blind and the halt, beggars, publicans, soldiers, artisans, women, and children? Would he disdain to be read by those whom he wished to have as hearers? If I had my way the farmer would read, smith and stonecutter would read, harlots and bawds would read, even Turks would read. If Christ did not keep them from his discourse, neither will I keep them from his books" ($a4_r$; in LB, VII, **2_v).[27]

25. I have used the edition of 1524, which was evidently set up from the first (1522) edition. See *EE*, IV, 609, introduction to *ep*. 1248. In the 1524 edition the text occupies sigs. $a3_r$–$a8_v$; in LB, VII, **2_v–4_v. For Erasmus' depreciation, *EE*, V, 46.19–25.

26. Erasmus' critics.

27. "Me quidem auctore leget agricola, leget faber, leget latomus, legent et meretrices et lenones, denique legent et Turcae. Si hos non submovit a sua voce Christus, non ego submovebo eos ab illius libris."

Some Old Testament writings, for example Ezekiel and the Song of Songs, give unusual difficulty to *idiotae* (unlettered laymen) because of their obscurities, but Erasmus would not forbid the reading of them. As for reading the Gospels, "divine wisdom accommodates itself wonderfully to the comprehension even of the weak, so that no one is too ignorant to learn the Gospel teaching" (a4$_r$; in LB, VII, **2$_v$).

There are pastors, but these are not always reliable. The hungry sheep look up and desire to be fed. The laymen are sheep, yet sometimes sheep are wiser than shepherd. Accordingly, as it does not become a layman to rebel against priests, so it does not become priests to lord it over the flock. Good pastors are to be heard reverently, "tanquam angeli Dei," and perhaps some profit can be gained even from inferior ones; but if they neglect duty or teach false doctrine, then the Christian should resort to private reading of Scripture (a4$_v$–a5$_r$; in LB, VII, **3). Reverent inquiry there should be, and inquiring reverence, but never rashness and wilful self-assurance.[28] What you read and understand, believe with your whole heart. Do not bother with unanswerable questions that are only distracting, such as the manner in which Christ's body left the tomb or how it is present in the Eucharist. Such questions may lead to contentions and heresies. But reading the Scriptures should not be forbidden to laymen simply because there is danger of falling into error. Error is the fault of the reader, not the reading (a5$_r$–5$_v$; in LB, VII, **3).

Some people are horrified if Scripture is turned into French or English. Yet the evangelists did not shrink from writing in Greek what Christ spoke in Syriac, nor did Latin writers fear to put the speech of the apostles into the Roman tongue. Christ wanted his teaching to be as widespread as possible. He died for all; he wants to be known by all (a5$_v$; in LB, VII, **3$_v$). And that requires translations. "Why is it improper if someone speaks the Gospel in his native language, the language he understands—Frenchman in French, Englishman in English, German in German, Indian in Indian? Much more improper or ridiculous is it, in my opinion, for simple laymen and women to murmur their Psalms and Paternoster in Latin, parrot-fashion, not understanding what they say. Like Jerome, I would sooner rejoice in the glory of the Cross, and deem it a splendid victory, if the Gospel were sounded in every tongue and by every race of men—if the ploughman at the plough should recite something from the mystical Psalms in his own tongue, if the weaver sitting at the loom lighten his labor with something from the Gospel, the pilot bound to the tiller hum something from this source; finally, let a companion or kinswoman read something from it to the housewife at her spinning-wheel" (a6$_r$; in LB, VII, **3$_v$).

Was Tyndale's promise about "a boye that dryveth the plough"

28. "Adsit quidem pia curiositas, et curiosa pietas, sed absit temeritas, absit praeceps et pervicax scientiae persuasio."

inspired directly by Erasmus, that is, either by the passage in *Paraclesis* or by the 1522 statement in the preface to the Paraphrase of Matthew? We do not know. Tyndale was familiar with some of Erasmus' writings, and as a translator used his edition of the Greek New Testament and probably his Latin version. How early he read Erasmus is another question. That the words about the boy that driveth the plough are "an echo of those written in 1516"[29] in Erasmus' exhortation is entirely possible, even probable; but the source might have been Erasmus' letter of 1522, for Tyndale was acquainted with that as well. He mentions both at the end of the preface to his *Obedience of a Christian Man*, challenging his opponents to be silenced by them or "geve shamfull answeres."[30] What is important is that these two men, one the editor of the first Greek text of the New Testament to be published and translator of a new Latin version, the other the translator of the first and most influential English version of the New Testament to be printed and published, insist within a few years of each other that the Bible must be put into the vernacular for the use of the laity, even of ploughmen.

We shall not follow Tyndale's career, since our main interest is Erasmus' attitude toward the vernacular Bible, but we may remind ourselves that one significant aspect of the work of the earlier Tudor translators was their fervor in allying the Bible in English with their doctrines of obedience to rulers and with the rightness and duty of Henry VIII's opposition to the papacy. The Tyndale who gave us the first printed English translation of the New Testament was the reformer who also wrote *The Obedience of a Christian Man* (1528),[31] which drove home to Henry's subjects some hard truths about the duty of subjects to rulers. They could read for themselves the Scriptural injunctions about obedience (Romans 13 being one of the favorite proof texts) if they had the Bible in their own language. Coverdale, in dedicating his translation to the King, pointed out that the Pope had done more, and

29. J. F. Mozley, *William Tyndale* (London, 1937), p. 34. C. H. Williams, *William Tyndale* (London, 1969), p. 12, says of Tyndale's pronouncement and *Paraclesis*: "The reader may be tempted to wonder whether literary artifice [on Foxe's part?] is here at work to bring the ideas of the two men into line, or whether Tyndale is here unconsciously repeating words he had himself read and which had impressed him." This seems a fair statement but leaves the question pretty much as we found it. We do not know enough about Tyndale's reading, in the years before he left England, to decide the question.

30. *STC* 24446, c4v. Reprinted in *Doctrinal Treatises and Introductions to Different Portions of the Holy Scriptures* (Parker Society), ed. Henry Walter (Cambridge, 1848), pp. 161–162.

31. *Ibid.*, pp. 131–344; see esp. pp. 173–198.

better, than he realized in conferring on Henry VIII the title of "Defender of the Faith." For the King's duty was to defend the *true* faith, "no dreames, no fables, no heresie, no papisticall invencions, but the uncorrupte fayth of Gods most holy worde." The Scriptures made abundantly clear that the authority of kings is above that of all other earthly powers, including popes.

Who coulde than stonde agaynst the godly obedience of his prynce (excepte he wolde be at defyaunce with God and all his holy ordinaunces) that were well acquaynted with the holy scripture, which so earnestly commendeth unto every one of us the auctorite and power geven of God unto kynges and temporal rulers?[32]

Many readers of Erasmus must have asked themselves if passages so typical as those in *Paraclesis* and the 1522 prefatory letter and, in the case of the earlier one, so frequently quoted, had sources or models. Are they refinements of recollections of ancient texts, like some other memorable dicta in his writings? Or, at the least, are they illuminated by expressions of comparable sentiments in his favorite authors?

We may, I think, accept the passages in question as the product of Erasmus' editorial labors, recently completed, on the New Testament and on Jerome, labors that had occupied most of his time for several years before 1516. His convictions about the Bible in vernacular languages may have been held for many years, but the fact that they emerged so pertinently and emphatically in the *Paraclesis* of 1516 must have owed more to his recent work on the New Testament and Jerome than to anything else.

Are there specific sources or analogues? If so, our inclination would take us naturally to patristic writers. Preserved Smith thought the passage in *Paraclesis* may have been suggested by Chrysostom's Homily 35 on Genesis. This homily (which is not one of those later translated by Erasmus) begins with commendation of reading the Scriptures and includes a long passage on the Ethiopian eunuch of Acts 8, always a favorite text in discussions of Biblical study. The Ethiopian was not ashamed to ask for help in understanding what he read, and, thanks to Philip (moved by God), he obtained it. Reading of Scripture should be

32. 1535 Bible, pp. ii–iii. The passage is reprinted in *Works of Bishop Coverdale*, II: *Remains* (Parker Society), ed. George Pearson (Cambridge, 1846), pp. 4–7.

convenient at all times and in all circumstances, whether one is at home, in the forum, or in the army.[33] This passage has obvious bearing on *Paraclesis*, but it does not emphasize commoners or plebeians as much as Erasmus' does; on the contrary, Chrysostom calls attention to the fact that the Ethiopian, Queen Candace's agent, is a prefect, a man in authority.

Erasmus' sentiments in *Paraclesis* and the 1522 letter on the vernacular Bible have lines of relationship to many patristic loci, including some in Chrysostom, but the most likely source must be Jerome. He is not named in or near the passage in *Paraclesis*; but in the 1522 passage (translated above), immediately following the lines on allowing Frenchman, Englishman, German, and Indian to have the Bible in their own languages, and the absurdity of simple folk reciting prayers in a language they do not understand, we meet this: "Like Jerome, I would sooner rejoice in the glory of the Cross, and deem it a splendid victory, if the Gospel were sounded in every tongue and by every race of men." Though interesting, this remark does not make clear whether the writer has a specific text or several texts in mind. It associates Jerome's name with Erasmus' opinions, nothing more.

Another text, however, may throw some light on this question. When replying in 1525 to Sutor's denunciation of his Latin version of the New Testament and disapproval of his pleas for the Gospels in the vernacular tongues, Erasmus writes: "Hieronymus gratulatur Religioni Christianae, quod etiam apud Scythas et Britannos arator aliquid e Psalmo decantet ad stivam."[34] What we notice at once in this passage is the repetition of certain words from the 1516 and 1522 passages under discussion. Scythians and Britons are named in 1522 and 1525, as are the Psalms; *decantet* and *stivam* appear in 1516, 1522, and 1525; *agricola* of 1516 is repeated in 1522, but *arator* is also used in 1522 and 1525. On this topic, then, Jerome is still the Father who comes first to mind when, nine years after publication of *Paraclesis* and three after the 1522 letter, Erasmus defends what he had written on vernacular trans-

---

33. J. P. Migne, ed., *Patrologia Graeca* (Paris, 1857–66), Vol. LIII, cols. 321–324. A passage closely resembling this one occurs in Chrysostom's third sermon *De Lazaro* (trans. Erasmus, LB, VIII, 77B–80A). Cranmer quoted from the latter passage in his preface (1540) to the Great Bible, in the issue appointed to be read in churches (*Miscellaneous Writings*, Parker Society, ed. J. E. Cox [1846], pp. 119–121).
34. LB, IX, 784D.

lation and reading. I have not found in Jerome a specific source for this 1525 sentence just quoted,[35] but I believe Erasmus' sentence can be clarified. We may conjecture that when writing the 1525 passage Erasmus was thinking of Jerome in general terms, but more precisely of what he himself had written in *Paraclesis* and in the 1522 prefatory letter, especially in the latter. Anyone familiar with Erasmus' habit of rapid composition, his failure from time to time to check sources or to quote them exactly, and his fondness for paraphrasing instead of quoting, will be likely to agree, I think, that this is a plausible explanation of his attribution of "quod. . .stivam" in the 1525 sentence to Jerome. That attribution is not altogether incorrect, to be sure, but it is unsatisfactorily vague to a modern reader who expects a footnote or assumes that if Jerome is named there must be a single, particular passage Erasmus had in mind. On the contrary (if I am right), Erasmus is thinking, and allows the reader to think, of Jerome not in terms of a particular passage but of Jerome's lifelong labor of making the Scriptures available in what was *his* vulgar tongue. At the same time Erasmus recalls, but has not looked up or remembered accurately, his own words in *Paraclesis* and the 1522 letter.

Although our concern is the vernacular Bible, it is nevertheless useful to keep in mind in this inquiry that Erasmus' Latin translation of the New Testament (most of it finished by 1509;[36] modified version printed with the first edition of his Greek New Testament, 1516; full version with the second edition, 1519) drew as much attention, favorable and unfavorable, as his Greek edition itself. It was an event of importance at the time.[37] It cost Erasmus some prolonged and tiresome controversies, but raised timely questions about the nature of the Bible, its transmis-

---

35. Mention of Scythians and Britons as examples of remote and still largely barbarous tribes who have lately been turning to Christianity does occur in Jerome's writings; see *ep.* 107: Migne, *PL*, Vol. XXII, col. 870; and compare *ep.* 106: Migne, *PL*, Vol. XXII, col. 837. In a letter to Marcella, purportedly written by Paula and Eustochium but now thought, as indeed it was by Erasmus (see his edition of Jerome's letters [1524], I, 124), to have been written or drafted by Jerome, we read: "Divisus ab orbe nostro Britannus, si in religione processerit, occiduo sole dimisso, quaerit locum fama sibi tantum et scripturarum relatione cognitum. Quid referamus Armenios, quid Persas, quid Indiae, et Aethiopiae populos, ipsamque iuxta Aegyptum, fertilem monachorum, Pontum et Cappadociam, Syriam Coelen, et Mesopotamiam, cunctaque Orientis examina. . . . Vox quidem dissona, sed una religio. Tot pene psallentium chori, quot gentium diversitates" (*ep.* 46; Migne, *PL*, Vol. XXII, col. 489).

36. See *EE*, II, 182–183.

37. Thomas Bilney, the Cambridge martyr, wrote in 1527 that it had changed his life. See Foxe, *Acts and Monuments* (1563), p. 468.

sion and translation. Certain critics carped at it for years,[38] but on the other hand such valued friends as William Latimer, Bishop Foxe of Winchester, and Thomas More praised it. More argued that to have more than one Latin version was not a disadvantage or disaster, that one version may throw light on one passage, another on a different passage.[39]

No discipline is more dependent on languages than theology.[40] For a theologian's *understanding* of Christian doctrine, study of Hebrew, Greek, and Latin is required: a conviction basic to Erasmus' own theological and Biblical studies and to his support of the trilingual colleges.[41] For *preaching* Christian doctrine it is necessary to know vulgar or barbarous languages. Here and there in his *Colloquia, De Pronuntiatione,* and letters Erasmus makes interesting though brief comments on vernacular languages. In his late treatise on preaching, *Ecclesiastes* (1535), he advises preachers to acquaint themselves with vernacular writings, for there is no language so barbarous but has "suam peculiarem elegantiam et emphasim, si fuerit exculta." That is why Dante and Petrarch are esteemed by Italians; and they say the same thing is true of the English language.[42] To Erasmus all vernacular languages were in a sense corrupt in his day, as "modern" Latin was corrupt in comparison with ancient Latin. The speech (*sermo*) of the apostles who preached the Gospel was not that of scholars but of common people—tailors, weavers, sailors, yes, and of pimps and bawds.[43] Here in a letter of 1529 he mentions just those social types he had written of in *Paraclesis* and the prefatory letter of 1522. And the letter implies the question, "Why should not the New Testament be

38. One of the most persistent was the Englishman Edward Lee. See *EE*, III, 203; 312–330; IV, 108–111; 139–152; 159–179; 198–201. One reply to Lee, not included in LB, IX, is printed by Wallace K. Ferguson in his *Erasmi Opuscula* (The Hague, 1933), pp. 225–303.

39. *EE*, II, 242.22–23; 371.21–23; 420.19–24. On some who did not approve, see More's comments, *EE*, II, 371.31–372.54. For his defense of Erasmus' Biblical studies, see *Correspondence of Sir Thomas More,* ed. Elizabeth Frances Rogers (Princeton, 1947), pp. 27–74, 165–206; translation in her *Sir Thomas More: Selected Letters* (New Haven and London, 1961), pp. 6–64, 114–144.

40. *Apologia ad Latomum,* LB, IX, 85E, 82A–B. See G. Chantraine in *Scrinium Erasmianum,* ed. Joseph Coppens (Leiden, 1969), II, 51–75, and his *"Mystère" et "Philosophie du Christ" selon Érasme* (Namur, 1971).

41. On these, P. S. Allen, *Erasmus: Lectures and Wayfaring Sketches* (Oxford, 1934), pp. 138–163.

42. LB, V, 856A–B. On Erasmus and vernacular languages, see R. Giese in *Romanic Review,* 28 (1937), 3–18; L. E. Halkin in *Revue des langues vivantes,* 35 (1969), 566–579.

43. *EE*, VIII, 259.35–39.

accessible to laity today, when in ancient times the laity had it in their own tongues?" Christ spoke not pure Hebrew but Syriac, a mixture of languages. The first Latin translator of the Gospels employed the common language of the people, but this was perfectly intelligible to the educated. If the Latin language then had been as corrupt as it is now among French, Spanish, and Italians, the translator would probably have used the vulgar tongue despite its corruption, "just as today those who preach the Gospel in French or Spanish or Italian use an exceedingly corrupt language if you compare it to Latin."[44]

Who should make vernacular translations? On this subject Erasmus is disappointingly vague. When attacked by Beda and Sutor for his opinions on Biblical translation, he is careful to say that *he* has not made a vernacular version, nor has he encouraged anybody else to do so.[45] He wins a debating point here but scarcely faces up to the question. Either this question could be safely postponed until the Church made official provision for it, or Erasmus thought the question would answer itself. No doubt his own preference would have been for a commission of learned men. In 1521 he suggested such a commission to arbitrate the Lutheran controversy.[46] A Biblical commission would have to be appointed by, and be responsible to, authority, but if it consisted of superior and devout scholars it might be the best means of providing accurate versions of the Bible. This, in fact, was the policy that produced the important English versions after Coverdale's. On one occasion Erasmus was scornful of the argument that textual criticism could be left to councils.[47] Would a committee of translators be more acceptable? If properly qualified, the commission would have at least some of the marks of the *consensus* he prized.[48] But he does not go into these matters far enough to satisfy us.

More, in his controversy with Tyndale, insisted that the Bible needed interpreters. Ignorant people must not meddle with the mysteries. He allowed (1529) that there was no good reason the Bible should not be translated into English, provided this version (1) were made by "some

44. *EE*, VIII, 259.42–52.

45. *EE*, VI, 105.739–740; LB, IX, 783E.

46. The commission was to be appointed by Charles V, Henry VIII, and Louis II of Hungary. See Ferguson, *Erasmi Opuscula*, pp. 352–361.

47. LB, VI, *** v.

48. On some applications of the idea of *consensus* in his writings, see James K. McConica, "Erasmus and the Grammar of Consent," *Scrinium Erasmianum*, ed. Joseph Coppens (Leiden, 1969), II, 77–99.

good catholike and well learned man, or by dyvers dividing the labour among them, and after conferring theyr several parties together eche with other"; (2) were authorized; and (3) were distributed under strict control of the bishops.[49] Erasmus would surely have agreed to the first condition and probably to some form of authorization, but he never hints, I believe, at the sort of episcopal control of the published translation that More thought necessary.[50] After all, who authorized or controlled his own uncommissioned Latin translation?

In England the constitution of Oxford (1407, 1408) effectively prevented unauthorized translation and circulation of the Bible. Erasmus says nothing, and doubtless knew nothing, about that constitution, but

49. " . . . all the copies should come whole unto the bysshoppes hande. Which he may after his discrecion and wisedom deliver to such as he perceiveth honest, sad, & verteous, with a good monicion & fatherly counsell to use it reverently with humble heart & lowly mind, rather sekyng therin occasion of devocion than of despicion. And providing as much as may be, that the boke be after the decease of the partie brought again & reverently restored unto the ordinarye" (*Dialogue Concerning Heresies*, III, xvi; *The English Works of Sir Thomas More*, ed. W. E. Campbell, R. W. Chambers, A. W. Reed [London, 1931], II, 245).

50. Texts of the controversy between More and Tyndale over Church and Bible are (1) More's *Dialogue Concerning Heresies* (London, 1529), reproduced in facsimile and with modern transcription in *The English Works of Sir Thomas More*, ed. Campbell, Chambers, and Reed (see n. 49, above); (2) Tyndale's *Answer unto Sir Thomas More's Dialogue* (Antwerp, 1531), ed. Henry Walter, Parker Society (Cambridge, 1850); (3) More's *Confutation of Tyndale's Answer* (London, 1532), now available in the exhaustive edition by Schuster, Marius, Lusardi, and Schoeck (New Haven and London, 1973). For an initial critique of Tyndale's doctrines on Scripture and on an English Bible, see the *Dialogue Concerning Heresies* (*English Works* [1931], II, 75–80, 87–91, 114–124, 230–253 of the transcription). The issues were then fought out in Tyndale's *Answer* and More's *Confutation*.

How closely did Erasmus and More agree on the Bible? Fundamentally, in my judgment, but not completely. The evidence for saying anything further is mostly *ex silentio*, though with respect to episcopal control of the distribution of vernacular translations, Erasmus' silence is significant. Erasmus seems not to be named in the *Dialogue* and is mentioned in only three passages in the *Confutation* (pp. 177–179, 185, 256 of the Yale edition). We recall how vigorously More had defended Erasmus' Biblical and patristic work in letters to Dorp and the monk Batmanson (n. 39, above), but what we would like to have are More's comments on Erasmus' proposals for vernacular translation of the Bible and Erasmus' comments on More's arguments against Tyndale concerning such translation. Unluckily for us, those arguments were in English and therefore, we must surmise, unread and unreadable by Erasmus. The extant correspondence of More and Erasmus has nothing of interest on the subject, and only eight letters written after 1520 survive.

In their quarrel over such words as "ecclesia," "church," and "congregation," a quarrel into which Tyndale brought the name of Erasmus, More declares that the essential difference between Tyndale and Erasmus is simply that Tyndale means heresy and teaches heresy, whereas Erasmus means none and teaches none. This is the passage that includes More's asseveration that if he knew anyone was likely to be harmed by a translation of Erasmus' *Moria* or by any of his own writings, he would help to burn those books with his own hands (Tyndale, *Answer*, pp. 13–16; More, *Confutation*, pp. 176–179).

Consult also Germain Marc'hadour, *The Bible in the Works of St. Thomas More* (Nieuwkoop, 1969–72), pts. iv and v.

More's own translations of passages from the New Testament are so interesting that it is a great pity he did not make an English version of at least one entire Gospel.

he does say more than once that he is unaware of any decree by the Church forbidding the laity to read the Scriptures in their own languages, and that if there ever was such a decree it was not obeyed.[51] He recalls that when he was young, French and German versions were in use.[52]

They are right who warn laymen against making rash judgments of Scripture, but I know not by what spirit those are led who simply snatch the sacred books from the hands of laymen. Certainly their decision is at odds with that of Christ and the apostles; and what they forbid is urged by the most approved doctors of the Church, who think most praiseworthy what those denounce as impious.[53]

Evidence abounds that the Fathers, unlike some "modern" theologians, had no dread of the vernacular.[54] So far were they from fearing the consequences of private reading of Scripture by the laity that they—for example, Erasmus' favorites, Chrysostom and Jerome—urged it strongly. They knew Scripture has depths simple minds cannot fathom, yet they emphasized the laity's duty of reading and the profit of doing so.

Controversies between Erasmus and his opponents over new translations of the Bible, Latin or vernacular, were dominated by two pervasive facts: the intervention of a millenium of ecclesiastical history and hierarchy between Jerome and Erasmus, and the unquestioned authority during that epoch of the so-called Vulgate. The triumph of the vernacular in the sixteenth century is still such a commonplace of religious history, especially with non-Catholics, that there is some danger of underestimating the arguments *against* vernacular translations and the circulation of those translations. A man of More's piety and learning insisted that the Bible was the possession of the Church; it came from the Church and was to be used by the Church for the good of her children. A man of Tyndale's piety and learning insisted that the New Testament was a gift, a legacy inherited by all Christians, possessed by them without restriction. Irreconcilable differences in antecedent assumptions about the Bible persisted throughout the Reformation controversies. Yet both sides appealed to Jerome, who translated the

51. LB, IX, 456E, 785B; *EE*, VI, 105.732–735.

52. See n. 7, above.

53. *Vidua Christiana*, LB, V. 729C–D; and see More, *Dialogue Concerning Heresies* (*English Works* [1931], II, 214).

54. Adolf von Harnack, *Bible Reading in the Early Church*, trans. J. R. Wilkinson (New York and London, 1912).

Bible but often warned of the difficulties. For translation is a supremely difficult art, demanding both reverence and learning.[55] Seer and scholar, prophet and translator have different gifts and serve different functions.[56] Read the Scriptures, but with due humility. If you do not understand a passage, inquire of him whose life, age, and reputation commend him. "Or, if there is no one who can explain it, better to be safely ignorant than to learn at your peril."[57] Like the Ethiopian of Acts 8, Christians need guides. Do not listen to those who tell you Genesis needs no explanation, that the Pentateuch is easy to understand.[58]

This theme of the depth and difficulty of Scripture is common in the arguments against new translations, and proof texts from Jerome, Chrysostom, Augustine, and other ancient authorities are invariably cited. The contrast between the mysteries of the sacred page and the limited capacities of unlettered men and women to cope with such matters was stressed, for instance, in the oft-quoted condemnation (1199) of private Bible-reading by Innocent III, who commended the motives of the people of Metz but ruled against them.[59] When the Scriptures were finally printed in German, Geiler von Keiserberg, the celebrated preacher of Strasbourg, objected for the same reasons advanced by other opponents in the fifteenth and early sixteenth centuries: Bible truths must be understood correctly; ignorant persons cannot understand them correctly; therefore the German Bible can harm readers.[60] When Archbishop Berthold of Mainz (1485) forbade publication

55. Jerome, *ep*. 57; Migne, *PL*, Vol. XXII, cols. 568–579.

56. "Aliud est enim vatem, aliud esse interpretem. Ibi Spiritus ventura praedicit; hic eruditio et verborum copia, ea quae intelligit, transfert" (*Praef. ad Pent.*; Migne, *PL*, Vol. XXVIII, col. 151A). On this passage, *EE*, VIII, 260.79–93. On Jerome's principles and methods of translation, W. Schwarz, *Principles and Problems of Biblical Translation* (Cambridge, 1955), pp. 26–37.

57. *Ep*. 22; Migne, *PL*, Vol. XXII, col. 415.

58. *Ep*. 53; Migne, *PL*, vol. XXII, cols. 540–549. With the vast subject of Erasmus' judgments and practices concerning the literal and non-literal interpretation of the Scriptures there is no space to deal in this essay. The most important statements of his opinions are found in *Enchiridion* (1503, 1518), LB, V, 29B–F; *Ratio Verae Theologiae* (1518 ff.), LB, V, 117A–127F; *Ecclesiastes* (1535), LB, V, 1028D–51E. These passages are the more valuable because they are in major writings from the earlier, middle, and final phases of his career. For his practice we must go to his notes on the New Testament and to his Paraphrases (LB, VI and VII). For some recent observations, see Craig R. Thompson, "Better Teachers Than Scotus or Aquinas," *Medieval and Renaissance Studies*, 2, ed. John L. Lievsay (Southeastern Institute of Medieval and Renaissance Studies: Durham, N. C., 1968), pp. 119–128; John B. Payne, "Toward the Hermeneutics of Erasmus," *Scrinium Erasmianum* (Leiden, 1969–70),II, 13–49; G. Chantraine, "Érasme, lecteur des Psaumes," *Colloquia Erasmiana Turonensia*, ed. J. C. Margolin (Toronto, 1972), II, 691–712.

59. *Quellen zur Geschichte des Papsttums und des römischen Katholizismus*, ed. Karl Mirbt (3rd ed. rev., Tübingen, 1911), No. 268, pp. 136–137.

60. "It is dangerous to put a knife into the hands of children and let them slice their own bread.

of any translation not approved by the Church, one of his reasons was that the German language was incapable of rendering suitably the profound meanings of the Greek and Latin writers. This was the sort of argument Luther dismissed with contempt.[61]

The passage in *Paraclesis* on the vernacular Bible follows, immediately and appropriately, an exhortation to accept the precepts of the Gospels, most of which, declares Erasmus, are clear and simple. One need not be learned but only devout and receptive. The Gospels, like the sun, are meant for everyone.[62] True, the Scriptures, especially the Old Testament, have obscurities that have puzzled commentators for ages. There are even a few sayings in the Gospels that Christ evidently did not intend his hearers to understand (for example, John 2:19) or that at any rate are unintelligible (Mark 3:29, 13:32).[63] Nevertheless, the essence of the Gospels, the message of salvation, is characterized by *simplicitas*. "Ipsa veritas, cuius quo simplicior, hoc efficacior est oratio."[64] We read the New Testament for substance, not for style; and although Erasmus strove for correctness of language in making his translation, he did not sacrifice the *simplicitas* of apostolic diction.[65] We do not demand eloquence of the apostles, any more than we look to them for Aristotelian or Platonic philosophy.[66]

A good will and sincere desire to learn will enable the ploughman of Erasmus' or Tyndale's pages to understand the Gospel sufficiently.

They can only wound themselves with it. So also the Holy Scriptures, which comprise the bread of God, must be read and interpreted by people who have requisite knowledge and experience and who are able to determine its true sense" (quoted by W. J. Kooiman, *Luther and the Bible*, trans. John Schmidt [Philadelphia, 1961], p. 86).

61. Mirbt, *Quellen*, No. 332, p. 184. Berthold praises the "divine" art of printing but does not permit unauthorized translations, whether of Scripture or other books, in his diocese. Luther, after defending his rendering of Romans 3:28, adds: "We do not have to inquire of the literal Latin, how we are to speak German. . . . Rather we must inquire about this of the mother in the home, the children on the street, the common man in the marketplace. We must be guided by their language, the way they speak, and do our translating accordingly. That way they will understand it and recognize that we are speaking German to them" (*On Translating: An Open Letter*, trans. Charles M. Jacobs, rev. E. Theodore Bachmann, in *Luther's Works*, American Edition [Philadelphia, 1955 ff.], XXXV, 189).

62. LB, VI, *3v; Holborn, 141.28–29; 142.7–9.

63. *EE*, V, 6. 43–56. Erasmus' notes on these passages in LB, VI, are not helpful, but his paraphrases of two of them are (LB, VII, 517F–518A; 184F–185B). On linguistic and rhetorical problems in the interpretation of Scripture, see *Ratio Verae Theologiae*, LB, V, 117A–126B; *Ecclesiastes*, LB, V, 1051E–56E.

64. LB, VI, *3; Holborn, 140.6–7.

65. *EE*, III, 381.35–37.

66. *EE*, III, 316.138–144, 154–160.

Other laymen, depending on their degree of education, are encouraged by Erasmus, as by Tyndale, to discuss passages. "The scriptures conferred togither expowne them selfe as saith S. Austen." So Tyndale.[67] "Conferring," comparing passages, is said by a speaker in Erasmus' *Convivium Religiosum* to be an excellent method of clarifying an obscure passage.[68] Origen and Augustine agree on this method.[69] Erasmus warns elsewhere, however, that it yields different results to different investigators; he warns also against lifting passages out of context, against ignoring the circumstances of composition and disregarding the writer's intentions.[70]

These become technical matters for theologians and exegetes. They seldom concern housewives, ploughmen, weavers, and other laborers for whom Erasmus, in *Paraclesis* and the 1522 preface, wanted translations to be prepared. When such uneducated or poorly educated laity have the Scriptures in their own tongues, they will at least be better off than they are now. They can and ought to concentrate on the essence of the Gospel, leaving the rest to theologians and preachers. "In the Scriptures alone, " says Erasmus, "what I do not understand I nevertheless revere,"[71] and he advises others to do the same.[72] The course of religious controversy in the sixteenth century shows that such advice was ignored as often as it was observed, for if there is one lasting impression we get after wading through some of the innumerable polemics it is that Selden was more right than wrong: almost everyone would claim the right to interpret.

To complete our examination of the passage in *Paraclesis* and the letter of 1522, advocating vernacular translation of Scripture, we may now refer to Erasmus' replies to three of his most formidable critics, Peter Sutor (Cousturier), Noel Beda (Bédier), and the Faculty of Theology at Paris. These rebuttals[73] show us how Erasmus defended or explained his 1516 and 1522 statements some years after they were

67. *The Supper of the Lord* (1533), STC 24468, c3ᵥ. This is printed with the *Answer* to More's *Dialogue* in the Parker Society edition (see n. 50, above); for the passage quoted, see p. 249. Augustine, *De Doctrina Christiana*, III, xxvi–xxvii, 37–39.
68. *The Colloquies of Erasmus*, trans. Craig R. Thompson (Chicago and London, 1965), p. 61.
69. LB, V, 131B–32A.
70. LB, V, 128B.
71. *Paraclesis*, LB, VI, *4; Holborn, 147.20–21.
72. LB, V, 1173D–E.
73. All are available in LB, IX. I have consulted the 1525 edition of Sutor's work, Erasmus' 1526–27 replies to Beda, and the 1532 text of his answer to the Theological Faculty.

printed. Even though these comments on translation occupy only a small portion of his replies, they are unfortunately far too long to be given in full; instead, some parts will be summarized or quoted.

Sutor, who became a Carthusian after his Paris career, condemned new Latin translations in his *De Tralatione Bibliae* (1525). In the final chapter he denounces the temerity of those who translate, or advocate the translating of, the Bible into vernacular tongues. Such versions are not needed. Knowledge of the whole Bible is neither necessary to salvation nor without danger if allowed to everyone. Common people have enough with Creed, Paternoster, Commandments, and precepts of the Church (q4r–q4v). Many parts of the Bible they cannot understand. Vernacular translations would promote irreverence (r1v–r2r).

In reply (LB, IX, 783E–787E), Erasmus concedes that learning Scripture *viva voce* may be the best way if a good teacher is available, but he has argued against those who think Christianity is finished if the populace has access to Scripture (783E–F). Jews read the prophets—yet Christians are kept from reading the sacred books! Jerome rejoiced that Scythians, Britons, and other barbarians were reading the Scriptures (784A–D). Sutor exaggerates the difficulties. Reading is the first step, even for theologians. If there was any decree by the Fathers against the common people having the Bible, that was a measure required by the nature of the times and issued to curb the arrogance of certain individuals. It was not directed against others, for the people in the ancient Church had the Bible in their own languages and read it openly (784F–785D). Sutor's argument that a woman who spends her time reading Scripture will neglect her household duties is nonsense. Why does he not worry about the dangers of pagan philosophy, which theologians study assiduously? It is nonsense, too, to blame the Lutheran tragedy on the cultivation of languages and literature (785E–787D).

Natalis Beda, of the Faculty of Theology at Paris, listed the many errors he found in Erasmus' writings in a *Censura* (1525), which he printed in May 1526 as *Annotationes*. Erasmus' *Supputationes Errorum in Censuris Beddae* (1526–27) consists of *Prologus* and *Divinationes*, from 1526 (LB, IX, 442C–514F), and *Supputationes*, from 1527 (515A–720C).

Erasmus repeats that he knows of no decree forbidding the laity to read the Bible, and that if any was issued it was not generally accepted. In advocating Biblical reading by the laity he stipulates a devout disposition (456E–F). "I assert that laymen should not be entirely forbidden to read the sacred books, but warned and instructed not to abuse them." Beda does not appreciate that Greek and Latin were vulgar languages in antiquity. Latin was understood by weavers (both male and female) throughout Italy, Spain, France, Africa. When later the languages (Latin, Greek, Hebrew) degenerated in popular usage, their pure forms became the preserve of theologians. There is no difference between reading the Gospels in French if you know French and reading them in Greek or Latin if you know grammar. If Beda's logic held, the Bible should not be read in church, because many boys and laymen present know Latin. Even the Song of Songs is read there; indeed, nuns learn it and read it out publicly in churches. If they understand it, so much the worse for them; if they do not, to whom do they chant it—the angels (552C–553C)?

If reading the Bible is dangerous, ignorance of it is far more dangerous. Priests should exhort the laity to read Scripture. Pastors should instruct the lower classes diligently. Then reading it may not be necessary. Or at least it will be rewarding. Chrysostom rebukes laymen for not having the Bible; Beda does not permit them to have it (553D–554A).

The Faculty of Theology at Paris issued a *Determinatio* against certain writings by Erasmus in December 1527, but this was not published until 1531. Early in 1532 Erasmus replied with his *Declarationes ad Censuras Lutetiae Vulgatas*. The Faculty held that Erasmus' proposal to let ignorant laymen read the Bible would do more harm than good. But, says Erasmus, since Scripture was translated into the common tongues in antiquity when even weavers and sailors understood Greek and Latin, when Chrysostom commended Bible-reading and Jerome translated, it would be a pity if Christians today were deprived of the same privilege. Far more profit than peril will result from giving the Bible to the laity. And if there is danger in reading it, there is greater danger in being ignorant of it. The agitations of our time are caused not by the laity but by the learned. (For example both Luther and Oecolampadius are Scholastic doctors.) People are barred from the Scriptures but not from the writings of philosophers (LB, IX, 871A–F).

Objecting to Erasmus' assertion that he would have farmers, smiths, and other artisans read the vernacular Bible, the Faculty told him the uneducated (*simplices*) are like babies in these matters, unable to digest solid food. No, says Erasmus; no one is so ignorant that he cannot grasp the meaning of the New Testament. As for the Old Testament, he would not urge, but also would not forbid, reading it (VII, $**2_v$; IX, 872F). Christians should not always remain babes. The Holy Spirit often divulges to children what it conceals from the wise. The same Scripture is milk for the weak and solid food for the strong, but whoever deprives them of the Bible offers neither milk nor solid food (872C–873B). He thinks it ridiculous for women to recite Psalms or Paternoster in Latin they do not understand when they could say them in French. However devout these persons, they would be even more devout if they said prayers in the vernacular tongue they understood. Erasmus holds with Paul (I Corinthians 14:19) that "in the church I had rather speak five words with my understanding, that by my voice I might teach others also, than ten thousand words in an unknown tongue" (874A–F).

We have seen that the passage in *Paraclesis* on vernacular translation of the Bible does not stand alone. It is amplified in the prefatory letter to the 1522 Paraphrase of Matthew and defended by Erasmus in replies to critics of those two works. Examination of all these passages leads to the conclusion that Erasmus is consistent in his principal theses: that what he means by Scriptures insofar as desirable versions in the modern languages are concerned is mainly the New Testament and the Psalter, for he readily concedes that some parts of the Old Testament give inordinate difficulty to the common reader; that hearing good instruction by good teachers would profit laity as much as reading for themselves—only he implies doubt that enough capable and dutiful teachers are accessible; that even the humblest people, however slight their education, can derive some profit from reading the Gospels; that if such reading is dangerous, as his critics contend, ignorance of the Bible is more dangerous; that the prevalent reluctance or refusal of authority to provide and circulate the vernacular Scriptures is a painful contrast to the practice of the ancient Church; and that his opponents fail to grasp that in antiquity the Bible was read in what were then vernacular tongues.

Neither Erasmus nor any other of the reformers could have foreseen how many differences of interpretation the reading of the freely circulated vernacular Bible would bring, or the influence of interpretation on polity, dissent, and sectarianism. Whatever one's opinions on those matters, the point to be emphasized here is that, despite all the criticism his proposals received from academic adversaries, and despite the admitted risks, Erasmus was more than willing to give the laity access to the Scriptures in their own languages. And by laity he included *idiotae* and *mulierculae* of the humblest kinds. He did not share More's notions about limiting copies to proper persons approved by bishops.

It may be true that the worsening of the Lutheran schism impelled Erasmus to write more cautiously than he wrote in *Paraclesis*. He would not have admitted changing his positions on major questions of interpretation, authority, and the like; nor, in my judgment, did he change them. But the increasingly vexatious controversies with academic theologians and others made more evident the advantages of prudence, definition, qualification, and forensic tactics. "Suspense loquor ac de meo sensu," as he says in his rebuttal of the Theological Faculty's censures (LB, IX, 873C). Contrast the tone of *Paraclesis* (1516) with that of *Hyperaspistes I* (1526). In criticizing Luther's conception of the Scriptures in the later work, Erasmus stresses the authority of the Church in a manner not prominent, and not urgent, in 1516.[74] On many occasions after 1522 he took pains to clarify statements, even to make (or appear to make) minor tactical retreats. Certainly he emphasized the authority of the Church more clearly. But he did not retract his advocacy of vernacular translations of the Bible for the laity. He continued to believe that the Scriptures should speak with many voices and that translations should be provided for the spiritual benefit of Christians. On this, as on so many religious topics, he found steady guidance in Jerome: "Vox quidem dissona, sed una religio."[75]

---

74. See C. Augustijn, "*Hyperaspistes I*: La doctrine d'Érasme et de Luther sur la 'Claritas Scripturae,'" *Colloquia Erasmiana Turonensia*, II, 737–748.

75. *Ep.* 46; Migne, *PL*, Vol. XXII, col. 489. Heinz Holeczek's *Humanistische Bibelphilologie als Reformproblem bei Erasmus von Rotterdam, Thomas More und William Tyndale* (Leiden, 1975), was announced too late for me to consult in this study, which was submitted in 1974.

II. Petrarch and Modern Lyric Poetry

O. B. Hardison, Jr. · *Director, Folger Shakespeare Library*

Francis Petrarch has the reputation of being the most autobiographical of poets. His fondness for confession, for the *cri de coeur* and the pageant of the bleeding heart, is evident in all his work—his voluminous correspondence, his imaginary dialogues and letters to ancient authors, his *Triumphs*, and his eclogues. Most especially it is evident in the *Canzoniere*, the collection of lyrics he wrote to describe his love for the lady Laura.

The trouble is that Petrarch was never content to describe his experience and leave it at that. We know that he was in bondage to Laura for twenty-one years and that he spent the rest of his life preoccupied with her memory. Far from concealing his passion, he went to great pains to publicize it to all the world. Yet in the autobiographical *Letter to Posterity*, written at the end of his life, Petrarch dismisses Laura in two blunt sentences:

I struggled in my younger days with a keen but constant and pure attachment, and would have struggled with it longer had not the sinking flame been extinguished by death—premature and bitter, but salutary. . . . As I approached the age of forty, while my powers were unimpaired and my passions were still strong, I not only abruptly threw off my bad habits, but even the very recollection of them, as if I had never looked upon a woman.[1]

This from the poet who continued to revise his poems to Laura until the time of his death!

Goethe, who wrote what is probably the only honest autobiography before Freud, called it *Dichtung und Wahrheit*—fiction and truth. What makes Petrarch especially puzzling is that nothing he wrote—or almost nothing—exists in its original form. He was a tinkerer, a nitpicker, probably the first fully documented neurotic author in history. Having written something, he could never let it go. His letters, his prose works, and his *Canzoniere* look like autobiography, but the more one studies the evidence of revision, the internal contradictions, and the

---

1. *Selected Sonnets, Odes and Letters*, ed. Thomas G. Bergin (New York, 1966), p. 2.

multiple variants, the less biographical they appear. He revised not only phrases and lines, but whole sequences. The *Canzoniere* seems to be a chronological record of his love affair, but many of the poems that can be dated through their allusions to historical events are obviously out of order. What we have, evidently, is not a chronological sequence but a mosaic of fragments arranged for maximum artistic effect.

According to Ernest Hatch Wilkins, the foremost authority on the subject, the *Canzoniere* went through no less than eight different stages dating from 1325, two years before Petrarch met Laura, to 1374, the year of his death. Even the last, beautifully written holograph, now one of the major treasures of the Vatican library, is not absolutely definitive since we have marginal numbers, evidently written after the manuscript was completed, proposing yet another arrangement of the last thirty poems. In Wilkins' words, "It is not a collection made toward the end of his life in a single editorial effort, nor is it a mere gradual accumulation of poems: it is a selective and ordered collection, the fashioning of which, begun in his youth, continued to the day of his death."[2]

To attempt to reconstruct Petrarch's life from his writing is therefore like following a thread through an increasingly dense tangle. Certainties tend to end in a confused body of probabilities, conjectures, and sheer guesses.

If biography is at best frustrating, the alternative is to accept a single text and to deal with it in its own terms as a work of art. This is an important point. Shakespeare's insignificance in the brilliant pageantry of Elizabethan London gave him anonymity, and Petrarch's constant tampering with the records of his life provides almost the same thing. Just as Shakespeare the Stratford burgher disappears behind the text of *As You Like It* or *Hamlet* or *The Winter's Tale*, Petrarch gradually assimilates himself into his work. We know all about the heart that bleeds so profusely in the *Canzoniere* and the Latin poems and letters, but it is not Petrarch's heart. The poems are drawn from Petrarch's experience, but the experience stands apart from his life as objectified experience, experience transformed into the shape of art.

Even the most basic facts about the *Canzoniere* are ambivalent. Was Laura really Laurette de Noves, married (with some historical irony) to Hugues de Sade, mother of eleven children, and dead of the plague in

2. *The Making of the "Canzoniere" and Other Petrarchan Studies* (Rome, 1951), p. 145.

1348? Or is she a montage of the several women in Petrarch's life, one of them the mother of his two illegitimate children? Or is she, in spite of his vehement protests to the contrary, an allegory of Lady Truth or a symbol of the allure of secular learning and poetry to a man who had almost, but not quite, lived past the Age of Faith, or simply a Freudian dream growing out of the tensions between Petrarch's sexuality and the ideal of celibacy? Did he meet her on 6 April 1327, as he states explicitly in Sonnet 176 and elsewhere, or was it, as he states in Sonnet 3, on Good Friday, 1327, which happened to be 10 April? If on 6 April, did he favor Good Friday because it was on a Good Friday that he felt inspired to write his Latin Epic *Africa*; and if on Good Friday, did he sometimes refer to 6 April as the date because Laura died on 6 April 1348, and the two dates created a neat frame within which to place the love affair? Does the *Canzoniere* contain 366 poems because that happens to be the number he composed, or because 365 is the number of time, being the number of days in the year, with the concluding poem, a hymn to the Virgin Mary, taking the sequence out of time into eternity?

At one extreme of art there are the confession and the diary. At the other there is the artifact that exists wholly independently of the artist. The writer of confessions is like an aeolian harp, passively waiting to be played by the winds from the world beyond, or a grubby chronicler of life's commonplaces like Samuel Pepys or James Boswell, or a Pavlovian man, salivating a poem each time the gong of experience is rung. The artisan, on the other hand, is an anonymous craftsman placing gargoyles over the buttresses of Chartres or a being separate from his work, who retires from it, to quote Stephen Dedalus, like God paring His fingernails after completing the six days of Creation.

These polarities are universal. They apply to the art of Petrarch's age for the same reason that men obeyed the law of gravity and behaved in psychological ways long before Isaac Newton and Sigmund Freud were born. If we consider the disappearance of Petrarch the man into his work, it is tempting to consider him as a member of the second group—as an artisan, a forerunner of modern symbolist poets, and hence in the aesthetic tradition. After all, art for art's sake is as old as Eratosthenes, and the notion that the artist is less important than his creation is pervasive in the classical authors whom Petrarch admired. Again, to a whole generation of historians, including Burckhardt and Symonds as well as Walter Pater, the Renaissance was a reaffirmation of

the absolute value of the here and now. Beauty—the beauty of land-
scape, of the nude human body, of artificial creations—is valuable in
itself and not because it is a cloudy vision of a more perfect beauty to
come.

There is something in this, but it is not a point of view that Petrarch
would have understood, much less approved. Officially Petrarch believed with Horace that the purpose of art is to delight and instruct or to
delight while instructing or to delight as a means of instruction. Petrarch
knew in his heart that there was something more. He referred to this
extra *je ne sais quoi* in the oration he delivered when he was crowned
laureate in Rome on 8 April 1341 as the mysterious love of art that
draws the poet up the difficult and lonely slopes of Parnassus. He knew,
too, that poets often speak in blind parables and that the myths of Ovid
conceal an ancient wisdom that may have survived in pagan literature
from the age before the Tower of Babel. But he never discussed inspiration or the hidden truths of mythology with the enthusiasm of his friend
Boccaccio. Evidently his understanding of art was much narrower and
more practical than the art itself.

The war between understanding and feeling is clear even in the
Canzoniere. Is this work the record of a glorious, ennobling love, which
is what Petrarch's heart told him, or a series of lyrics about a soul
ensnared by lust, which is what his understanding, drawing on a
tradition that goes back to St. Augustine and earlier, kept whispering?
In Sonnet 47 Petrarch exclaims:

> Benedetto sia 'l giorno e 'l mese e l'anno
> e la stagione e 'l tempo e l'ora e 'l punto
> e 'l bel paese i 'l loco ov'io fui giunto
> da' duo begli occhi che legato m'ànno . . .
>
> e benedette sian tutte le carte
> ov'io fama l'acquisto, e 'l pensier mio,
> ch' è sol di lei, sì ch' altra non v'à parte.[3]

One sonnet later the mood is reversed:

> Padre del ciel, dopo i perduti giorni,
> dopo le notti vaneggiando spese

---

3. Quotations from the sonnets are from *Rime, trionfi, e poesie latine*, ed. F. Neri *et al.* (Milan,
1951).

con quel fero desio ch' al cor s'accese,
mirando gli atti per mio mal sì adorni,

piacciati omai, col tuo lume, ch' io torni
ad altra vita et a più belle imprese,
sì ch' avendo le reti indarno tese,
il mio duro adversario se ne scorni.

The ambivalence runs through the *Canzoniere*. As we have seen, in the *Letter to Posterity* Petrarch disposes of the whole love affair in a few harsh words: "As I approached the age of forty, . . . I not only abruptly threw off my bad habits, but even the very recollection of them, as if I had never looked upon a woman." It is a baldfaced lie, but as a judgment it is no less severe than the verdict of St. Augustine, who appears in Petrarch's *Secretum* and dismisses both the *Canzoniere* and the hunger for fame that is so much a part of it with a phrase echoing Ecclesiastes—Vanity, vanity, all is vanity.

Nothing is fixed in Petrarch. It is all flux and contradiction; more so the more honest he tries to be, the more deeply he looks into his own heart. He was, I think, a fundamentally restless man. What makes him remarkable is that time after time in his quest for meaning in his life he comes back to a few central moments that are linked, at least in the imaginary world of his art, to symbolic dates and festivals and themes. Other men of his age had intense experiences. Petrarch is unique because he could not let them go. He constantly reexamined them in his prose and poetry and confessional dialogues. Since he was never of the same mind about them, he kept seeing them in a new light, adding new versions to the old or revising what he had already written. In Sonnet 43 he quotes the grim motto of Aeschylus: "Call no man happy until the day he dies." For much of his life Petrarch was miserable or claimed he was. When he was dying he may have found some consolation in the fact that his great work carried the stamp of his latest and presumably his sagest insights; but it is more probable that he died indignant that he would not have time for more revisions.

Long before we come to the final version of the *Canzoniere* it becomes apparent that the two themes between which the poems alternate are the world as illusion and the world as fact. St. Augustine speaks in the *Secretum* for the world as illusion, buttressed by the twin authorities of Socrates and the Bible. Life is a dream, the shadows that play across the walls of a cave or a prison. What we see now in a glass darkly we will

later see face to face. Only the invisible world is unchanging. Earthly
beauty is a snare, and mortal love is a trap invented by Satan. The
Augustinian note is dominant in Sonnet 25:

> Quanto più m'avvicino al giorno estremo
> che l'umana miseria suol far breve,
> più veggio il tempo andar veloce e leve
> e 'l mio di lui sperar fallace e scemo.
>
> I' dico a' miei pensier: Non molto andremo
> d'amor parlando omai, ché 'l duro e greve
> terreno incarco, come fresca neve,
> si va struggendo, onde noi pace avremo;
>
> perché con lui cadrà quella speranza
> che ne fe' vaneggiar sì lungamente,
> e 'l riso e 'l pianto, e la paura e l'ira:
>
> sì vedrem chiaro poi come sovente
> per le cose dubbiose altri s'avanza,
> e come spesso indarno si sospira.

It recurs more powerfully in the sonnets on Laura's death, such as
Sonnet 303:

> E' mi par d' or in ora udire il messo
> che madonna mi mande a sé chiamando;
> così dentro e di for mi vo cangiando
> e sono in non molt' anni sì dimesso
>
> ch'a pena riconosco omai me stesso;
> tutto 'l viver usato ò messo in bando;
> sarei contento di sapere il quando,
> ma pur devrebbe il tempo esser da presso.
>
> O felice quel dì che del terreno
> carcere uscendo lasci rotta e sparta
> questa mia grave e frale e mortal gonna,
>
> e da sì folte tenebre mi parta,
> volando tanto su nel bel sereno
> ch' i' veggia il mio Signore e la mia Donna!

The second theme is the one everybody knows and remembers. It is
the theme that appealed to Petrarch's imitators, who made it into the
central theme of modern poetry. It is the theme of the here and now. Life

is important; the fleeting experience of beauty, love, and vitality is important; this particular moment and this particular woman, framed in this particular blend of sunlight and shadow, are important, more important than all the syllogisms of the philosophers and all the pieties of the schoolmen. It is a theme that echoes in Marvell's lines, "But at my back I always hear/Time's winged chariot hurrying near;/And yonder all before us lie/Deserts of vast eternity," and ramifies into the obsessive particularities of Impressionist painting. It explains why Petrarch was fascinated with dates and anniversaries and particular moments of vivid experience:

> Era il giorno ch' al sol si scoloraro
> per la pietà del suo fattore i rai;
> quando i' fui preso, e non me ne guardai
> che i be' vostr' occhi, Donna, mi legaro.
>
> (Sonnet 3)

At night Petrarch meditates on death, only to interrupt the flow of commonplaces with a passionate exclamation:

> Con lei foss'io da che si parte il sole
> e non ci vedess'altri che le stelle,
> sol una notte, e mai non fosse l'alba!
>
> (Sestina 1)

He repents, but the stubborn reality of beauty pulls him back to the earth:

> Misero me, che volli,
> quando primier sì fiso
> gli tenni nel bel viso,
> per iscolpirlo, imaginando, in parte
> onde mai né per forza né per arte
> mosso sarà fin ch' i' sia dato in preda
> a chi tutto diparte?
> Né so ben anco che di lei mi creda.
>
> (Canzone 5)

Her memory haunts him:

> Erano i capei d'oro a l'aura sparsi
> che 'n mille dolci nodi gli avolgea. . . .
>
> (Sonnet 90)

Even after her death, he remembers and catalogues her particular beauties:

> Oimè il bel viso, oimè il soave sguardo,
> oimè il leggiadro portamento altero!
> Oimè il parlar ch' ogni aspro ingegno e fero
> facevi umile ed ogni uom vil gagliardo!
>
> Et oimè il dolce riso. . . .
> $\qquad$ (Sonnet 267)

In old age, in spite of the invisible reality just beyond his reach, he is still drawn back to the flesh:

> Tornami a mente, anzi v' è dentro, quella
> ch'indi per Lete esser non po sbandita,
> qual io la vidi in su l' eta fiorita
> tutta accesa de' raggi di sua stella;
>
> sì nel mio primo occorso onesta e bella
> veggiola, in sé raccolta e sì romita,
> ch' i' grido: "Ell' è ben dessa, ancor è in vita",
> e 'n don le cheggio sua dolce favella.
> $\qquad$ (Sonnet 290)

Here I think we are close to the essential Petrarch. Not in poems expressing passion—the Goliards and the Troubadours knew all about passion—but in poems that remain attached to the world and the flesh within the context of other poems reminding us that the third member of the trinity of the world and the flesh is the Devil. This is what makes Petrarch unique. It can be explained only by a kind of chemistry within Petrarch himself. He knew better. He had read St. Paul and St. Augustine and St. Thomas and Dante, and he had learned their lessons. Everything in his heritage testified to the superior reality of the invisible world, but though he tried for a lifetime, he could not deny the reality of what he felt or allow the people and events that caused the feelings to be absorbed into a sponge of neat scholastic abstractions. His view of history is like this. In the *Africa*, Scipio Africanus is a symbol of virtue and patriotism, but there are moments when he is a man living at a particular moment in history rather than a figure in a secular morality play. Laura is far more complex. She moves bewilderingly in and out of the world of abstraction. At times she is Lady Truth misunderstood by a youthful poet whose vision is clouded by his sexuality. At other times she represents the lure of fame and at others the attraction of secular as against religious art. She is distanced further by her involvement in the myth of Daphne changed to a laurel tree, the symbol of poetic fame, when pursued by Apollo, the god of poetry. And if the myth of Daphne absorbs her in a secular allegory, her virtue and her spirituality relate her to the world of angels and of the Virgin Mary. She is all of these things because the habit of mind that Petrarch inherited explained everything by making it into a series of abstractions. Beyond all of these symbols and myths and abstractions, however, she remains the Laura who demolishes myths and abstractions. Not necessarily Laurette de Noves, mother of eleven children, but the Laura of the *Canzoniere* who broke in on Petrarch's world on 6 April 1327 and of whose image he wrote:

> Misero me, che volli,
> quando primier sì fiso
> gli tenni nel bel viso,
> per iscolpirlo, imaginando, in parte
> onde mai né per forza né per arte
> mosso sarà fin ch' i' sai dato in preda
> a chi tutto diparte?
> Né so ben anco che di lei mi creda.
>
> (Canzone 5)

If Laura had been only a figure out of *The Marriage of Philology and Mercury* Petrarch might have written the *Triumphs* and he would probably be remembered as a talented author "in the school of Dante" or "the school of Guillaume de Machaut." He would not, however, be remembered for what he is: the founder of modern lyric poetry.

Here I need to clarify what I meant by my earlier reference to Petrarch's inner chemistry. Everyone knows that Descartes wrote the basic definition of modern consciousness: *Cogito ergo sum*—I think, therefore I am. Descartes' *cogito* applies nicely to the modern scientific consciousness (probably to the medieval scholastics as well). The essence of this scientific approach is to subsume the particulars of experience under the most general of all abstractions, the abstractions of mathematics. A falling apple is dehydrated to $S = \frac{1}{2} gt^2$. The hooks and deflected paths of the atoms of Democritus are abstracted to quantum mechanics, while a glass of port is reduced to a formula: C_2H_5OH plus minor impurities.

By contrast, the formula for the modern sensibility—our way of experiencing reality as against conceptualizing it—could be summed up as *sentio ergo sum*—I feel, therefore I am. For Wordsworth on Westminster Bridge, London is not a case study in sociology but an experience:

> Earth has not any thing to show more fair:
> Dull would he be of soul who could pass by
> A sight so touching in its majesty. . . .

And for Wallace Stevens, a jar is not simply a small vessel but a potential focal point through which the world can become coherent in human terms:

> I placed a jar in Tennessee,
> And round it was, upon a hill.
> It made the slovenly wilderness
> Surround that hill.

In every way a biographer could list, Petrarch was a child of his age. It was an age of abstraction, and he learned all the formulas. He learned the seven parts of speech and the ten difficult tropes and the names of the nine worthies and the seven deadly sins and the three cardinal virtues and the twelve labors of Hercules and the names of the Attic orators and the myths of Ovid and the date when the world began—all before he left grammar school. Later he learned about the nine spheres and the seven wandering stars, the varieties of disjunctive syllogisms, the four humours, and the signs and influences of the zodiac, and later still he studied Roman and canon law at Bologna, and the wisdom of the Fathers from his own reading.

I stress this context because in order to appreciate the greatness of Petrarch's achievement we need to remember how deeply such formulaic learning was impressed on him. What he achieved was the affirmation of his own irreducible and unabstractable reality—the validity of his inner chemistry—in spite of and, as the lyrics testify, frequently in open defiance of the abstractions that he had been given by his culture to explain it. He refused to allow the *sentio* to be absorbed by the *cogito*. I do not mean that no one before Petrarch had feelings that refused to yield to neat explanations; I mean something more important. I assume that men of Petrarch's time commonly had experiences that could not easily be squared with their concepts of experience. What is remarkable about Petrarch is that he did not dismiss his sense of conflict between the *sentio* and the *cogito* or record it in a single poem and then move on. Instead he made it the center around which his whole life revolved for the nearly fifty years that followed his first sight of Laura in 1327.

The result was a vision of reality surrounded by and threatened by abstractions, but always resisting them, always circling back to the month, the day, the moment of that first meeting, when his life was fundamentally changed. A twentieth-century critic would call it an epiphany. Just as Descartes, having discovered the *cogito*, found he could deduce the created world from it, Petrarch, having experienced a particular beauty at a particular moment, found that it organized his life in the same way that Wallace Stevens' jar organized the slovenly wilderness in Tennessee. To put it differently, Petrarch, having experienced the reality of the *sentio*, was never able to forget it or leave it alone.

Not that he didn't try. The penitential theme in the *Canzoniere* and the endless revisions extending to the effort to reorder the last thirty poems show how hard he tried. The curious thing is that the harder he tried—the more he revised, the more he added orthodoxies and symbols and numerological grace notes, the more he emphasized the reality of the invisible world—the more real the sequence became. As Horace could have told him: *Naturam expelles furca tamen usque recurret*— push Nature out of the front door and she comes in at the back. The point is that nobody before Petrarch had tried so valiantly and persistently to push Nature out of the front door, and consequently in no major poem before the *Canzoniere* does she make such a triumphant and visible entrance at the back.

In spite of himself Petrarch created the first modern homily on the text *sentio ergo sum*, and no version of the *Canzoniere* illustrates the text more persuasively than the final version. In doing this Petrarch created the picture frame within which modern sensibility was destined to view the world.

This is my last point and it is an important one. I use the metaphor of the picture frame to recall the view of art developed by Ernst Cassirer. As a latter-day disciple of Kant, Cassirer regards consciousness as a shaping force, a frame or perspective that influences the way reality is perceived. The particular frame that a society or an individual uses is a symbolic form. The most basic symbolic forms are language and religion. In advanced cultures these basic forms are influenced by science and art. Every art work—every poem—is a symbolic form in that it invites the reader to view experience from a perspective not his own. The effect of symbolic forms can be explained in part, but only in part, because in determining the shape of consciousness they determine the way that experience presents itself to the mind for analysis. This is why at least part of the experience of art is, to use Susanne Langer's term, non-discursive.

Individual poems normally affect individuals. Occasionally, however, a work is created that influences a whole culture. Here we return to Petrarch. Petrarchism and the vogue of Petrarchan imitation extended from the fifteenth to the seventeenth century. It was the dominant mode of European lyric poetry for this period, and most subsequent lyric poetry is indebted to it, although the subject matter shifts from love between man and woman to other kinds of experience. This is another way of saying that the form of consciousness objectified in the *Canzoniere*, which began with Petrarch's first meeting with Laura and was developed slowly and painfully through a lifetime of creative effort, was a discovery so important that it swept Europe. It taught Europeans a new way of responding to experience, which is the same thing as saying that it gave Europeans a new framework within which to live their lives.

In this sense the *Canzoniere* is as much a discovery as the discovery of the New World. We are still living in the reality that Petrarch created. If the *Canzoniere* occasionally seems familiar and even commonplace, this is because even if we have not read it, we have lived it. To read a Petrarch sonnet is like looking into an antique mirror. The image is a little strange, a little distorted, but it is familiar because it is our own image. It was duplicated a thousand times, with endless variations, by the imitators who domesticated it in every European vernacular—in English by Wyatt and Surrey, by Gascoigne and Spenser and Shakespeare and John Donne, among others.

Petrarch is tagged as a love poet in the literary histories. He is a love poet, of course, but love is the subject, not the motive of the *Canzoniere*. The motive is an epiphany, the intense moment of experience associated with 6 April 1327, around which the sonnets—and much of Petrarch's life—revolved. The Renaissance took the motive and the subject matter together. They are both present, for example, in Shakespeare's Sonnet 116:

> Love is not love
> Which alters when it alteration finds,
> Or bends with the remover to remove:
> O, no; it is an ever-fixed mark,
> That looks on tempests and is never shaken;
> It is the star to every wandering bark,
> Whose worth's unknown, although his height be taken.

We have the same motive, extended to cover the whole spectrum of human experiences, in romantic poetry. The opening lines of Keats's *Endymion*, for example:

> A thing of beauty is a joy for ever:
> Its loveliness increases; it will never
> Pass into nothingness. . . .
> Therefore, on every morrow, are we wreathing
> A flowery band to bind us to the earth. . . .

We are reminded of Petrarch's fourteenth canzone:

> Da' be' rami scendea,
> dolce ne la memoria,
> una pioggia di fior sovra 'l suo grembo,
> ed ella si sedea
> umile in tanta gloria,
> coverta già do l' amoroso nembo. . . .

It is perhaps enough for my thesis to stop here with the flowery band that binds us to the earth and the image of Laura covered with the petals of real flowers in a real garden at a real moment in time. I would not object to adding a reference to modern love poetry, but I would prefer out of sheer sentiment to defer until another time a consideration of the *sentio* as it is objectified in the poetry of the wasteland and the city of dreadful night.

III. Italian Tributes to Cardinal Pole

George B. Parks · *Professor Emeritus of English, Queens College, City University of New York*

Probably no Englishman in Italy before or since his time has been paid such tributes there as those received by Reginald Cardinal Pole (1500–58). Pole lived in Italy for twenty-six years (1521–26, 1532–53), nearly half his lifetime. Aided by being a second cousin of Henry VIII, he achieved intimacy with leaders in both church and state in Italy and was created cardinal in 1536. To escape Henry's subsequent wrath at his acceptance of this office, he remained in Italy in exile until the accession of Queen Mary permitted his return home to effect the reunion of the English Church with that of Rome. In his varied roles of scholar, prince, cardinal, and potential victim (as his family was actual victim) of a ruthless king, and finally as primate of England, Pole was the recipient of much praise. A good deal of it is highly mannered in expression, of course, but the earnestness of many of the tributes that were paid to him attests the strong appeal of his character.

The most striking tribute to Pole was paid in the papal conclave of 1549–50 when a majority of the cardinals, but not the required two-thirds, voted to elect him pope. He had had no appreciable experience of administration, he had not proved himself a spiritual leader, and he was not yet even a priest. Yet those who knew him all praised his spiritual nature. To Bishop Jovius, the historian, he was "il divin Reginaldo,"[1] and to Vittoria Colonna, poet and noblewoman, he was "il santo Polo."[2] Girolamo Seripando, experienced administrator and judge of men as general of the Augustinian monastic order, called him "non hominem, sed Angelum de Coelo" when Pole spoke of religious matters.[3] The mighty of this world spoke highly of him. Paul III, who had created him cardinal as one who would be useful in the reform of

---

1. Paolo Giovio, *Lettere*, ed. G. G. Ferrero (Rome, 1956—), Vol. II (1958), no. 218, 29: written 10 October 1545.

2. *Le Rime di Vittoria Colonna*, ed. Pietro Ercole Visconti (Rome, 1840), Parte seconda, sonnet 197, p. 357.

3. *Epistolarum Reginaldi Poli Collectio*, ed. A. M. Quirini, 5 vols. (Brescia, 1744–57), Vol. II (1745), "Praefatio," 4. This work hereinafter will be referred to as *Epistolae Poli*.

the Church, noted later that in the eyes of the world Pole was "superiore agli altri di nobiltà, bontà e dottrina."[4] Charles V is reported to have said that he did not know in all Christendom a better priest than the Cardinal of England.[5] Even the King of France, Henri II, at the very moment when he was blocking Pole's election because Pole was a protégé of the Emperor, recognized his "sincerity and integrity."[6]

To trace the growth of Pole's reputation to these heights, we return to the beginning of his long stay in Italy. At the age of twenty-one he went on from Oxford to Padua, where he read privately with a senior classical scholar, Leonico Tomeo. What he was like then may be judged in small part by the somewhat condescending remarks made of him by a scholar of some renown, the Belgian Christophe de Longueil (or Longolius), whom Pole generously befriended in his poverty by taking him into his house. Though grateful, Longolius could not help writing to a former patron, an older and worldlier person than Pole, that the young Englishman "is, it is true, a bright and certainly a learned youth, with acute perceptions; but he would not like our sort of talk and discussion, and he is notably reserved and silent."[7] What he did not find at Pole's table was the "good times" of the past, "occasions for laughing, talking, guessing, joking, and for all sweet and friendly discussion." Later in the letter it slips out that Leonico Tomeo dominated the conversation, and we can infer that Pole was unused to the give-and-take of student company, probably because he had lived at Oxford in the house of the president of Magdalen, and still perhaps spoke only when he was spoken to. Later witnesses were to note the complete ease and appeal of Cardinal Pole in any company.

4. Cited by Ludwig von Pastor from Lodovico Frati, *Archivio Storico Italiano*, 5 ser., Vol. 35 (1905), 449. Frati dates the remark before 1540, but Pastor after 1546 (*History of the Popes*, [London, 1951], XIII, 12).

5. Cited by Pole's biographer and longtime friend the Archbishop Lodovico Beccadelli in his *Vita*, in *Epistolae Poli* (V, 391): "Io non conosco in tutto il Christianesimo il miglior Prete del Cardinale d'Inghilterra. . . ."

6. The King's instructions to his agent D'Urfé in Rome, in Guillaume Ribier, *Lettres et mémoires d'estat* (Blois, 1666), II, 258.

7. *Christophori Longolii Orationes duae* (Florence, 1524; facs. ed., Farnborough, Hants., 1967), fol. 119[r], letter to Stefano Sauli:

Nam Polus noster est quidem ille ingeniosus et mehercule doctus, et elegantissimi iudicii adolescens, sed qui neque istius modi disputationibus ac nunciis magnopere capiatur, et mira quadam etiam tum modestia tum taciturnitate sit praeditus. . . . Dii immortales, quae tempora, quos risus, quantam sermonem coniecturarum, iocorum, amicissimarum atque suavissimarum inter nos concertationum facultatem amisimus. Quod ipsum hoc molestius tuli quod nemo fere hic fuit, quicum his de rebus familiariter communicarem. . . .

It may be that this shyness which we here infer also made a first impression on Bembo, the leading man of letters in Venice, to whom Longolius introduced Pole. Toward the end of Pole's first Paduan stay, Bembo wrote of "Monsignor d'Inghilterra" that he was "il più virtuoso e dotto e grave giovane che oggi forse sia in tutta Italia."[8] It is of course the "grave" (serious) that suggests a certain diffidence; the other epithets suggest that Bembo did not forget that the young man was of royal blood. At any rate, he became one of Pole's sponsors, and six of his extant letters to Pole before 1526 include highly complimentary remarks, as do three more after Pole's return in 1532. Another letter to a third person may carry Bembo's frank judgment of Pole on the latter's appointment as cardinal in 1536. "I take loving pleasure," he wrote, "in the creation of Mons. Pole, whose excellence in learning and whose infinite virtue deserved no less distinguished an honor."[9]

So the chief qualities of Pole seem to have been perceived as learning and virtue. This was the official view of the Republic of Venice, as seen in the Doge's letter of congratulation on the cardinalate. He "whom we have always highly valued and held most dear, " he wrote, was now rightly honored by his new place among those "outstanding in either learning or virtue."[10] Since Pole had as yet no achievement to point to, the tribute could hardly say more, as its "either . . . or" could hardly say less. Pole must have been grateful for the assurance that he had always been welcome in Venice. At any rate, he praised both the unmatched excellence of the University of Padua and the warm friendship of the Venetians.

Pole's special Italian friends were churchmen of an earlier generation. He was born in 1500, when Contarini was seventeen, Sadoleto twenty-three, and Bembo thirty. The former two were among the new cardinals specially chosen like Pole as devoted to reform of the Church, and they became his personal friends and sponsors. We should add to these the devoted Bishop of Verona, Gianmatteo Giberti; Gregorio Cortese,

---

8. *Lettere*, III, [iv], written 17 July 1526, to Cardinal Cibò, in *Opere* (Milan, 1809), V, 89–90.

9. *Lettere*, III, [xviii], to Francesco Maria Molza, written 1 January 1537, in *Opere*, VII, 108: "m'è dolce e cara stata la creazione di Mons. Polo a cui per la sua eccellente dottrina e per l'infinita bontà non si conveniva men chiaro ed illustre grado."

10. *Epistolae Poli*, II, "Epistolae" i, p. 1: congratulating him, "quem plurimi semper fecimus, charumque in primis habuimus," who has been chosen cardinal, joining "tales viros, qualis ipse es, vel doctrina, vel morum sanctitate excellentes. . . ." The date is 5 January 1536[–7].

Benedictine abbot; and of course Bishop Carafa of Chieti, who was, paradoxically, to become Pole's bitter enemy.

It was Bembo who introduced Pole to both Sadoleto and Giberti, who were then, early in the 1520s, in Rome. When Pole returned from England in 1531, stopping in Avignon until late 1532, Sadoleto became closely acquainted with the Englishman. Strong affection at once developed between Pole and Sadoleto, and the latter wrote to Giberti that Pole exhibited "high intelligence and an excellent knowledge of Greek and Latin, with an exceptionally high standard of behavior and excellent manners."[11] Pole had become adult and we do not hear again about any obvious stiffness of manner.

Sadoleto's affection grew yet warmer after the two men had further association, both now cardinals, in Rome and Carpentras. "Our affection," wrote Sadoleto in 1540, "is lodged not in paper or in ink, but in both our hearts, and not merely written there but burnt in so that it cannot be erased."[12] To esteem and affection Sadoleto was to add a picture of happy friendship. In sending a letter of greeting to Pole on the latter's return to Rome in 1540, he rejoiced that "immediately on arrival you have met the two luminaries of our order, Contarini and Bembo, and you have been received with great joy and mirth by these best, most affectionate, and most distinguished men."[13] A little later Sadoleto was to praise not merely "la dolcissima, & utilissima conuersatione del Reverendiss. sig. nostro Polo," but also "quei nostri virtuosi, & dolcissimi compagni"[14] in the household of Pole at Viterbo, where Pole spent his most congenial years (1541–47). And to all this assurance of warm and congenial friendship Sadoleto had added still another tie, that of pitying sympathy. When Pole received news of the execution by Henry VIII of Pole's kinsmen—his brother, his cousin, and eventually his mother—Sadoleto wrote to Contarini:

11. *Ibid.*, I, 276: "cum summum ingenium, & excellentem in Graecis Latinisque scientiam, tum vero summam in moribus & congressu elegantiam, atque humanitatem."

12. *Jacopi Sadoleti Opera* (Verona, 1738), II, "Epistolae," bk. xiii, epist. [v], p. 49, written 3 kal. Feb. 1540: "non est in chartis, neque in atramento positus noster amor: sed in cordibus utriusque nostrum, non tam inscriptus ille quidem, quam inustus, ut deleri non possit."

13. *Ibid.*, "Epistolae," bk. xiii., epist. [v], p. 50: "quod ipse primo in introitu in duo lumina nostri ordinis incideris, Contarenum & Bembum, quod fueris ab optimis, amicissimis, praestantissimisque hominibus summa cum laetitia & hilaritate acceptus, & gratulor tibi, & mihi plurimum gaudeo." The letter was written on 24 April 1540.

14. *Lettere di XIII Huomini Illustri* (Venice, 1571), p. 221.

Our Pole, who has just departed, left me with so great a sense of loss that I cannot summon my thoughts from reflection and sorrow. I am moved not only by affection for him, but by pity for his most undeserved fortune. That such a man should be so bitterly tried makes fortune appear a total enemy of virtue.[15]

The same and even stronger pitying affection will be apparent in Vittoria Colonna.

A still more intimate friend of Pole was Bishop Giberti of Verona, who like Sadoleto was much admired for his devotion to the duties of his diocese. Pole traveled with Giberti to Rome in October of 1536, and Giberti accompanied Pole on his long diplomatic mission to Paris and Liège, which took up most of 1537. Although no statement of Giberti's affection for Pole appears to be extant, we must infer a strong feeling from Pole's own expression in 1539 of his desire to leave Rome and retire to Verona, where he could "enjoy solitude, yet [be] favored by the affection and infinite kindness of this excellent bishop."[16]

As Bembo was Pole's first sponsor in Venice, Contarini was his principal sponsor in Rome. Many letters passed between them as Pole followed the efforts of Contarini in a hoped-for rapprochement with the Protestants. The letters generally concerned business, however, rather than friendship. It was in late 1534 that Pole wrote to Sadoleto that he was leaving Padua for Venice and the company of two men: Bishop Carafa, "vir sanctissimus, & doctissimus," and Contarini, not yet cardinal, who had "full knowledge of all the most eminent arts, whether invented by the human mind or given us by divine benevolence: he possesses also every ornament of virtue."[17] Contarini's impression of Pole is first revealed in a letter of 1535 to the Emperor, to whom he had been Venetian ambassador. He called the young Englishman the model of a pious Christian, desirous of being a fighter for the true faith,

15. *Opera*, II, "Epistolae," bk. xiii, epist. iii, p. 46, written 8 October 1539:

Polus noster, qui a nobis hinc discessit, ita magnum sui mihi reliquit desiderium, ut a cogitatione & dolore avocare animum non possim. Non solum enim benevolentia erga illum moveor, verum etiam indignissimae illius fortunae misericordia: quae talem virum tam acerbe opprimit, ut omnino virtuti inimicam se offerre videatur.

16. *Epistolae Poli*, II, "Epistolae," lxxxiv, 200, 17 October 1539: "godendo la solitudine accompagnata dall'amorevolezza, e bontà infinita di questo dabenissimo Vescovo."

17. *Ibid.*, I, "Epistolae," xvi, p. 417, dated "15 kal. Octobr." 1534: "Contarenus, Patricius Venetus. . . .qui ad praestantissimarum artium omnium, quaecunque vel humano genio inventae, vel divino beneficio nobis datae sunt, perfectam cognitionem, omne virtutis decus adjunctum habet. . . ."

fearless, ready to suffer like the first Christians for the Savior.[18] This is a decidedly limited portrait of Pole, and we realize that Contarini was here writing a covering letter for one of Pole's to the Emperor, which proposed rather desperate missions to England to save it for the Church. Surely we may wonder whether the veteran diplomat took Pole altogether seriously, since the Emperor in turn did not, and even forbade Pole to travel through his domain toward England.

What Contarini really thought of Pole is a matter of deeds, not words. As a leader of Church reform, and made so officially by the cardinalate, he brought Pole to Rome to serve on the reform commission, and it is fairly certain that he proposed Pole for the cardinalate. His relations with Pole were not only official, however, and we may certainly discover warmth and affection in their relationship. When in 1537 Pole returned from the mission to the Low Countries, Contarini's brother and brother-in-law hastened to meet him as soon as they learned that he had arrived in Verona. "I embraced them," wrote Pole, "with as great joy, and I felt my soul pour forth, as I used to feel with relatives and neighbors when I saw them after a long interval; these your relatives seemed to have been transformed by God into the likeness of mine."[19]

I have already quoted Sadoleto's forecast of the joyous meeting in Rome in 1540 of Pole with Contarini and Bembo. By that time Pole's first missions to France and Spain had proved ineffective in restoring the Roman Church in Britain, and he was presently (1541) to accept a sinecure in Viterbo. We hear less about him now from his seniors, who begin to die off, and Pole's personal qualities become more evident. It is true that the poet Marco Antonio Flaminio, whom Pole took into his *familia* to save him from heresy, and who lived with him until his death in 1550, made only passing references to Pole, but doubtless Pole would not have wished more formal ones. Flaminio's inscription for Pole's portrait has only four lines:

> Si velut egregia pictura, maxime Pole,
> Est expressa tui corporis effigies:

---

18. *Calendar of . . . State Papers, Spanish*, ed. Pascual de Gayangos, vol. V, i (London, 1886), item 172, pp. 485–486, an English version of the Contarini letter, written in Italian, in the Simancas archives.

19. *Epistolae Poli*, II, "Epistolae," xxxvii, p. 90, written 30 September 1537: "haud alio, mihi crede, genere gaudii illos amplexans animum mihi profundi sentiebam, quam quo solebam perfundi parentes, & propinquos ex longo intervallo videns, quos in horum similes Deus transtulisse videtur."

> Sic divina tuae potuisset mentis imago
> Pingi, nil oculi pulchrius aspicerent.[20]

Quite as conventional, if more ingenious, is the one full statement on Pole in a poem about the summer heat. This allows Flaminio to say,

> malim aduri
> Ardenti Libyae, Indiaeve ab aestu,
> Quam magni alloquiis carere Poli,
> Qui virtute sua, suoque miro
> Cepit sic animum meum lepore,
> Ut illo sine mella amara, Soles
> Obscuri, nivea atra, ver amoenum
> Horridum mihi sit, diesque longo
> Anno longior.[21]

Another mannered poem urges the summer breeze to seek out and cool the fiery heat that threatens Pole's tender limbs (I, xxxvii, "Ad Auram de Reginaldo Polo," pp. 39–40).

We may find more interest in records that suggest the quality of life of the Pole household. Several of Flaminio's verses to friends offer a cool retreat at Viterbo, the company of friends, and books in profusion in both Latin and Greek. An earlier account of the daily life of Pole's mission to the Low Countries in 1537, when the envoys were refused admission to court and had little to do, may set the pattern of the routine. It is the work of Pole's devoted friend and follower, the Venetian patrician Priuli.[22] The scene is Liège. After mass, the company dined; St. Bernard was read aloud during the meal, and there was discussion; afterward Bishop Giberti read a chapter of Eusebius for

20. *Carminum Libri VIII* (Padua, 1727), bk. ii, xvii, p. 73:

> Great Pole, your body's image shows
> Impressive in this picture's pose;
> Could the painter show your heavenly soul,
> Eyes could not find a fairer scroll.

21. *Ibid.*, bk. v, xiii, p. 157:

> I would rather burn
> In the ardent heat of Libya or India
> Than miss the talk of our great Pole,
> Whose virtue and admirable charm
> Have so taken me that without him
> Honey is bitter, the sun dark, snow black,
> Gentle spring rough, and one day longer
> Than a whole year.

22. *Epistolae Poli*, II, "Diatriba," pp. civ–cv.

further discussion, which may have gone on for more than an hour. After vespers in midafternoon, Pole read aloud until suppertime from the Epistles of St. Paul. "This holy reading," wrote Priuli, "is done by this holy man with so great reverence and humility and judgment that I could ask nothing better, and I am sure that I was not misled by affection."

A Flemish clerical visitor added an important comment. After reading aloud,

Pole talked to the company, and although they might go on to other matters, yet these were matters of religion and learning, so that one came away either better or more learned, indeed both better and more learned. . . . It is pleasanter to talk of this Pole, of his household which is like him, modest, quiet, perfectly schooled in the three tongues. . . . If the other Fathers in Council [of Trent] are like him, I shall be surprised if the Council will not indeed assemble with the Holy Spirit as its inspiration. . . .[23]

The visitor was clearly impressed by the reading and the discussion during and after meals, a custom which was common in Italy, though apparently not in the Low Countries.

At Viterbo Pole arranged his afternoons, as he wrote to Contarini in 1541:

The rest of the day I pass in the religious and useful company of Signor Carnesecchi and our Marco Antonio Flaminio. I call it useful because in the evening Messer Marco Antonio gives . . . to me and to most of my *familia* . . . that food which is immortal . . . so that I do not know when I have felt greater consolation or edification.[24]

The "food" furnished by Flaminio may have been his continuing work on the Psalms, the commentaries that supplemented his earlier translations into Latin, or else the "Carmina Sacra," the last section of his verse. We may hope that the Cardinal enjoyed also the cheerful poems written by Flaminio for Pole's kitten, especially the "Catella ad Reginaldum Polum" (I, xxxv, p. 37). The kitten complains that Pole, despite his benignity, will not let her ride to Rome with him in his litter.

23. From a letter by Gerard Morinck, ed. Henry de Vocht, in *Monumenta Humanistica Lovaniensia* (Louvain, 1934), pp. 577–578. I translate from his Latin.

24. *Epistolae Poli*, III, xxiii, p. 42: "Il resto del giorno passo con questa santa & utile compagnia del sig. Carnesecchi, & Mʳ Marco Antonio Flaminio nostro. Utile io chiamo, perche la sera poi Mʳ Marco Antonio da pasto a me, & alla miglior parte della famiglia de illo cibo, qui non perit, in tal maniera che io non so quando io abbia sentito maggior consolatione, ne maggior edificatione."

> Cur me, Pole, tua venire ad urbem
> Lectica prohibes? tuae quid, oro,
> Summae participem benignitatis
> Esse non pateris?

The dogs of heroes accompany them to the heavens, she argues, and why are not cats treated correspondingly? Why is she not allowed to ride in a corner and keep his feet warm? Clearly the kitten adds an intimate touch to a somewhat too contemplative picture.

Before proceeding to opinions of Pole as a spiritual leader, we should have a summary view of his private personality. I quote such a statement by his biographer Lodovico Beccadelli, himself an influential prelate and longtime friend. Despite Pole's small income, wrote Beccadelli,

when he needed to display splendor in some fashion, he did it lavishly according to his means, revealing the lordly character which he showed from infancy. He was above all the soul of modesty, and never angry: so much so that to some he appeared at times too humble; but following a great example, that is the blessed Jesus Christ, he took no offense and did not put himself forward. He was friendly, gay in speech, and because of familiarity with worldly matters and much reading, he could be entertaining in a fine way, and was so, among other things. I have never known a man with such *bons mots* and figures of speech; they flourished in his style with no sign of affectation, and their seed is evident in his writings. . . . He was a truly sincere friend, an enemy of adulation and of dissimulation, but he spoke his mind with such grace that he never offended those whom he spoke against. . . . His courage was so great that I am almost bold to say that he had no equal in our day. It was not a philosophical courage or a military, but entirely founded in God. . . . And he therefore endured calumny, exile, persecutions, and death of friends and family with intrepid courage.[25]

---

25. Beccadelli, *Vita Poli*, in *Epistolae Poli*, V, 384–385, 386, 388:

Et quando occoreva usar magnificenza in qualche maniera, lo faceva secondo il poter suo splendidamente, mostrando l'animo signorile, che dalle fasce portava. Modestissimo fu sopra tutto, & senza ira: talchè ad alcuni parve alcuna volta d'animo troppo humile, ma esso c'haveva un grande exempio innanzi, ch'era Jesu Christo benedetto, non si risentiva delle offese, nè si metteva innanzi. Era piacevole, & di conversatione gioconda, & per esser molto pratico nelle cose del mondo, & haver letto assai, con bella maniera sapeva intrattener ognuno, & lo faceva. Et fra l'altre cose non conobbi mai huomo c'havesse più pronti bei motti, & comparationi di lui; pareva che nella sua bocca fiorissero senza affetatione alcuna, & se ne vede ancho il seme sparso per le sue scritture. . . . Era veramente amico sincero, nimico della adulatione, & della bugia, ma diceva le opinioni sue con tanta grazia, che nè anco offendeva quelli a cui contradiceva. . . . La fortezza dell'animo suo fu di tal sorte, che forse ardisco dire, che non hebbe pari a' dì nostri; non era fortezza filosophica, o militare, ma tutta fondata in Dio. . . . Et per questo supportava calunnie, exilio, persecutioni, & morte d'amici, & parenti con animo intrepido.

If we now put together these several judgments of Cardinal Pole, we find a man of easy manner, affable, tactful, and gifted; modest, however, and even humble, given over to study and prayer; a man upright, truthful, and possessing the natural courage and endurance of a martyr; a man appropriately called saintly. There remains the consideration of Pole as leader, whether in spiritual appeal or in public accomplishment, a man who might be thought of as *papabile*, a possible pope. We do not know when Pole was first looked at in this light, but it would certainly not have been before the 1540s.

In this respect we discover two enthusiastic witnesses whose tributes to Pole pass beyond praise to exaltation. One enthusiast was a poet, Vittoria Colonna, the long-widowed Marchesa of Pescara. She was nearing the age of fifty in the late 1530s when she met Pole in Rome; he was ten years younger. In 1540 she mentioned her acquaintance with him: "I speak often with the Most Reverend Pole, whose conversation is always of heaven, and only to help others does he see and note earth."[26] This is the significant note of otherworldliness that befits the spiritual leader, and the Marchesa was presently to define the leader's complete role. Meantime, she discovered that he had his own earthly trials: a brother and a cousin executed in 1538, and his mother in prison from May 1539 to her execution in May 1541. The Marchesa offered her consolation, suggesting even her willingness to be a second mother to him.[27] A recent biographer of Pole, Wilhelm Schenk (1950), discovered the theme in one of her sonnets; and I find that another sonnet sounds the same theme. I give the sonnets here, also venturing an English translation of both poems.

> Figlio e signor, se la tua prima e vera
> Madre vive prigion, non l'è già tolto
> L'anima saggia, o 'l chiaro spirto sciolto,
> Nè di tanta virtù l'invitta schiera.
>
> A me, che sembro andar scarca e leggiera
> E 'n poca terra ho il cor chiuso e sepolto,

26. *Carteggio di Vittoria Colonna*, ed. E. Ferrero and G. Müller (Turin, 1889), epist. cxii, p. 187, 15 February 1540: "Ne ragiono assai col reverendissimo Polo, la cui conversazione è sempre in cielo, et solo per l'altrui utilità riguarda et cura la terra. . . ." The letter, to the Queen of Navarre, was first published in Venice in 1542 in *Lettere volgari di diversi nobilissimi huomini*, fol. 126ᵛ.

27. No extant letter of hers bears this message, but Pole's answer refers to it: *Epistolae Poli*, III, "Epistolae," xlvi, pp. 77–80, n.d.; also in *Carteggio di Vittoria Colonna*, no. cxxxix, pp. 231–235.

Convien ch'abbi talor l'occhio rivolto,
Che la novella tua madre non pera.

Tu per gli aperti spaziosi campi
Del ciel cammini, e non piu nebbia o pietra
Ritarda o ingrombra il tuo spedito corso.
Io grave d'anni aghiaccio! Or tu, ch'avvampi
D'alma fiamma celeste, umil m'impetra
Del commun Padre eterno omai soccorso.[28]

   Con un'immagine del Redentore

Perchè la mente vostra, ornata e cinta
D'eterno lume, serbi la sembianza
Del gran motor nella più interna stanza
Ove albergar non puote immagin finta;
Forse da quella ardente voglia spinta,
Che mai non s'empie, anzi ad ognor s'avanza,
Con esser suol di veri amanti usanza,
Aggradir la potrebbe anco dipinta.

Ciò pensando, signor, la vostra umile
Nova madre ed ancella ora v'invia

28. *Le Rime di Vittoria Colonna*, Parte seconda, no. 199 (Rome, 1840), p. 359:

> My son and lord, even if your first and real
> Mother lies in prison, yet her wise soul,
> Her clear and nimble spirit, have not left her,
> Nor the invincible army of her virtues.
>
> To me, who may seem to be free and not bound down
> (Although my heart is buried in a grave),
> Yet I am bound to my new obligation
> To keep your new mother ever at her task.
>
> You travel through the open and spacious fields
> Of Heaven, where neither rocky ways nor clouds
> Will slow or hinder your inevitable way.
> I, now heavy with years, have turned to ice,
> While you burn with heavenly flame: pray now for me
> To our common Father eternal for His aid.

Another edition (*Rime e Lettere*, Florence, 1860) gives the sonnet the heading "In Morte del Marchese Del Vasto." Del Vasto was a younger cousin, Alfonso (1502–46), of Vittoria's husband (died 1525), and had inherited from him the title of Marchese of Pescara. The sonnet could not have been addressed to him after his death since he would not then need an earthly mother. It would not have been addressed to him before his death because he is not likely to have had a mother in prison, and because he was a most successful soldier and imperial official rather than devoutly other-worldly. For the same reasons, the sonnet would not have been addressed to his son Ferdinando Francesco (died 1571), of the same name as Vittoria's husband.
   The sonnet fully fits an ascription to Pole; his mother lay in prison from 1539 to 1541, and Vittoria is known by other evidence to have offered to be his second mother.

L'opra ch'in voi miglior mastro scolpío;
Pregandovi ch'a dir grave non sia,
Se questa in parte a quell'altra è simile,
Cui sempre mira il vostro alto desio.[29]

It is to be noted that in the first sonnet the real mother is still living, in prison, while in the second sonnet she is not mentioned. For that matter, the role of the second mother is merely to look at the male figure, whose abode in heaven requires his heroic journey, or who on earth is inspired by the image of Christ in his heart and by the flame in his soul. A third sonnet (no. 197, p. 357) in memory of Archbishop Federigo Fregoso (died 1541), brings in

il divin Polo
Che va sopra le stelle altero e solo,

also on his journey above the stars. So far he is a remote and heroic figure. Intimacy appears, however, in the letter of the Marchesa on the death of Cardinal Contarini (in 1542), written to his sister Serafina Contarini, lamenting

quel perfettissimo fratel suo et signor mio, hor che altra spiritual servitù non mi resta, che questa dell'illustriss. et reverendiss. monsignor d'Inghilterra, suo unico, intimo et verissimo amico et più che fratello et figlio. . . .[30]

"Servitù" may translate as "obedience," which she owes to her one remaining spiritual guide.

29. *Ibid.* (the 1840 edition), Parte seconda, no. 205, p. 365.

With a Portrait of the Redeemer

Because your spirit, adorned and girded with
Eternal light, ever preserves the likeness
Of the divine Mover in that inmost mind
Which could not harbor a fictitious image:
Perhaps to one urged on by that flaming will
Which is never content but always presses on,
As reality shows in the practice of true lovers,
Even a picture could give the spirit pleasure.

It is with this thought, my lord, that your own humble
New mother and servant now sends on to you
A picture (outdone by the better artist who shaped you).
She begs you not to reproach her if this picture
Only slightly resembles that heavenly one
Which always claims your first devoted love.

I am indebted to my colleague Professor Daniel J. Donno for aid in these translations.
30. *Carteggio di Vittoria Colonna*, epist. cxlvii, pp. 251–252: autumn 1542.

We can imagine that Pole was much averse to this continuing language of exalted praise. Certainly he had tried to reduce it in his reply to the Marchesa's letter of condolence on his mother's death. Her letter is not extant, but the length, and we may say also the breadth, of his reply point to indirect rebuke.[31] He thanked "Your Excellency" for her prayers as well as for those of the nuns in whose convent she lived, as if they were of equal importance. For her offer of maternal aid, he called himself in some degree fortunate that though he had lost a mother to a raging Pharaoh, he had not been abandoned, but, like another victim-to-be of Pharaoh, Moses, had indeed been rescued by the daughter of the Great King. This complicated reply certainly disclaimed any pretense of filial intimacy.

What the Marchesa was allowed to say further to the heroic journeyer beyond the stars may be seen at length in a letter of the year 1543 in which she explained to him the nature of her dependence.

Our Lord above knows, however, that my desire to speak with your lordship is not excessive, because I see in you an order of spirit of which only spirit is aware, and which always draws me up to that fullness of light. It does not allow me to dwell too much on my own wretchedness, but rather with much high substantial thought reveals to me the greatness of things above and our lowliness and nothingness, and it sees that we ourselves and all created things serve us to this end, that we must find ourselves only in Him who is all things. And when, helped by this grace, I hasten toward Him, so much the more need have I to speak to your lordship: not because of anxiety or doubts or trouble which I have or fear to have, because His kindness is sure; but because whenever your lordship speaks of that most stupendous sacrifice, of eternal destiny, of being loved from the beginning, of what has been hidden and now is found in these mountains, harbors, and fountains; and when you write, you always turn the sword of the Word against every [vain] confidence of ours: always you cause the soul to rise on wings, assured of flying to the desired nest. So that speaking with your lordship is like speaking with an intimate friend of the Spouse, Who will prepare me by this means, Who calls me to Him, and desires that your lordship speak to kindle me and to comfort me. . . .[32]

31. *Epistolae Poli*, III, "Epistolae," xlvi, pp. 77–80: written 1542.
32. *Carteggio*, epist. cliv, pp. 263–264:

sa il Signor Nostro che per altro non desidero excessivamente di parlar con V. S., se non perchè vedo in lui un ordine di spirito, che solo lo spirito lo sente, e sempre mi tira in su a quell' amplitudine di luce, che non mi lassa troppo fermare nella miseria propria, anzi con sì alti substanziosi concepti mi mostra la grandezza di lassù e la bassezza e nihilità nostra, che, vedendo noi stessi et tutte le cose create servirci a questo, bisogna trovarci solo in colui, che è ogni cosa. Et quanto io per gratia sua caminassi presto verso lui, tanto più ho di bisogno di

She summed up what he had done for her otherwise: "I . . . am indebted to his reverend lordship for both the salvation of my soul and the health of my body."[33]

Such tributes from the Marchesa of Pescara affirm the capacity of Cardinal Pole for private spiritual leadership. For his capacity for public spiritual leadership we call upon the testimony of the energetic churchman Girolamo Seripando, later a cardinal. Seven years older than Pole, he was the intellectual in action, being general of the Augustinian order, a skillful drafter and harmonizer of doctrinal statements in the Council of Trent, and the effective leader of the reform delegates.[34] Making Pole's acquaintance presumably in the early 1540s, he wrote to a friend in 1544 his high appraisal of Pole:

Pole . . . is a man of proven virtue, of truly Christian piety, of outstanding learning: his civilized character and holiest virtue are so approved by all good men that whoever does not revere and esteem him cannot be counted among good men. Certainly I will never in anything think myself more fortunate than that this man eminent in all manner of virtue has honored me with his domestic intimacy and admitted me to his friendship. As often as I hear him speak of divine matters, I seem to be listening not to a man but to an angel from heaven bringing the eternal gospel to mankind. I would never fall silent if I tried to tell all the thoughts that come to mind in thinking of his uprightness and saintly life and his patience in adversity, which is the distinguishing virtue of a Christian.[35]

parlare alla Vostra Signoria, non per anxia, nè dubbi, nè molestia, che abbia, nè tema d'havere per bontà di colui, che ne assecura, ma perchè ogni volta che la Vostra Signoria parli di quel stupendissimo sacrificio della eterna destinazione, dell'essere preamati e di quel viene ascondito trovato su quelli monti, porti et fonte [sic], che scrive, con sempre convertire il gladio del verbo contra ogni nostra confidentia, fa star l'anima sull'ali, sicura di volar al desiderato nido; sì che tanto è a me parlare con Vostra Signoria come con un intimo amico del sposo che mi prepara per questo mezzo, et mi chiama a lui et vol che ne ragioni per accendermi e consolarmi. . . .

33. *Carteggio,* epist. cxlii, p. 239: to Giulia Gonzaga, 8 December 1541: " . . . sono a Sua Signoria reverendissima della salute dell'anima e di quella del corpo obbligato." (He had advised her against excessive fasting and other mortification.)

34. Hubert Jedin, *Girolamo Seripando* (Würzburg, 1937, 2 vols.). The English version (London, 1947) lacks some of the documentation.

35. Seripando to St. Thomas de Villanova, Archbishop of Valencia, 28 November 1544, in *Epistolae Poli,* II, "Praefatio," p. 4:

RAYNALDUS POLUS, Angliae Cardinalis, Vir spectatae virtutis, pietatis vere Christianae, & doctrinae singularis; de cuius humanitate, & sanctissimis moribus, tanta est apud bonos omnes opinio, ut qui hunc non colit & observat, in bonorum numero haberi non possit. Ego certe nulla re unquam me existimabo feliciorem, atque hac, quod Vir hic in omni virtutum genere maximus, sua me consuetudine domestica dignetur, & in suam admittat familiaritatem: quem quoties de divinis loquentem audio, non hominem, sed Angelum de Coelo Evangelium aeternum ad homines afferentem, mihi audire videor. Numquam silerem, si quaecumque mihi in mentem veniunt de Raynaldi Poli innocentia, & vitae sanctimonia, ac patientia in rebus adversis, quae una Christiani hominis egregia virtus est, enarrare vellem.

At the start of the Council of Trent, Seripando kept a diary of some scope. Looking back thence to the attempted beginning of the Council in 1542, he wrote of Pole as one of the three directing legates: "Pole, a man remarkable for virtue, holiness, and his knowledge of a pure and holy theology. . . ."[36] Thinking of him again, he wrote: "Pole, whom a little earlier we described in full colors as well as we could; to explain his uprightness and holiness no eloquence would suffice."[37]

If Pole's private talk excited Seripando to this extent, his public speeches at the Council of Trent aroused the same excitement in many delegates. Seripando wrote in his diary a long account of Pole's first official speech, the opening sermon, on 6 January 1546, a "keynote speech" as we would call it.[38] It challenged each delegate to consider that churchmen themselves were responsible for the plight of the "almost fallen" Church. Seripando exclaimed of this "divinae orationis" that it aroused the delegates to think of the larger issues; he himself "was so animated and inflamed" that he resolved to take only truth and God for his guides, and to defy either fear or favor in his voting. Pole's "admonitio" to the delegates was at once published.

On 13 January, Pole joined the other legates in denouncing the "disgraceful and wretched ambition of trivial men, disturbing most important matters" by dwelling on technicalities. Seripando wrote that Pole,

though he spoke sparingly, was both avidly looked to by all, and most attentively heard. His speech was pure, wise, adorned by choice words and solemn thoughts, and (as rather divine than human) filled not only our ears but our hearts and minds. For what he presented here, among other things, how true, how sincere, how effective! . . . All good men were greatly pleased by this speech. The few others, though they had been most talkative, were overcome, and remained silent.[39]

36. *Concilium Tridentinum* (Freiburg, 1911), II, 404: "Polum denique, virum innocentia, sanctitate, sanctaeque et purae theologiae doctrina insignem. . . ."
37. *Ibid.*, II, 406: "Polum denique illum, quem paulo ante quoad potuimus suis coloribus depinximus, in cuius explicanda probitate et sanctimonia eloquentia ipsa deficeret."
38. *Ibid.*, II, 415–416, 7 January 1546.
39. *Ibid.*, II, 422–423, 13 January 1546:

qui cum parcius et rarius loqueretur, et ab omnibus avidissime expectabatur et attentissime audiebatur. Erat eius oratio pura, prudens, selectis verbis gravissimisque sententiis tanquam luminibus ornata, et, quod divinum est potius quam humanum, non in aures modo, sed in corda atque animos influebat. Illud enim, quod hoc loco inter caetera attulit, quam verum, quam sincerum, quantae fuit efficacitatis! . . . Bonis omnibus haec oratio vehementer placuit. Pauci illi, tametsi loquacissimi essent homines, obstupescentes obmutuere.

Another diarist, Severolus, also summarized Pole's speech, ignoring the other two legates, because the English Cardinal spoke "piously, as always."[40] This time, it is clear, pious or not, Pole denounced where before he had exhorted.

Since Seripando soon gave up his extensive note-taking, we have less information on the effect of Pole's personality at Trent during the six months before he resigned. At any rate, Seripando amply demonstrated the spiritual leadership that made Pole seem *papabile*. That Seripando was to be to a degree the voice of Pole in the later sessions of the Council is perhaps the strongest sign of his admiration.

A less subtle observer was Giovanni Della Casa (1503–56), Archbishop of Benevento and a frequent papal nuncio. The author of *Il Galateo*, Della Casa twice paid high though undistinguished compliments to Pole. The first was published in 1533 in a verse prefatory to the Latin version of the Psalms by the Fleming Campensis. This scholar was favored by Pole, as we learn from Della Casa's poem:

> Praecipue magnus Polus, quo doctior alter
> Non est, aut melior, nec erit post tempore longo.[41]

In 1550, at the height of Pole's fame, Della Casa returned to the task. In his *Vita Bembi* he linked Pole with several of the newer cardinals and referred to him as "a man brought undoubtedly by the will of immortal God from farthest Britain, or rather dropped from heaven (if one may say so): . . . no one will ever sufficiently praise his distinguished and clearly divine virtue."[42]

The climax of literary tributes to Pole in his *papabile* years is perhaps to be found in a sonnet by Bernardo Cappello, a Venetian poet (1495–1565) in exile in the Papal States. The poem, in a collection of largely occasional *Rime*, is skillfully climactic and apt in focusing on the spiritual leadership of the Cardinal. Because it suggests that Pole was destined to be pope, it should doubtless be dated about 1549.

> Due Poli ha'l cielo: & l'uno & l'altro degno
> D'altera lode, & d'immortal honore:
> Poiche ciascun col chiaro suo splendore

40. *Ibid.*, I, 19.
41. *Epistolae Poli*, I, 335.
42. *Ibid.*, p. 330: "tum vero praecipue a Reginaldo Polo, homine, Dei immortalis, dubio procul, beneficio, ex ultima usque Britannia ad nos vecto, vel de coelo potius, si modo dictu fas est, lapso; cujus . . . de tam praeclara, ac plane divina virtute nemo satis digne umquam loquetur. . . ."

È di chi scolca l'onde amico segno.
Un n'ha la terra; che di Pietro al legno
Scorta prepare il saggio alto Fattore;
Di piu bel lume, & di maggior ualore,
Et di charità vera ornato, & pregno.

Questo non, come quei, sua luce porge
A chi'l mondo ueder procaccia, & farsi
Trauagliando nel mar ricco, & possente:
Ma di bell'opre entro a la nostra mente
Thesor facendo, al ciel co i rai la scorge:
C'haue in lui Dio, come in suo specchio, sparsi.[43]

There was to be more Italian praise of Cardinal Pole on his mission to England to restore the English Church to Roman allegiance. Before passing on to that matter, however, we should note the appearance of serious danger to him within the Roman Church itself, a danger that in the end threatened not only his liberty but his very life. We do not need to repeat here the history of Pole's outspokenness at the Council of Trent, which at once led to the charge of heretical doctrine close to Protestantism. The story of Pole's thought has now been ably told by Dermot Fenlon,[44] and we note here only the consequent disparagement as anti-tribute. The public attack on Pole as heretic was made by Cardinal Carafa at the opening of the conclave of 1549–50 and must have helped to bar Pole from election to the papal throne. Moreover,

43. Cappello, *Rime* (Venice, 1560), p. 175. The word "scolca" in the fourth line is presumably an error for "solca." I am indebted to Professor Donno for this note and for help in translation:

Heaven has two Poles, and both are counted worthy
Of highest praise and of immortal honor:
For each one in his ever-shining splendor
Is a friendly sign to him who ploughs the sea.
One is on earth, and the great and wise Creator
Prepares his escort to the bark of Peter.
He is of brightest light and greatest worthiness,
Stored and adorned with truest charity.

He does not shed his light only to aid
The traveler who sails the world to grow
Wealthy and powerful by his toil at sea;
Our star lights up the good deeds in our hearts,
And guides them heavenward in those bright rays
Which capture as in a mirror God's own light.

A colleague has pointed out to me that the sonnet derives its background from the image in Petrarch's Sonnet 4 of "questo e quell' altro emispero."

44. *Heresy and Obedience in Tridentine Italy: Cardinal Pole and the Counter Reformation* (Cambridge, 1972).

this attack speedily became public knowledge, as we learn from the
pasquinades on the conclave. In one collection Pole was freely called
"Lutheran," "l'Inglese/Ch'è Lutherano palese" (openly Lutheran).[45]
Moreover, Italian Protestants in exile blamed him as a "nicodemist"—
that is, a secret Protestant who refused to acknowledge his Protestant
faith by choosing exile.

One ironic echo much later of these Italian controversies may be
noted here. The life of Pole by his successor as Archbishop of Canterbury, Matthew Parker, was to record that Pole had upheld at Trent the
Protestant view of man's salvation as achieved by faith alone rather than
the Roman view of salvation by faith and righteous works, though he
still kept the Roman allegiance. Since he thus maintained one view in
Rome and another in Trent, the Italians ascribed to him, as Parker
wrote, "*Dapocagine*, by which name they describe one who, lacking
opinions of his own, depends entirely on other persons; they consider a
man of this kind useless and unsuitable for rule or magistracy."[46] What
Italian in England passed this story and this epithet on to the English we
cannot say. Nor can we forget that, two pages earlier, Parker had called
Pole an "Anglus italianatus, diabolus incarnatus," a current English
saying to describe an ungovernable man. Pole's crime, according to
Parker, had been that originally, "as if he had drunk the cup of Circe, . . .
[he] had been changed from an Englishman to an Italian, from a
Christian to a Papist."[47]

Thus doubted or hated by the followers of both churches, Pole was in
special danger from the Inquisition in Italy after 1549 and was fortunate
only in the opportunity of the English mission on the accession of
Queen Mary in 1553. Even today Italian historians may report him as
anxiously and luckily escaping to this mission as if for safety, a willing

45. I have consulted the collection of nearly a hundred pasquinades in BM MS Royal 14.A.ii.
The expression quoted is on fol. 34ᵛ.

46. *De Antiquitate Britannicae Ecclesiae* (London, 1572; 2nd ed. Hanover, 1605). The Pole
biography occupies pp. 344–358 in the second edition. "Dappocaggine" means "worthlessness,"
and the reference occurs on p. 348:

Haec Poli varietas & inconstantia vt aliud Romae, aliud alibi de religione sentiret, effecit vt
neque sibi, nec alteri cuipiam constare videretur, veniretque ipsis Italis in eius vitii suspicionem,
quod illi *Dapocagine* vocant, quo nomine designant eum qui proprii consilii inops, totus
pendet ab aliis, cuiusmodi virum imperio aut magistratui gerēdo prorsus inutilem & ineptum
statuunt.

47. *Ibid.*, p. 346: "tanq̄ Circaeo exhausto poculo ex Anglo in Italú, ex Christiano in pontificium
conuersus."

fugitive.[48] It was one of his contemporaries who, in my view, best understood his success and his misfortune:

And Pole might have seemed to be a happy man, because he had not only regained his native land but had also recalled it to the way of salvation; but a stain darkened the last part of his life, the imputation laid by Paul [IV, Carafa], that he had gone astray in his faith in the sacred doctrines.[49]

Regarding Pole's return to England, we note that the move led to a flood of encomia. Pamphlets were published in Rome, Antwerp, and London concerning (I give a sample title) *Il felicissimo Ritorno dal Regno d'Inghilterra alla Catholica Unione* (London, 1 December 1553). Not least in praise of Pole was the *Orazione* (1555) by Alberto Lollio, emissary of Ferrara to England, which contains this outburst: "Tu dunque o generoso Polo, gloriar ueramente ti puoi, d'hauere con l'industria, sollecitudine, & diligenza tua, aperto il polo del Regno del Cielo, al nobilissimo & fioritissimo Regno d'Inghilterra. . . ."[50]

We suppose a number of such encomia, and are therefore grateful for one competent appraisal of Pole on his English mission made by an Italian official. The Venetian ambassador Giovanni Micheli, in England from 1553 to 1557, reported on the state of England in the formal Venetian manner on his return home. Out of nearly one hundred printed pages, Micheli gave Pole four. He does not mention specific actions of Pole, but describes his role in the government and his qualities in office. His judgment is in the highest degree laudatory.

Certainly in both offices [as in effect head of the Church and of the state under the Queen] he has not deceived nor does he deceive the promise of integrity and sincerity and great value: wherefore we see that the cause [of this success] was that he was deprived of the papacy to which he came so close, God having reserved him for the return of this kingdom to its obedience to the Church and its liberation from schism. For this work [could be done solely by] a subject of

48. "Quasi fuggiasco" is the expression used by Giuseppe Toffanin of Pole in "L'Umanesimo al Concilio di Trento," the introduction to a Latin edition with Italian translation by Antonio Altamura (Bologna, 1955) of Vida's *De Rei Publicae Dignitate*, p. 23.

49. Antonio Maria Gratiano (Graziani), *De Casibus Virorum Illustrium*, written before 1611 (ed. Paris, 1680). The fates of Englishmen are discussed (Henry VIII, Wolsey, Fisher and More, Pole, Queen Mary, Northumberland, four kings); Pole's story is given on pp. 209–229. Fourteen other contemporaries are also discussed. The Pole passage reads as follows (p. 229): "Et Polus quidem felix videri poterat, non receptâ modo patriâ, sed ferme per ipsum ad salutis rationem revocatâ, nisi & ultimam vitae partem inusta a Paulo errantis in fide sacrorum sententiae macula inobscurâsset."

50. The pamphlets were to be reprinted in *Epistolae Poli*, vol. V, this passage at p. 401. Note the recurrent pun on the Cardinal's name.

as great character, adding to station and rank so great learning and so great goodness as to lead this people to such new ways. . . . In this task he continues daily to gain marvelous success by the model and example which he sets in his deeds and his life, being completely unmoved, as those who know him know, by every sort of human prejudice and material interest in whatever concerns his office, whether the authority of important persons or family appeal or that of friendship or any other: he is totally severe in this respect, and without equal. For these characteristics he is loved and revered by King and Queen and by the clergy; while in secret he is envied and hated by some of those in high position because they can no longer, as they were accustomed, obtain advancement by authority and favor, since all are referred to him, [and the Queen will relieve of rank or office any of whom he complains; he is in effect king and ruler, though with all modesty of behavior; Priuli relieves him of much of his correspondence, and is a twin soul and mind]. The Cardinal is always grateful to and proud of Venice, and says commonly, *Altera me genuit, altera me excepit.*[51]

Pole had come into his own.

---

51. Condensed in translation from the "Relazione di Giovanni Micheli" (1557), in Eugenio Albèri, ed., *Relazioni dello Impero Britannico . . . Scritte da Veneti Ambasciatori* (Florence, 1852), pp. 49–140. Pole is discussed pp. 109–113.

Addenda

Tributes to Pole that were published at the time also need to be recorded. It should be noted that except for the first few he was not sought out as patron until he returned to England—that is, until he finally achieved a noteworthy success.

1. Venice, 1524: dedication to Pole as patron of the *Dialogi* of Leonico Tomeo, Pole's tutor at Padua. The book consists of lectures on such topics as prophecy, immortality, the invention of names, and the mastering of grief. The dedication addresses Pole as "eruditissime" and "humanissime."

2. Venice, 1537: Antonio Brucioli, *Dialogi della philosophia morale*, bk. ii, "Dialogo xi, Della Virtù" (fols. lxxxii^v–lxxxv^r). In this second edition of the work (originally published in Florence in 1527), "Signor Renaldo Polo" in effect delivers a lecture on the acquisition of virtue, addressing a young English nobleman, Teogeno. (In the first edition the speakers were Hermeo and Teogeno.) The simple Stoic formula of training in the habit of virtue has a schoolmasterish quality, and no reason is shown for the choice of Pole as lecturer.

Brucioli had been exiled from Florence on suspicion of heresy, and he made a living in Venice by writing. He had translated the Bible into Italian, and he was in constant trouble with the Venetian Inquisition. Pole's relation to him is not known, and his name does not appear in the published records of the Pole inquiry by the Roman Inquisition.

3. Venice, 1538: Antonio Brucioli, *Dialogi della metaphisicale philosophia*, bk. iv, "Dialogo xvi della prescientia di Iddio" (fols. 44^r–47^v). "Rev.^{mo} Polo," now Cardinal, is reported by the Duchess of Urbino as discussing with a philosopher the function of God's foreknowledge, which does not impede, but indeed is the source of, man's seeking to do good. Again there is no apparent justification for assigning the topic to Pole, except that he was now a notable like the other speakers.

4. Venice, 1554: Jovita Rapicius of Brescia (1476–1533), *De Numero Oratorio . . . ad Reginaldum Polum, Cardinalem Amplissimum.* The reason for the dedication is "animi tui candor et celsitudo." The book is an essay on rhetoric by a respected humanist, once chosen by

Bembo to be his son's tutor. Paraphrases of the Psalms are added at the end.

5. Bologna, 1555: Achille Bocchi, *Symbolicarum Quaestionum de Universo Genere . . . libri quinque.* This is a collection of 151 copper engravings by Giulio Bonasone presenting allegorical figures; no. 77, on page clxiii, shows Ganymede carried off by an eagle, both figures relaxed to illustrate the line "Pacati emblema hoc corporis atque animi est," the peaceful union of soul and body. The engraving is inscribed on the facing page (clxiv) to Cardinal Pole; the first inscription reads "Pax est laeta piis usque domi et foris" ("Peace is joyful to the pious both at home and abroad"). After six lines explaining the picture as illustrating body and soul in "otia laeta," a second inscription to Pole reads

> Tota mente Deum ac pura nosce, & cole, prestò
> Laeta domi, atque foris pax erit usque tibi.

("Know and adore God with pure and complete mind, and glad peace at home and abroad will surely be yours.")

The late Delio Cantimori considered this collection to be a vehicle of "nicodemism," or concealed Protestantism, beginning with the dedication of the book to Renée of France, Duchess of Ferrara, protectress of Protestants. See "Note su alcuni aspetti della propaganda religiosa nell'Europa del Cinquecento," in *Aspects de le propagande religieuse,* Travaux d'Humanisme et Renaissance, No. 28 (Geneva, 1957), p. 347 for Bocchi.

6. Paris, 1555: *Palladii . . . Historia, et Theodoreti Religiosa Historia,* translated into Latin by Gentian Hervet, dedicated to "Renaldo Polo Cardinali Amplissimo." Though Hervet was not Italian, and had once been a tutor in the Pole family, he attended the Council of Trent in the suite of Cardinal Cervini, who had induced him to do this translation. He was now in the suite of Juan Morillo (Moruillerius), Bishop of Orléans, who had been Pole's theological adviser at the Council. Hervet's Italian experience was therefore a main reason for the work, and it was Morillo's suggestion that Pole be the recipient. (Cervini, who should have received it, was elected Pope as Marcellus II in this year, but lived only a few days thereafter.)

Hervet's dedication of this important scholarly work on the lives of the early monks justified his choice of patron with two reasons:

Primum quidem, quod ij qui de monachis scribunt auctores, nescio ad quem
mitti debeant convenientius, quam ad eum, qui . . . vel in mediis gravissimarum
rerum agendarum occupationibus, antiquam illam vitam prope agit monas-
ticam. Accedit his, quod cum multis iam seculis lapsam veterem ecclesiasticam
disciplinam in integrum restitui cupere, magnopere semper prae te tuleris, & ut
fieret, quantum licuit, pro viribus contenderis. . . .(sigs. a iii^v–a iv^r)

"First because those who write about monks ought to dedicate their
work to none more appropriately than to him who . . . lives like a monk
of the ancient pattern in the midst of duties requiring the most serious
activity. In addition, you have always been greatly concerned with and
desired to restore the ancient discipline of the church which has fallen
away during these many centuries, and, as far as has been permitted,
you have vigorously striven to bring [the revival] to pass. . . ."

7. 1556: Giulio Pogiano, translator into Latin of St. John Chrysostom, *De Virginali Laude*, dedicated to the Cardinal of England "quod
& reliquarum virtutum specimen & illustre exemplum castitatis habuit
haec aetas." Before Pogiano got the book published (Rome, 1562), the
Pope had died. The intent to dedicate is noted in a letter of Pogiano
dated 6 December 1556; it is cited by Pio Paschini, *Cinquecento
romano e riforma cattolica* (Rome, 1958, p. 231), reprinting an article
published in 1937.

8. Venice, 1556: Bernardinus Tomitanus, *Clonicus, sive de Reginaldi Poli Card. Ampliss. Laudibus*, 359 hexameters, dedicated in
prose to Pietro Carnesecchi, Protonotarius, of the Pole circle, destined
to burning at the stake as a heretic. The encomium ignores the life or
nature of the Cardinal, praising in vague terms the restoration of the
English Church to Rome.

9. Antwerp, 1556: *Di Orlando di Lassus il primo libro de mottetti a
cinque & a sei voci. . .*, No. 10, fol. xx^v. "Te spectant Reginalde
poli. . . . tibi sidera rident, Exultant montes, personat oceanus Anglia
dum plaudit quod faustus [*sic*] excutis ignes Elicis et lachrimas ex
adamante suo."

10. Basel, 1556: Joannes Pierius Valerianus, *Hieroglyphica, sive de
Sacris Aegyptiorum commentarii literis. . .*, fifty-eight books, of which
no. 53 is dedicated to "optime clarissimeque Reginalde" because of his
love of "bonarum literarum optimarumque"; among his virtues are

"admirabilis morum suavitas," "summa benignitas et singularis humanitas," his "pietas integerrima," and "divinarum rerum studia fervida," and so forth. The book is actually a dictionary of symbols in classical literature; Pole's book concerns the symbolism of olive, grape, and fig. Priuli and Pole's biographer Beccadelli are each recipients of the dedication of a book (54, 57).

11. Cremona, 1556: Marco Girolamo Vida, Bishop of Albi, *Dialogi de Rei-Publicae Dignitate.* The work debates the value of organized society, especially that governed by Christian principles, as against that of the state of nature in which man is free. The speakers are Vida himself, with an easy victory for government over the poet Flaminio, both citing their illustrations from classical history and literature. The scene is Trent before the start of the Council, and the listeners are the three legates, including Pole; he has little to say, but displays a general benevolence. The *Dialogi* begin with a long introductory address to Pole, noting Vida's familiar terms with him, praising him for his "divina virtute" and his "maxima conciliatione ac diligentia," which have persuaded the whole English nation to return to Rome, and which have overcome the new spirit of revolt against civilization. He asserts that Pole must then "omnium saeculorum praeconio usquequaque clarum fore, ac semper laudibus florentem, nullamque posteritatem ullo unquam tempore tui immortalis beneficii ac singularis facti immemorem aut ingratam futuram."

IV. Opposed Tudor Myths of Power: Machiavellian Tyrants and Christian Kings

Robert P. Adams · *Professor of English, University of Washington*

In late Elizabethan times those who pondered the meaning of such an event as the Massacre of St. Bartholomew's (1572), the work of legitimate kings, may have sensed uneasily an incompatibility between the traditional view that history was tragedy ruled by divine providence, and the radical view that tragedy was history ruled by *raison d'état*. With the tragedies of Greville, Marston, Shakespeare, Chapman, and Ben Jonson (ca. 1596–1603), the older view may be seen as losing credibility, the newer tending to displace it. The great tragedies of state of the late English Renaissance, now seen as "myth-historical," [1] represent attempts to cope with the haunting question, why is there so much seemingly needless, man-made evil and suffering in the world? Inevitably the focus came to be upon the workings of the modern power-state. The Pandora's box of fateful questions about kingship and the rights of subjects, opened after St. Bartholomew's, could not be closed despite all the censorship efforts of the establishment. What is here termed the myth of Machiavellianism, which of course many Elizabethans took to be a major political reality, antedates the Massacre but gained from it both sharpened focus and increased momentum. [2] Laski observed how radical were the implications of the questions raised by the 1579 *Vindiciae contra tyrannos*:

The sixteenth century is pre-eminently a century of *raison d'état*. The poison of Machiavelli was in its blood, and, as the reign of Henry VIII makes evident, a cynical utilitarianism is its predominant temper. Expediency is a basis of rights; it can never become an effective basis of right. [3]

---

1. F. Smith Fussner, *Tudor History and the Historians* (New York, [1970]), p. 231.

2. E.g., anti-Machiavellianism is said to have grown "for reasons which have little direct connection with Machiavelli himself, such as . . . St. Bartholomew" (N. W. Bawcutt, "Machiavelli and Marlowe's *The Jew of Malta*," *Renaissance Drama*, ed. S. Schoenbaum, N.S. 3 [1970], p. 10).

3. Junius Brutus (pseud.), *A Defence of Liberty Against Tyrants* (trans. 1689), introd. by Harold J. Laski (London, 1924), p. 27; cited hereinafter as *Vindiciae*.

The myth of Machiavellianism was and is above all an expression of the realities and fantasies of those who actually control the power-to-destroy and of those, including real or potential victims, who sense that the great men-of-respect do have such capabilities. By late Elizabethan times the myth was a force in being, one able to inspire extraordinary "repulsion and horror," partly, at least in England, linked to a "genuine moral repulsion at some of Machiavelli's doctrines."[4] Some evidence suggests that writings which reflected the horror felt after the Massacre circulated at first "only among the more intellectually minded," but that the assassination in 1588 of the Duke of Guise, a chief leader of the Massacre, soon made ordinary people more aware than ever before of Machiavellianism, which Marlowe's Prologue to the *Jew of Malta* asserts was common knowledge in England (the first recorded performance was in 1592).[5]

The myth of Machiavellianism in late Elizabethan times reflected an emerging tragic vision of life in the modern power-state. All across Europe, with the Reformation and the rise of would-be absolutist, monarchic regimes, there dawned the first modern century to forgo nearly all pretense that international law (itself a mythic and nostalgic medieval notion) had living force. The shifting power-spaces between nationalist kings tended to be filled with anarchy, a trend that indeed was obvious even before the Reformation.[6] As the worn-out myth of "Christendom" collapsed, the normal relationship between major European princes became one of warfare.

From late nineteenth- or twentieth-century critical perspectives it seems at times simpler than it was in late Elizabethan days to estimate realities then apparent. Gentillet's critique of Machiavelli, Englished by 1577 though not now known to have been printed until 1602, refers bluntly to "our Machiavelistes of France, which were authors and enterprisers of the massacre of S. Bartholomew. . . " (*STC* 11743, p. 348). Meyer, however, thought that in late Elizabethan times there was such a "scare" that Machiavelli "came to be regarded as an incarnation of the Evil One himself."[7] Meyer's study (no less a scholar than Mario Praz termed the work "epoch-making") held that the "gist of the whole

4. Bawcutt, p. 10; Felix Raab, *The English Face of Machiavelli* (London, 1964), pp. 30–34.
5. Bawcutt, pp. 29–30.
6. Robert P. Adams, *The Better Part of Valor* (Seattle, 1962), pp. 207–211.
7. Edward Meyer, *Machiavelli and the Elizabethan Drama* (Weimar, 1897), p. x. The idea seems to persist, e.g., in the "satanic figure of the Machiavel" (Robert Ornstein, *The Moral Vision of*

matter" was that "Shakespeare and his contemporaries ... simply dubbed all the horrors and cruelties invented by themselves for their tyrant heroes, 'Machiavellism'; and for this very reason their use of the Florentine seems to us unskilful and clumsy" (p. 57). Praz spoke with similar ease of a "popular legend of Machiavelli, the wicked politician," which grew out of France and then spread to Scotland and England. It was clear to Praz, however, that "Machiavelli was no more the inventor of Machiavellianism than Graves is the inventor of Graves's disease." Nevertheless, he thought that most of the Machiavelli quotations gathered by Meyer amounted to no more than "echoing a popular cliché; their import does not reach beyond a superficial passing record of a fashionable byword." [8]

For some thoughtful writers, from Fulke Greville to Jonson, during what seems to have been a turning point in tragedies of the power-state, the greatest interest centered upon political analysis and, insofar as censorship permitted, upon representation in tragic drama of what great men in history actually did with power, not what they ought to have done. It now appears false that Gentillet's *Against Machiavell* "became the arsenal from which future would-be combatants drew their weapons." Equally false is the idea that the popular Elizabethan concept of Machiavellianism as an embodiment of active political evil can be traced to Gentillet, "the source of all the Elizabethan misunderstanding" (Meyer, pp. x, 9). Meyer's reference to "so-called 'Machiavellism' " would, I suggest, have dumbfounded Marlowe, Greville, Marston, Shakespeare, Chapman of the first *Bussy d'Ambois*, or Jonson of *Sejanus*. [9]

Gentillet indeed identified himself with the cause of just government and opposition to tyranny, and in the late sixteenth century in Europe and England these were live questions with many implications for the tragic sense of life. The French title of Gentillet's book was *Discours sur les Moyens de Bien Gouverneur* (1576). The short English title of Patericke's 1577 translation is *A Discourse upon the Means of Well Governing, Against Nicholas Machiavell*. Gentillet knew that the arts of

---

Jacobean Tragedy [Madison, 1960], p. 24). On some recent views that Machiavelli seems the victim of a "legend" that grew about his name, cf. Bawcutt, p. 10.

8. Mario Praz, "Machiavelli and the Elizabethans," in *The Flaming Heart* (New York, 1958), pp. 90, 96, 127.

9. Cf. Bawcutt, pp. 3–49; and his " 'Policy,' Machiavellianism, and the Earlier Tudor Drama," *English Literary Renaissance*, 1 (1971), 195–209.

tyranny were not Machiavelli's creation. In his preface he said he meant to confute Machiavelli's maxims by examples drawn from Roman and French history (sig. Aii^r). He grants that if well governing were taken to be the way to chronic tyranny and civil war, Machiavelli would be useful. Otherwise, he thought the Florentine a glib novice in political power, an inexperienced greenhorn who had no direct executive knowledge. Machiavelli's *Art of War* (in English by 1574) was a pointed example. What did this "simple Secrethrie or Towne-clarke" know about war at firsthand? For practical purposes, he knew nothing anyone in his right mind need respect:

and in truth it sheweth an exceeding great pride and rashnesse in Machiavell, that hee dare speake and write of the affaires of warre, and prescribe precepts and rules unto them that are of that profession, seeing he had nothing but by heare-say, and was himselfe but a simple Secrethrie or Towne-clarke, which is a trade as far different from the profession of warre, as an harquebush differs from a pen and inckhorne. (sig. Aiii^{r-v})

This passage brings to mind an expert soldier's later ridicule of another mere military theoretician, "a Florentine" (*Othello*, I.i.20). In Gentillet's view, Machiavelli taught not an art of governing well, "but a Tyrannicall science," and he "understood nothing or little" else (sig. Aii^r). The chaos and tyranny of post–St. Bartholomew's France, under its Italianized court, were proof to Gentillet that the employment of "the doctrine of Machiavell" in the royal power-games was a disaster to the people.

But now by the Italian government of this time, the good and auncient lawes of the realme are abolished and suppressed; cruell warres and dissentions are maintained in France; peace alwayes broken; the people destroyed and eaten, and trafficke decayed; subjects are deprived of their auncient liberties . . . , yea, and brought into such confusion and disorder, that none knowes well what is his owne, and what is not. . . . (sig. A4^v)

St. Bartholomew's, as gradually became clear to many Englishmen, very emphatically by the time of Marlowe's grim *Massacre at Paris* (played as new in January 1593) showed for one thing a new tragic role for the people in a technically legitimate but monstrously corrupt power-state. When, before their eyes, tragedy had become history ruled by those who possessed the power-to-destroy, or *raison d'état*, the people's part was to be "eaten" by viciously great men-of-respect such as the Duke of Guise. I think Marlowe's *Massacre at Paris*, with its Guise-figure, as well as *Tamburlaine I* (first played before 1588), challenged audiences actively to experience this role. Such sinister great men, stripped of all would-be masks of self-righteousness, could be seen as terrible predators prowling a Machiavellian jungle called the state, ever searching for victims. Sometimes, by a peculiar irony, it seems that the people unconsciously *demanded* to be "eaten," but in any case, when great power is greatly abused, they *are* "eaten." "And why should Caesar be a tyrant, then?" asks Cassius rhetorically in *Julius Caesar*. "Poor man! I know he would not be a wolf / But that he sees the Romans are but sheep" (I.iii.103–105).

One thing that made the Massacre an ominous turning point was exactly that it was the work of completely legitimate rulers. Hence, their monstrous crime for political power, from the view at least of Elizabethan Protestants, was diametrically opposed to what tradition and Elizabeth's establishment assured the people was the truth. For when Elizabethans conventionally thought of tyrants, they tended to begin with images of the illegitimate usurper and, upon this basis, to build ever more formidable characterizations of criminal greatness through oddly plausible uses of Seneca and Machiavelli as they knew them.[10] Since these conventional views were widely known, they posed no tragic problem, except perhaps to radical thinkers who, in late Elizabethan times, began to find the providential idea of history increasingly incredible, because it could not be reconciled with the harsh and evident facts (e.g., the Massacre) of how power really worked in the modern state.

The figure of Richard III is a case in point. When Shakespeare wrote *Richard III* about 1593, he himself apparently still took the providential idea to be valid. As an illegitimate tyrant, Richard fitted perfectly the most popular Elizabethan concepts of a "mirror of usurpation and tyranny." But Richard had been accepted as a Machiavellian before Gentillet's *Against Machiavell*, and "he continued to be associated with Machiavellianism." Campbell thinks it clearly shown that audiences at *Richard III* "would probably have current applications of history in

---

10. What is now often taken to be the conventional wisdom is summed up by W. A. Armstrong, "The Elizabethan Conception of the Tyrant," *Review of English Studies*, 22 (1946), 161–181 (cited as Armstrong 1946); W. A. Armstrong, "The Influence of Seneca and Machiavelli on the Elizabethan Tyrant," *RES*, 24 (1948), 19–35 (cited as Armstrong 1948). These two studies were cited as nearly definitive by Eugene M. Waith, *Ideas of Greatness* (London, 1971), p. 119.

mind." [11] One such application, and one of the most bizarre of Shake-spearean developments, is that of a belated attack of conscience (V.iii) in which the tyrant is haunted by the ghosts of his victims. While such tales were common, Campbell shrewdly suggests that politicized audiences may have been meant to sense a parallel between Richard and the notorious Charles IX of France. "If Shakespeare did have a Machiavellian Richard in mind, it would have been fitting to accord him a death copied from the death [in 1574] of the arch-representative of Machiavellian evil":

The ghosts have been attributed to Senecan influence; they have been regarded as Shakespeare's interpretation of the workings of conscience, which the chronicles recorded; they have been attributed to the influence of *The Mirror for Magistrates* with its ghostly speakers. . . .

[Charles IX], the son of Catherine de Medici, . . . was at least technically responsible for the massacre of St. Bartholomew's eve which had so shocked the Protestant world, and which was constantly recalled to Englishmen when Elizabeth proposed to marry first one and then another of Catherine's sons. Charles was said to have died horribly. His pores exuded blood. He dreamed of the massacred corpses which filled the streets of Paris. He had a hot fever, and the images of his victims passed before him. Such were the tales of the divine vengeance exacted from the sinner, who, according to the Protestant writers of Shakespeare's day, had sinned in accordance with the teachings of Machiavelli (Campbell, pp. 332–333).

It is an egregious historical error to assume, with Meyer, that late Elizabethan playwrights crudely invented "horrors and cruelties" for their "tyrant heroes" and called the gross result "Machiavellism." The best writers between ca. 1596–1603 went to history, often quite recent history, for their mirrors of the power-state at work, and history amply provided them with horrors and cruelties. Conventional minds, like John Foxe's, took comfort that divine providence had meted out justice to Charles IX. Sir Philip Sidney could hope that such justice would "fear" kings out of being tyrants. Unfortunately, by the time Marlowe's *Jew of Malta* was first staged (1592), no such fears had deterred Catherine de Médicis from having one son, Charles IX, killed in favor of another, nor had it deterred Catherine and Henri III from having the

---

11. Lily B. Campbell, *Shakespeare's Histories, Mirrors of Elizabethan Policy* (San Marino, Calif., 1958 [1st ed., 1947]), p. 332. See also David Bevington, *Tudor Drama and Politics* (Cambridge, Mass., 1968), pp. 1–26.

infamously great Duke of Guise murdered at Blois in 1588—an event to which the *Jew of Malta* alludes as common knowledge.

For some critical minds the providential idea of history and of tragedy had lost credibility by the 1590s. Machiavellianism, far from being, as Praz thought, a "superficial, passing record of a fashionable byword," should rather be seen as one means by which creative men strove to understand and to dramatize how the power-to-destroy actually worked in absolutist states. Greville (in the first *Mustapha*), Marston (in his two *Antonio* plays), Shakespeare (in *Julius Caesar* and *Hamlet*), Chapman (in the original *Bussy d'Ambois*), and Ben Jonson (in *Sejanus*) were intensely conscious of recent and ancient history's man-made horrors. Their radical tragic vision of ca. 1596–1603 did not form adventures in *Grande Guignol* for jaded coterie audiences. As all these imaginative mirrors of the power-state came into being, they were complicated, I think, by an emerging if uneven awareness that there was a very real and tragic resemblance, monstrously ironical, between two titanic myths or images of the power-to-destroy that towered over the sixteenth century. Between them there was an officially irreconcilable conflict. The seemingly total opposition may be suggested by the titles of two famous books written in the same year: Erasmus' *Christian Prince* and Machiavelli's *The Prince* (cf. Adams, Chap. 7). "We are no tyrant, but a Christian king," says Shakespeare's Henry V (I.ii.241), unhistorically, to the French ambassadors. Before Damascus, Marlowe's Tamburlaine does not bother with such politic ploys; he simply promises that unless the city surrenders on his terms, he will annihilate it, and then he proceeds to do so.

The inevitable conflict between these rival myths of supreme state-power—the illegitimate tyrant versus the legitimate Christian king—in late Elizabethan times helped to create a radically new kind of tragic vision and with it strikingly altered concepts of human greatness or heroism.

II

Some of the best Elizabethan minds were moved to examine the problems of the evil of political power—what Campbell termed "political sin"—in the contemporary state. As this movement developed, two tremendous historic myths came into full confrontation. Eventually

those supreme images of the power-to-destroy—such as Henry V and
Tamburlaine—tended, ironically, to coalesce, at least from the viewpoint of politicized audiences who, when they empathized with the
victims of these great men of power, came to sense that their own role in
the power-games of such princes was to be "eaten." When such a fusion
of supposedly polar opposite mythic power-figures takes place, tragic
uneasiness, not to say tensions and terrors, may be experienced by
audiences.

To critics such as E. M. W. Tillyard and his followers, who feel certain
what orthodox Elizabethans believed and did not—or almost could
not—doubt, there is presumably no tragic contradiction to be seen in
Henry V's arrogant "We are no tyrant, but a Christian king." Elizabeth's
propagandists regularly assured the people that the difference between
these mythic figures and England's actual rulers was both polar and
absolute. Indeed, the Tudor myth and the entire establishment of
Elizabeth depended on massive acceptance of the ideal that the Queen
herself was the supreme embodiment of the legitimate and just Christian prince. Armstrong recalls to us the officially respectable ideology
that all true subjects were supposed to believe. In the most extreme
instance, any king who lawfully succeeds, even if he becomes evil and a
tyrant, must be endured and obeyed by the people. No right of rebellion
can possibly exist against God's anointed. Not so for the usurper or
power-snatching Machiavellian prince, such as Shakespeare's Richard
III. Such satanically wicked tyrants have no just right to rule. Hence,
rebellion against them is not sedition (a favorite Elizabethan establishment attack word). When the true Christian prince was identified—or
when he identified himself, as Shakespeare's Henry V did—as the agent
of God, and when the Machiavellian tyrant was identified as the agent
of Satan, all was clear to the orthodox. So Armstrong and others have
found in the drama the hardening of what he thought became "a
definitive dramatic convention" in which "the worst stage tyrants are
always presented as usurpers and . . . the legitimate princes who invariably defeat or supersede them possess the moral virtues of model kings."
Shakespeare is said only to have touched up the standard convention by
imaging the "beastlike fury" with which Richard III as "usurping tyrant
. . . defends his infamous regime" against the "just claimant to the
crown," the first Tudor, Henry of Richmond, who is said to appear "as

virtually an avenging angel, divinely appointed to conquer the forces of evil." [12]

A similar establishment line is alleged to have come into existence through use of ideas drawn from Seneca and Machiavelli. Thus, characterizations of tyrant figures are said to have been "controlled and directed by [orthodox] contemporary moral and political theories, and the result is not so much imitation as adaptation" (Armstrong, 1948, p. 20; Waith, p. 119). Most curiously, however, profoundly radical exceptions are laid aside without apparent, adequate explanation. For example, the extraordinary and nearly contemporaneous Soliman of Fulke Greville's first *Mustapha* (1596–1600; Q. 1609) is simply noticed as "the only fully-drawn stage tyrant who avoids the fate of violent death after committing unnatural crimes . . . [and] is likewise a lawful king." [13] By one of the latest opinions, which chimes with Armstrong's, Marlowe's figure of Tamburlaine is said to be "no tyrant—he is, in fact, the special enemy of tyrants," the "polar opposite of the tyrant heroes," and fully opposed to the figure of Shakespeare's Henry V (Waith, pp. 50, 99).

The conventional wisdom on such supreme men-of-respect as Soliman, Tamburlaine, and Henry V may be in error, especially when an effort is made to sense the experience of these plays as they impinged upon the consciousness of their readers or audiences. Merely to determine that the bulk of Elizabethans were tradition-bound and may well have believed the establishment "line" on good kings versus tyrants only demonstrates that, for a time, the people can be hoodwinked. But the great illusion about the theoretically ideal king must be maintained with at least apparent consistency, like a seamless and immaculate garment of the power-state, lest it begin to unravel once it is torn. Laski accurately sees that St. Bartholomew's "destroyed the mutual faith of prince

---

12. Armstrong 1946, pp. 161–171 *passim*. Official Tudor historians early set this "line": in his *Anglicae Historiae Libri* (1534) the historian Polydore Vergil, brought to England by Henry VIII, saw Richard III's death as representing "part of divine justice, that the wicked by their carelessness provoke the punishment which they merit" (cf. Denys Hay, *Polydore Vergil* [Oxford, 1952], p. 142).

13. Armstrong 1946, p. 177; cp. Waith, p. 119. Largely ignoring the original *Mustapha*, perhaps too striking an exception to his alleged set rule, Armstrong was pleased to see that, by the elaborately recast posthumous 1633 form of *Mustapha*, "additions . . . declare that God will treat Soliman as he deserves, and, at the end of the play, in the midst of a disintegrating kingdom, the emperor faces the threat of a hostile mob" (*loc. cit.*). A detailed critique of the original *Mustapha* forms part of a larger study of which this essay is an offshoot.

and subjects, and so uprooted the foundations of the state. It made necessary the abandonment of the fiction that the powers of the King were not a fit subject for discussion. . . . Men . . . had no longer any faith either in the theory of absolutism, on the one hand, or its corollary of passive obedience upon the other."[14] A parallel effect of St. Bartholomew's was not only to politicize English dramatic audiences but fatefully to show people that their usual role in the great kings' power-games was to be "eaten," which does not mean that they had to enjoy such tragic experience any more than did the victims in Marlowe's *Massacre at Paris*, with whom Protestant audiences were meant to empathize.

These events and tendencies of the times, I think, intensified and spread among many late Elizabethans an uneasy sense that tragedy was becoming history, ruled not by divine providence but by ruthless *raison d'état*. Elizabeth herself, as well as the establishment censorship that reflected her at times almost despotic will, showed an unmistakable tendency to over-reactions, especially apparent in a recurrent hysteria about "seditious" words and a tendency to smell conspiracies in many places.

Indeed, in late Elizabethan times the so-called "definitive dramatic convention," which comfortably opposed the mythic figure of the angel-king to that of the devil-tyrant, was turning out to be too simple, except perhaps for those who may have been incapable of questioning the officially sacrosanct Tudor myth. Certain awful historical facts, then widely known, suggest that it may be unwise to give unquestioning critical faith to such a dramatic convention and that apparent exceptions to such rules should not be brushed aside. Charles IX, one of the legitimate royal powers who masterminded St. Bartholomew's in 1572, soon met a nasty death, which at the time was interpreted by English Protestants (like John Foxe) as a demonstration of divine justice at work. Nevertheless, his co-conspirators, Catherine de Médicis and Henri III, remained masters of French royal power-games until 1589, even managing the murder of the great Duke of Guise in 1588. Soliman the Great, who died a natural death in 1566 while engaged in war, was to Elizabethans about as recent a figure when Greville portrayed him in his original *Mustapha* (ca. 1596–1600), as Stalin, who also died a

14. *Vindiciae*, pp. 22–23.

natural death, is to us. Soliman and Stalin, as supreme men-of-respect, are like Tamburlaine in that their only victorious opponent was finally death itself.

In the most notable tragedies of state, with Kyd and Marlowe as the pioneers from about 1586 onward, great tyrants are by no means (as Armstrong would have it) "always presented as usurpers," nor are they "invariably" defeated and replaced by morally virtuous "model kings." To believe so now appears fallacious to me. Such establishment-approved thinking on tyrants versus good kings in late Elizabethan times was, as Lever has said of the concept of the great chain of being, in "an advanced state of rust." When the best tragic writers went to history—often, daringly, to very recent history—for their mirrors of the modern state, what they and their politicized audiences could see depended not only upon what they had been officially instructed to see; their tragic vision also related to what they had grown *prepared* to see as an alternative. Doubtless the Queen herself would have applauded the flattering notion that the first Tudor, Henry of Richmond, in *Richard III* figures "as virtually an avenging angel, divinely appointed to conquer the forces of evil." At least in the aftermath of St. Bartholomew's, however, some writers began to grasp that the expert or merely fortunate use of the overwhelming power-to-destroy self-legitimizes the winner in the power-games of great princes. Thus, the future Henry VII legitimized his role in the state simply by destroying Richard III at Bosworth Field in 1485. Had the outcome been reversed, so would have been the legitimacy. Success at any cost had become the name of the game, and the winner took all. Similarly, Julius Caesar, by annihilating Pompey in the civil wars concluded shortly before Shakespeare's tragedy of state opens, had *de facto* legitimacy for his role in the state, with a rubber-stamp senate, at least according to Plutarch, agreeably confirming the obvious.[15] Even in the first court scene of *Hamlet* (I.ii), does not Claudius succeed in maintaining the outward appearance of legitimacy in his elected succession to power? If the election was corrupt and "rigged," no one with common sense says so out loud or where the King's spies can hear him. Even Hamlet himself, in some respects

15. Plutarch bitterly noted a symptom of rottenness in the state of Rome, namely the willingness of the Romans to choose Caesar "perpetual Dictator. This was a plain Tyranny: for to this absolute power of Dictator, they added this, never to be afraid to be deposed" ("Life of . . . Caesar," *Julius Caesar*, ed. W. and B. Rosen [New York, 1963], p. 140).

dangerously naïve in the ways of power-politics, can see harsh necessity sometimes: "But break, my heart, for I must hold my tongue!" (I.ii.159).

Nevertheless, the myth that the Christian prince should be taken to be a polar opposite to, and utterly irreconcilable with, the diabolical Machiavellian prince was a myth that died hard, if such mighty fictions of political power ever may be said to die. For Elizabethans to dare to doubt that divine providence ruled history was to open up limitless prospects of tragic terror, prospects of a state without safe guides to conduct men through a potential or actual Machiavellian jungle. Thus, to the orthodox, the Devil-as-Machiavellian prince played a continually updated role in a so-called "comedy of evil." [16]

III

Regimes like Elizabeth's, which are basically absolutist with recurring tendencies toward despotism, whether relatively benevolent or not, often depend upon political power-myths that supposedly brook no question. One standard pattern of power usage employed by the Tudors was designed to elicit apparent uniformity of support among subjects through such instruments as official homilies. Direct and outspoken public questioning was intolerable, though silence sometimes could win establishment approval. [17] In 1579 tragedy and history collided in a strange episode that brought into near-confrontation the rival myths of the Christian prince and the Machiavellian tyrant.

We may call it the *Gaping Gulf* affair, and its humble hero was a patriotic Puritan, one John Stubbs. The storm developed over Elizabeth's schemes for a French marriage, which were energetically renewed in the summer of 1579, the year in which the *Vindiciae contra tyrannos* was printed. Alençon (the supreme villain, Monsieur, in Chapman's original *Bussy d'Ambois*) secretly came to London with his entourage. Elizabeth seemed warmly sympathetic to his wooing, but her advisers were divided. Sir Philip Sidney dared to write a private letter to the Queen in which he emphatically opposed the marriage and

---

16. Douglas Cole, *Suffering and Evil in the Plays of Christopher Marlowe* (Princeton, N. J., 1962), p. 144. To him, *The Jew of Malta* "remains a comedy of evil—with a Marlovian twist."

17. Thomas More found that, in Henry VIII's service, he eventually lost freedom even to be silent; see Adams, pp. 181–184, 298.

referred to Catherine de Médicis as a "Jezabel." Luckily, he was well advised by Hubert Languet (a close friend who is often thought to have written the *Vindiciae*) "not to press his luck more than 'you can bear,'" sentiments with which his great friend Fulke Greville concurred.[18] Sidney escaped with no worse than a temporary banishment from court and a passing cloud over his career that provided the enforced leisure to work on his *Arcadia*.

Less favored and less fortunate, John Stubbs narrowly escaped complete political martyrdom. Sidney's opinions were given privately, but Stubbs's were printed in *The Discovery of a Gaping Gulf Whereinto England Is Like to Be Swallowed*, which was published anonymously and dated August 1579.[19] What followed gave Englishmen a striking and highly public example of a ruthless power-state at work.

By 27 September the *Gaping Gulf* had apparently become widely dispersed and, we infer, eagerly read. It provoked from the Queen an infuriated, if not almost hysterical, double-broadside Proclamation, "Given at Giddie Hall in Essex." Its style suggests that she wrote it herself. *Gulf* was a "lewde seditious booke . . . seditiously dispersed into sundry corners of the Realm," a "Fardell of false reportes, . . . false Lybel . . . like as by a trumpe of sedition. . . ." Wherever found it "shall be destroyed [i.e., burned] in open sight of some publike Officer."[20] The Queen, as J. E. Neale has observed, "was passionately angry" and with what seemed to her to be good and sufficient reasons. The establishment rolled into action almost as though a popular rebellion was at hand. The Proclamation was ordered to be read to all the City companies, and to the clergy by their bishops, while at Paul's a preacher was "put up . . . to extol the Queen's government."[21]

What did the *Gaping Gulf* contain to arouse such an amazingly infuriated response? A somewhat apologetic view is that Stubbs's booklet represented "the violence of a hot-headed professor of religion, the prejudice of an Englishman, the concern of a loving subject, spoke[n] in

---

18. Malcolm W. Wallace, *The Life of Sir Philip Sidney* (Cambridge, 1915), pp. 211–220. For the letter, which termed Catherine "that Jezabel of our age," Sidney's *Works*, ed. A. Feuillerat (Cambridge, 1923), III, 51–60; Fulke Greville, *Life of Sir Philip Sidney* (1652), ed. N. Smith ([Oxford], 1907), pp. 45–63.

19. *STC* 23400; see also John Stubbs's *Gaping Gulf*, ed. Lloyd E. Berry (Charlottesville, Va., [1968]).

20. The Proclamation (*STC* 8114) was reprinted in *All Such Proclamations, as Were Published During the Reign of . . . Elizabeth* (*STC* 7758), collected by H. Dyson (London, 1618).

21. *Queen Elizabeth* (London, 1934), p. 242.

outrageous language" (Neale, p. 242). It is an understatement to term
the piece merely "injudicious" (Wallace, p. 220). The anonymous author, soon known to be Stubbs, spoke in Biblical terms to oppose the
French marriage. "S. Paul speaking of contrary couplings together,
compareth them to the uneven yoking of the clean Oxe to the unclean
Asse, a thing forbidden in the lawe." Turning to the white-hot question,
whether or not Alençon would become a Protestant with the marriage,
he referred to "these [French] discoursers that use the word of God with
as little conscience as they do Machiavel." And he alluded to Catherine
de Médicis' ambitious and tireless "trotting betwene hir sonnes as a
broker of reconciliation" (STC 23400, sigs. A4^v, A6^v, E5^r). There were
uncomplimentary references to the French diplomats, like Simier, who
were actively promoting the match. And, for good measure, Stubbs
even alluded unfavorably to Richard II's French marriage (cf. Neale, p.
241). In plain fact, Englishmen abroad as at home felt the same fears
that Stubbs dared to express openly. Burghley, a leading initial advocate
of the marriage, heard secretly from Andalusia that "It is said here that
. . . if France and England join, it will grow to a foul piece of work. The
common people are afraid of their own shadow." [22]

As read today, the *Gaping Gulf* presented, certainly in less courtly
and diplomatic language, most of the same arguments used by Sidney in
his private letter to the Queen. What was intolerable to Elizabeth, I
suggest, was that *publicly* the *Gulf* raised officially forbidden questions
about kingship and the rights of subjects—the same sort of questions
that were nearly brought into open discussion in the wake of St.
Bartholomew's. By its very nature, Stubbs's book raised for public
debate traditionally unthinkable questions. A subject's right to discuss
public questions, not what Neale calls "outrageous language," was at
the heart of the matter. The author's principal offense in the Queen's
eyes was that his book offered a dangerous precedent. Any Englishmen,
"by these kind of popular Libels," might presume that they had "au-
thoritie to argue and determine, in every blinde corner, at their severall
willes, of the affaires of publique estate; A thing most pernicious in any
estate" (STC 8114).

Elizabeth's idea that the perpetrators of *Gaping Gulf* had issued a
trumpet of sedition, if not of treason, was rapidly acted upon by her

22. 12 Dec. 1579: *State Papers Domestic, Elizabeth*, VII, 572.

justicers. The speed with which the anonymous author, publisher, and printer were identified suggests for once an efficient informer system. By 13 October 1579 John Stubbs as author, William Page as "disperser" (i.e., publisher), and Hugh Singleton as printer of the *Gulf* were on trial at Westminster, *not* in the City. Stubbs's patriotic devotion to Elizabeth was not called into question in any account I have seen,[23] and yet his patriotism was by no means enough to save him.

The establishment's objective was evidently to make a crushing public example of the offenders. How this was done, despite the obscurity of the victims, vividly reveals the workings of what was but too clearly despotism. Under pressure from the top, the judicial authorities searched the statutes back to the time of that notorious Queen under whom, as John Foxe said, "moderacion had no place, but all was ruled by rigore."[24] Found in the statutes of 1 and 2 Philip and Mary was "An act against seditious words and rumors," with a special penalty of "Loss of the right hand" for "Writings against the king or queen, not being treason. . . ." However, the statute was to be in force only until the end of the Parliament which passed it.[25]

That the statute had expired did not deter Elizabeth's judicial authorities. They knew perfectly well what the Queen wanted done. In opposition to the legal proceedings against Stubbs and his compatriots, two honorable if daring lawyers publicly declared that the whole legal process involved was invalid because the statute brought to bear had died with Queen Mary and was therefore void. Camden, who was close to the events, states:

Some Lawyers storming hereat, said the judgement was erroneous, and fetcht from a false observation of the time, wherein the Statute was made, that it was only temporarie, and that (Queene Marie dying) it dyed with her. (Camden, Bk. III, 15–16)

The lawyers in question were summarily refuted, not by logic or law but by quick imprisonment and despotic power:

23. See Neale, p. 241; *DNB*, XIX, 118–119; William Camden, *Annales* (London, 1625; *STC* 4497), Bk. III, 14–16; John Stow, *Annales 1592* (London, 1592; *STC* 23334), p. 1181; Stow, *Annales 1605* (London, 1605; *STC* 23337), p. 1168. Stow repeats 1581 in error for 1579; so does Camden, III, 14–16. Cp. Neale, pp. 242–243. On Stubbs's life, see Berry, pp. xx–xlvi.
24. *Actes and Monuments* (London, 1563; *STC* 11222), p. 1708.
25. *The Statutes of the Realm* (London, 1739), IV, Pt. i (1547–85), 240–241, Sec. IV. Sec. X provided for the expiration of the Statute.

Of the which Lawyers, one Dalton for his clamorous speeches was committed to prison [1635: "the Tower"]; and [Robert] Monson, a Judge of the Common-pleas, was sharply rebuked, and his place taken from him.[26]

Elizabeth's chief legal advisers overpowered all opposition. The Chief Justice of England, Sir Christopher Wray, declared it "manifest by Law" that the statute in question was alive and in force: "yea, that Statute likewise in the first yeare of Queen Elizabeth was revived againe to the Queene and her Heires for ever" (Camden, Bk. III, 16). Sir Christopher, it seems, had one firm point, but then forced his interpretation so as to guarantee the conviction that Elizabeth desired. True, the questionable statute of 1 and 2 Philip and Mary had been renewed by Elizabeth's first Parliament.[27] What the crown's prosecutor overlooked or perhaps chose to overlook was that the original statute, to stay alive, required re-enactment by each successive Parliament and that none, save Elizabeth's first, had done so up to 1579.[28] "Neither would Queene Elizabeth bee perswaded," wrote a historian who almost revered her, "that the Author of this booke had any other purpose, but to bring her into hatred with her subjects, and to open a gap to some prodigious innovation. . . ."[29]

The sentence upon Stubbs and his associates was carried out in a manner worthy of the revenge drama of Kyd. As Camden, an eyewitness, described the event, a "stage" was set up in the marketplace before the Palace at Westminster on 3 November 1579. For such a *cause célèbre*, so elaborately publicized, a capacity crowd was assured—a crowd that might have included Fulke Greville (then aged twenty-five), Thomas Kyd (twenty-one), George Chapman (about nineteen), or just possibly even Marlowe or Shakespeare (both fifteen).

The dramatic scene recalls the stark woodcuts that often illustrated Protestant religious and political martyrdoms in Foxe's *Book of Mar-*

---

26. Camden, Bk. III, 16. *DNB*, XIX, 118, records that Judge Monson was "sent to the Fleet prison" when he would not retract his opinion that the statute "was abrogated by Queen Mary's death." Neale seemingly makes the establishment look better by asserting that Dalton "openly bawled out" his dissent, that both men earlier had been "obstreperous parliamentarians," and that both were imprisoned (pp. 242–243).

27. *Statutes of the Realm*, 1 Eliz. C. 6, vol. IV, pt. I, pp. 366–367.

28. *Statutes* . . . (1562–63), pp. 401–402; *ibid.* (1575–76), pp. 606–607. A new statute on seditious words appeared in 23 Eliz. 1580–81, Sec. XV, pp. 659–661, with provision that it should continue during the Queen's life.

29. Camden, Bk. III, 14–15; Camden, *Annales* (London, 1635; *STC* 4501): "she warned the people that the said booke was nothing else but a fiction of traitors . . . " (p. 239).

tyrs. Without avail Stubbs had pleaded to the Queen for mercy, saying that his only intent in writing had been to safeguard her and England's welfare. Camden was standing close by the stage, and his observation of the audience's experience of the tragic episode is particularly acute:

Hereby had Stubbs and Page their right hands cut off with a Cleaver driven thorow the wrist with the force of a beetle [heavy mallet], upon a scaffold in the market place at Westminster. . . . I remember (being present thereat,) that when Stubbs, having his right hand cut off, put off his hat with his left, and sayd with a loud voyce, *God save the Queene*; the multitude standing about, was *altogether silent, either out of horrour of this new and unwonted punishment, or else out of pitty* towards the man being of most honest and unblameable report, or else out of hatred of the marriage, which most men presaged would be the overthrow of Religion.[30]

This miniature tragedy's climax had many thrilling touches and surprises. Led to the chopping block were three convicted men, but the printer of *Gulf* was pardoned in the nick of time.[31] Each of the two remaining victims was allowed a few words, but neither retracted what the *Gaping Gulf* had said against the French marriage, although presumably both sensed that an abject recantation might gain them lesser punishment. Surgeons were ready with hot irons to sear their wounds lest they bleed to death.[32] Stubbs did not speak of Elizabeth's ruthlessness but, an orthodox man of his time, laid all to divine providence:

Before I was condempned, I might speak for my innocencie; but nowe my mouth is stopped by judgement, to the which I submitt myselffe, and ame contente patientlie to endure whatsoever it pleaseth God, of his secrett providence to laie upon me, and take it justlie deserved for my sinnes.[33]

With two blows Page's right hand was smitten off. "So, lifting up the stompe, he said to the people, 'I have lefte there a true Englyshmans haund.' And so went from the scaffolde [to prison] very stoutlie and with great corradge" (Harington, III, 183). In ironic contrast another

30. Camden 1635, pp. 238–239. Stow, *Annales 1592*, p. 1181, notes the event but not apparently as an eyewitness; cp. *DNB*, XIX, 118–119. Italics, other than for "*God save the Queene*," are here added.

31. In December 1579, fortunately for poetry, this Hugh Singleton printed the first edition of Edmund Spenser's *The Shepheardes Calender*. Disguised in some of its fables were the poet's own covert, liberal, Puritan attacks on the French marriage. See Berry, pp. li–lv.

32. Cp. *Merchant of Venice* (IV.i.257–262), where Portia urges Shylock "to have by some surgeon . . . / To stop his wounds, lest he [Antonio] do bleed to death," a plea of course rejected.

33. *Nugae Antiquae*, comp. by Sir John Harington, ed. Henry Harington (London, 1779), III, 179–181 *passim*. Cf. Wallace, p. 220.

chronicler, after noting this atrocious episode, tells us brightly that Alençon and other French nobles, two days before the sentences were executed, "came to London, and were honorably received, and reteined at the court with banketting and diverse pleasant shewes and pastimes" (Stow 1592, p. 1182). About six years after the *Gaping Gulf* affair Thomas Kyd wrote his epochal *Spanish Tragedy*. This powerful drama of cruelty, corruption, and seeming indifference to justice at the highest levels in the modern state was of course tactfully set in Catholic Spain, which was both hated and feared by most Englishmen.

Even though Elizabeth's regime is seen by most modern historians as a more or less benevolent despotism, the benevolence was staggeringly absent during the *Gaping Gulf* affair. This very important fact was apparent to the multitude who saw the sentences carried out. That the crushing triumph of a royal act of outrage, too thinly disguised as justice, had some aspects of a pyrrhic victory seems not altogether to have escaped the power-establishment. A well-known ploy in such regimes is to attempt to modify public opinion favorably by staging a new sensation hard on the heels of the unpopular act in hopes of obliterating or at least minimizing its negative impact. Thus, even while Alençon was still in England, "the Queen to take away the fear conceived by many, that religion should change," had the state trial of the Jesuit Campion for conspiracy and treason moved up quickly (Camden 1625, Bk. III, 16–18). In today's terms, this was an effort to repair Elizabeth's tarnished "image" as a Christian prince. In addition, to close a too obvious and embarrassing legal gap, the Parliament of 1580–81 enacted a new statute on "seditious" words, to continue during Elizabeth's lifetime.[34]

In connection with the *Gaping Gulf* affair, and considering rising new ideals of heroism and human greatness in the power-state, it may be useful to define the man-of-respect. Some remarkable Renaissance concepts, it seems, still queerly persist, at least in Sicily, among the *mafiosi* to whom the *uomini rispettati* remain a real force. Among them, according to Luigi Barzini, "Each man's individual rank is determined by the amount of *fear* he can generate."[35]

In any society, obviously, the supreme man-of-respect is he who by whatever means can and does generate supreme fear. And the evident

---

34. *Statutes of the Realm . . .* , IV, Pt. I, Sec. XV, pp. 659–661 for 23 Elizabeth.
35. Cf. Luigi Barzini, *The Italians* (New York, 1964), pp. 253–272; emphasis mine.

basis for this reality is ultimately the power-to-destroy that the ultimate leader, in this instance Elizabeth herself, has under command. The audience who experienced the climax of the *Gaping Gulf* affair had prima facie evidence that the legitimate sovereign not only could but would employ such power, with complete ruthlessness, when expedient.

One fateful consequence of that moment of truth on the stage before the palace at Westminster, before Stubbs fell unconscious, was, I suggest, that the age's supreme rival myths of power—those of the Christian prince and its allegedly polar opposite, the Machiavellian tyrant—for that historic instant appeared to fuse. After St. Bartholomew's it could not be, and was not, effectively concealed from English audiences that such political horrors as the massacre and the *Gaping Gulf* affair were the deliberate work of legitimate rulers. The "horror of this new and unwonted punishment" inflicted upon Stubbs could no more be concealed than the fact that it was the direct result of Elizabeth's abuse of her power-to-destroy. Too many people knew too much of the legal and political contexts of the event to believe that what they watched that day was anything but an outrageous corruption of the judicial process, cynical *raison d'état* almost transparently at work. Obligingly, the humbly heroic victim himself put forward the orthodox and quintessential idea that could alone then make the Tudor myth retain credibility—that his condemnation represented the result of God's "secret providence." Some may have believed it, but for a great many in that politicized audience this explanation could not be accepted any more readily than Charles IX's explanation to Queen Elizabeth that the victims of St. Bartholomew's were themselves to blame for their slaughter. In late 1572 the great Burghley and Archbishop Parker, dreading in England massacres like St. Bartholomew's, were in "great consternation" and frankly at their wits' end for fear.[36] Now, in 1579, expecting national disaster through Elizabeth's proposed French marriage, the multitude itself seems to have shared in a comparable consternation, "afraid of their own shadow."

At least three aspects of the "multitude's" experiences at the climax of the *Gaping Gulf* episode are of particular interest for the late Elizabethan tragic sense of life. First, as Camden reports, there was the

36. John Strype, *The Life and Acts of Matthew Parker* (Oxford, 1821), II, 118–120.

crowd's extraordinary silence when Stubbs cried "*God save the Queene.*" Second, there was the multitude's sense of horror, and third, its mingled sense of pity and fear. All three stimulated this audience to a sense of participation in the experience of tragedy as history ruled by *raison d'état*, even when their most apparent role—like Stubbs's—had become to be "eaten" in the power-games of ruthless princes.

First, the silence. His right hand chopped off, Stubbs "putt off his hat with his left, and sayd with a loud voyce, *God save the Queene.*" The traditional response from the English multitude should have been at the very least a murmured "Amen." The horror-struck silence that fell at the moment of dramatic and tragic truth is reminiscent of that moment in Shakespeare's *Richard II* when the lawless but politically effective man-of-respect usurps the crown. Like the obscure lawyers, Dalton and Monson, who openly declared Stubbs's conviction to be "erroneous," the brave Bishop of Carlisle, in Shakespeare's rearrangement of historic events, denounces Bolingbroke to his face as a great criminal; for his pains, Carlisle is summarily sentenced to prison, "put to silence," like the two tribunes who oppose Caesar's power-games (*Julius Caesar*, I.i). Haled before Bolingbroke, who has crowned himself, King Richard cries, "God Save the King!" On stage he says it into a silence comparable to that of the multitude at Stubbs's execution of sentence. "Will no man say amen?" Richard asks. "Am I both priest and clerk? Well then, amen" (*Richard II*, IV.i.172–173). The striking parallel between this episode and the *Gaping Gulf* affair may well have occurred to some members of Shakespeare's audience eighteen years later.

The members of the multitude at the execution of Stubbs's sentence, as Camden records it, were intensely engaged in the tragic experience enacted before them. Furthermore, the sense of horror and pity they felt was inextricably mingled with popular fear and hatred of the French marriage. Elizabeth's regime, in a fury of despotism, had demonstrated what fate any subject could expect if he openly crossed the will of the sovereign. The quasi-judicial process by which the establishment had created the outrage was common knowledge. The whole *Gaping Gulf* affair had received enormous and official publicity. I infer that the audience, thus politicized to understand how this princely power-game had actually been played, was also aware, and indeed was intended to be aware, of the enormous fear that the Queen and her lesser men-of-respect could generate, and that this feeling which permeated the multitude was based upon some understanding that the fear, like the horror, rested firmly upon the power-to-destroy. For at least a moment, as Stubbs and Page met the executioner's blows, the fiction or myth of the Christian prince fell away, to reveal only the harsh, modern reality of the Machiavellian tyrant.

The meaning of the *Gaping Gulf* affair cannot be dismissed by what amounts to a critical "numbers game." We are told that this *once* "Elizabeth's good sense deserted her" (Neale, pp. 242–243). We could be told that the event is now virtually forgotten and that anyway only two obscure Englishmen had their hands chopped off, which seems numerically insignificant compared to the fifty thousand estimated to have been slaughtered in the Massacre of St. Bartholomew's. Tragic truth cannot be annihilated so easily, however, for at its heart is a haunting question concerning the meaning of individual life, of suffering, and of outrages upon human dignity.[37]

The politicized audience at the climax of the *Gaping Gulf* affair clearly understood that at such crises of power the mythical Christian prince and the mythical Machiavellian tyrant figure had one thing in common: both depended upon the power-to-destroy and hence the capacity for generating fear to maintain control over the common people. Before Damascus, Marlowe's Tamburlaine, with ferocious candor, displays just such power; he demands that the city surrender on his terms or be annihilated. Shakespeare's Henry V does the same thing at Harfleur. As a matter of historical fact, "the men of Harfleur yielded to a mercy which was not recorded of Henry V, but was much praised in the behavior of the Earl of Essex toward the people of Cadiz in 1596" (Campbell, p. 287).

Not surprisingly in the wake of the *Gaping Gulf* episode, by the mid-1580s the Elizabethan regime was very busy trying to prohibit all printed criticism of itself, using methods that, some objected, too much resembled the Spanish Inquisition. In this campaign the Queen's chief man-of-respect was that authoritarian perfectionist John Whitgift, Archbishop of Canterbury. By 23 June 1586 he caused the high commission court to pass "an extraordinarily rigorous decree—known as the Star-chamber decree." This provided that "No manuscript was to be set up in type until it had been perused and licensed by the Archbishop

---

37. Cf. Herschel Baker, "The Renaissance View of Man," Pt. III in *The Dignity of Man* (Cambridge, Mass., 1947).

or the Bishop of London. The press of any printer who disobeyed the ordinance was to be at once destroyed; he was prohibited from following his trade thenceforth, and was to suffer six months' imprisonment." Those who muttered that this action was too much like the Spanish Inquisition (i.e., was a barely disguised act of tyranny) were ignored, and the rigorousness of Whitgift's action confirmed Elizabeth's faith in him.[38] The operation of this despotic system can be seen almost perfectly in the case of Sir John Hayward's *History of Henry IIII* in 1599, which gained him speedy incarceration in the Tower and might have ended with his execution for treason if Bacon had not bravely defended him to the enraged Queen.[39]

An implicit intent of all this machinery of repression was to make sure that no more dangerous political questions would be raised in print to stir up the kinds of political thought raised in England in the aftermath of St. Bartholomew's. Fortunately, no such despotic censorship is perfect. Almost reluctantly conceding that Elizabeth's regime was a "paternal despotism," one recent critic was cheered by the thought that "Elizabethan drama itself, in a way strangely unremarked, exonerates the regime: it could never have come into being under a tyranny."[40] What is more obvious is that Elizabethan tragedies after the time of Kyd focus upon great abuses of power in the modern state (however disguised for stage purposes), and that they probably could not have come into being if the late Elizabethan despotism had been as efficient as it wished to be. By an accident of the theater's modes of operation, playwrights seem usually to have had little or no special incentive to have plays printed. In the last years of Elizabeth's reign, playwrights who mirrored supreme state-power at work ran heavy risks. Even as highly placed a man as Fulke Greville, who deliberately wrote closet-dramas, burned his tragedy on Antony and Cleopatra, "Essex then falling," evidently fearing that if it "leaked" out, he might risk a charge of treason (cf. Greville's *Sidney*, pp. 155–156).

38. Arber, *Transcripts of Stationers' Company*, II, 810–811; *DNB*, XXI, 129–137 *passim*. John Milton, of course, powerfully stressed the parallels of the Spanish tyranny in *Areopagitica* (1644), when his own Puritan party proposed similar prior censorship.

39. For an account of the episode, see F. J. Levy, *Tudor Historical Thought* (San Marino, Calif., 1967), pp. 252–267. Tried twice but never actually convicted, Hayward simply stayed in the Tower, apparently until receiving amnesty under King James. S. L. Goldberg shows him a prisoner until Christmas of 1602, "but not in June 1603" ("Sir John Hayward, 'Politic Historian,'" *RES*, N. S., 6 [1955], 233–244, esp. 236 n.).

40. Alfred Harbage, *Shakespeare and the Rival Traditions* (New York, 1952), pp. 263–265.

But the ferment of thought on kingship, tyranny, and the rights of subjects that rose after the Massacre of St. Bartholomew's was like the fabled genie who, once escaped from his bottle-prison, could never again be induced back into it. Thus appeared, ironically in the Armada year, duly entered and licensed 26 April, the *Short Apologie for Christian Souldiours* (STC 15207). Now usually judged to have been the work of Sidney's friend Hubert Languet (possible author of the 1579 *Vindiciae contra tyrannos*), it appeared as the work of one Stephanus Junius Brutus. Seemingly pro-Protestant enough, it raised the question whether Protestants ought, "if need require, to defend by force of arms" their Church against "the tyranny of Antichrist and his adherents," which from a Protestant viewpoint, of course, meant, above all, Catholic Spain. Keeping on the safe side, the author warned marginally that "We must reade this advisedly, because we may not by the worde of God resist our own Prince if he be wicked" (sig. A6ᵛ). The question was, "When the Subjects of anie Prince are either afflicted for Religion, or oppressed with tyrannie, it is lawfull for the Princes inhabiting about them, to send them ayde" (sig. A2ʳ). And this, by a fine irony, is the fourth question raised in the *Vindiciae* itself, a book Whitgift thought to be not only dangerous but well known in England by 1600.[41]

When such popular audiences as that at the climax of the *Gaping Gulf* affair gradually realized their role in tragedy as it tended to become history ruled by *raison d'état*, they could never again be excluded from the power-games of princes, even if their role was often to be "eaten." Such audiences, or the more politicized among them, could sense at times that when those rival myths of power—the Christian prince and the Machiavellian tyrant—came into confrontation, they tended to fuse into a single, frightful image, one able to generate enormous popular fear because it expressed a real and even limitless power to destroy. This fusion of power-myths was explored by some bold dramatists in the 1590s, thus opening up a whole spectrum of radical questions about heroism, chivalric idealism, and human greatness. Some of the greatest

---

41. On Whitgift, see J. W. Allen, *A History of Political Thought in the Sixteenth Century* (London, 1960), p. 331. The authorship of both the *Vindiciae* (1579) and the *Short Apologie* has long been disputed. *Enc. Brit.* (13th ed., XVI, 181) notes divers attributions to Beza, Hotman, Casaubon, and Duplessis-Mornay, while favoring Languet, as *STC* does for *Short Apologie* (15207). Laski favors Duplessis-Mornay for both (his reprint of *Vindiciae*, pp. 59–60). The dispute over exact authorship is of no special consequence here, however, where the work's ideas count above all.

and most enduring characters in these dramas include Soliman the Magnificent of Greville's first *Mustapha*, the rival dukes in Marston's *Antonio* plays, Shakespeare's Julius Caesar and Marc Antony, King Claudius and Hamlet, Chapman's Monsieur (Alençon) and Guise in *Bussy d'Ambois*, and, finally, Sejanus, Tiberius, and Macro in Ben Jonson's mirror of a police-state, *Sejanus*.

V. Sir Thomas More: Personage and Symbol on the Italian Stage[1]

Beatrice Corrigan · *Professor Emeritus of Italian and Hispanic Studies, University of Toronto*

Much has been written of the fascination with Italy of Elizabethan and Jacobean playwrights . They convey a complex, double vision of that country, idyllic or dark with murder and treachery.[2] Seldom, however, is the interest of the dramatists historical. Familiar though they must have been with the rulers and issues involved in the Italian wars, in which England was often concerned diplomatically if not actively, the dramatists may borrow, as Massinger does, the name of Ludovico Sforza (*The Duke of Milan*), or show their knowledge of a recently created title (*The Grand Duke of Florence*), but they attach it to an imaginary ruler. Occasionally they dramatize an actual tragic event, but always of a domestic nature, such as the story of Vittoria Accoramboni or Bianca Cappello. Even then, murder is not enough, and they add to the original such condiments of incest, treason, sadism, and sacrilege as will give what seems to their audience an authentic Italian flavor. Machiavelli pervades the tragedy of the period, but a mythological Machiavelli, the genius of violence and treachery. The disastrous fortunes of Italy during the early sixteenth century seem to have excited in English playwrights no sympathy, indeed no interest. To parallel George Chapman's *Bussy d'Ambois* and *Byron*, Marlowe's *The Mas-*

[*The death of Professor Corrigan on 4 January 1977 is recorded here with sadness.*]

1. The editions used for this essay were: Hortensio Scammacca, *Tragedie sacre e morali*, Vol. XII (Palermo, 1648; microfilm, Biblioteca Nazionale, Palermo); Jacopo Rossi, *Il Tomaso Moro* (Lucca, n.d.; microfilm, Folger Shakespeare Library); G. A. Bianchi (under pseudonym of Farnabio Gioachino Annutini), *Il Tomaso Moro* (Rome, 1727; microfilm, Yale University Library); and Silvio Pellico, *Tommaso Moro* (in his *Opere complete*, Milan, 1864). I should like to express my thanks to the libraries mentioned for providing the microfilms. Palermo also supplied a microfilm of Luigi Natoli's *H. Scammacca e le sue tragedie: studio* (Palermo, 1885). The alternative spellings, Tomaso/Tommaso, Hortensio/Ortensio, Buonvisi/Buonviso, have been preserved as they appear in the texts. Full bibliographical details of Italian plays on More are given in Giovanni Salvioli's "Tommaso Moro nel teatro italiano," *Giornale degli eruditi e dei curiosi*, 3 (1885), 209–210.

2. This subject has been most skillfully analyzed by Mario Praz in "The Politic Brain: Machiavelli and the Elizabethans," "Shakespeare's Italy," and "Ben Jonson's Italy," in *The Flaming Heart* (New York, 1958).

sacre at Paris, or Peele's *Battle of Alcazar* there are no English plays that draw their basic situation from Italian history or politics.

On the other hand, when Italian playwrights wrote of England, they were interested in the dynastic and political murders, dignified by the name of executions, in which the Tudor monarchs seemed to be carrying out Machiavelli's advice to a new ruler to exterminate all rival claimants to the throne and all who might threaten his power. This policy King Henry VII and his descendants followed with a consistency unmatched by any Italian dynasty of the Renaissance or after. But during the sixteenth century no Italian tragedy was set in contemporary England. Giraldi Cinzio's *Antivalomeni* has an English setting and the scene of his *Arrenopia* is Ireland, but they are the mythical England and Ireland of the romances of chivalry, not of Mary Tudor and Thomas Cromwell.

Italian historians, on the contrary, were deeply interested in contemporary English history and a system of government so different from any other in Europe. The relations between the King and Parliament, and particularly between Church and State from the beginning of Henry VIII's dispute with Rome, were subjects for close study, based on the reports of the Venetian and Tuscan ambassadors and the commercial and intellectual interchange between England and Italy, only intermittently hampered by religious prejudice. Accounts of political events in England and of the rise and development of the Anglican schism,[3] accompanied by translations of works by English Catholic writers, began to appear in the sixteenth century and continued throughout the seventeenth. These in time were used for a series of historically based tragedies, the first of which was probably *Hidalba*, written by the Venetian Maffio Veniero before 1584, but not published until 1596.[4] *Hidalba* is set in Frisa, but its plot follows in unmistakable detail the fate of Lady Jane Grey, the rival and victim of her cousin Mary Tudor. Its source is a historical account drawn in part from the reports of the Venetian ambassador and composed by Luca Contile, Veniero's kinsman.

The most famous of these tragedies is Federico Della Valle's *La Regina di Scozia* (first version, 1591; final form, 1628). It was written at

3. For example, Girolamo Pollini's *L'Historia Ecclesiastica della Rivoluzion d'Inghilterra . . .* (1591) and the better known Bernardo Davanzati's *Storia dello scisma d'Inghilterra* (1602).

4. B. Corrigan, "Research in Italian Renaissance Drama," *Research Opportunities in Renaissance Drama*, 11 (1968), 11–12.

the request of the Conte di Moretta, ambassador of the Duke of Savoy at Mary Stuart's court, and hence it is a striking example of the intimate ties that united England and Scotland with Italy. Mary's story was an eminently suitable subject for Italian baroque tragedy: a royal heroine, a precipitous fall from high estate, and a religious element to associate it with the saintly protagonists fashionable during the Counter-Reformation. The execution of Mary, Queen of Scots, had been a staggering blow to Roman hopes of a Catholic succession, violent or peaceful, to the English throne, and Della Valle's play was followed by at least four others on the same subject during the seventeenth century.[5] Tommaso Campanella himself wrote a tragedy, now lost, on this same victim of Elizabeth's justice.

The Jesuit dramatists, encouraged to offer for the emulation of their pupils both early and modern Christian martyrs, found in another object of Tudor ruthlessness, Sir Thomas More, an opportunity for political as well as religious propaganda.[6] Thomas Stapleton's *Tres Thomae*, published in 1588 at Douai, seat of the famous college for the education of English Roman Catholics, was widely read in Latin and in translation. His three Thomases were St. Thomas the Apostle, St. Thomas à Becket, and Thomas More, who was thus admitted to the company of the saints over three centuries before his formal canonization.[7] This work was unmistakably the source of Ortensio Scammacca's trilogy, *Tommaso a Londra, Tommaso a Contorbia* [sic], and *Tommaso Moro*, published in Palermo as the twelfth volume of his *Tragedie sacre e morali*.[8] Two plays are about Thomas à Becket, the first dealing with his flight to France in 1164, the second with his murder and the repentance of Henry II. The theme uniting all three plays is resistance to royal encroachment on the prerogatives of the Church, and the con-

5. Karl Kipka, *Maria Stuart im Drama der Weltliteratur* (Leipzig, 1907), pp. 29 ff.

6. For Italian interest in More see Piero Rébora, "Tommaso Moro e l'Italia," in *Civiltà italiana e civiltà inglese, studi e ricerche* . . . (Florence, 1936); Luigi Firpo, "Tommaso Moro e la sua fortuna in Italia," *Occidente: rivista di studi politici*, 8 (1952), 225–241, particularly on the fortunes of the *Utopia*; Thomas Wheeler, "Thomas More in Italy: 1535–1700," *Moreana*, 27–28 (1970), 15–23.

7. More was beatified in 1886 but not canonized until 1935. In 1572 Gregory XIII declared him worthy of public veneration in the English College in Rome. A play bearing his name is listed as having been performed in the seventeenth century in the English College of St. Omers, possibly as a compliment to his great-grandson, Henry More, S.J., who was twice rector of the college. See William H. McCabe, "The Play-list of the English College of St. Omers 1592–1762," *Revue de littérature comparée*, 17 (1937), 374.

8. Scammacca's tragedies were published only in collected form, and the dates of composition are not known. Vol. XII appeared in 1648, shortly after his death.

stancy of More was particularly striking, as Stapleton pointed out, because he was a layman, not a priest. Consequently, his refusal to obey a temporal ruler whose policy defied Rome could be interpreted as a model for all Catholic citizens in conflict with Protestant rulers.

Under Spanish rule, Sicily had isolated itself from the erudite dramatic forms so early invented in continental Italy, and had clung stubbornly to the old *sacre rappresentazioni*, little more than spectacles and pageants. Scammacca, who had entered the Jesuit order in 1582 at the age of twenty, was educated in Messina at the Collegio Mamertino, where the custom of performing original tragedies in Latin as a formal part of the Jesuit curriculum had possibly originated.[9] He became convinced that he had been prepared by his classical education for an apostolate through the theater by writing similar plays in Italian, and during his long career he composed more than forty dramas, which won him the sobriquet of the Italian Euripides and were performed in Palermo and in Jesuit colleges elsewhere. *Tommaso Moro* is an excellent example of his method in dealing with a modern subject. The tragedy is in verse and is classical in form, with a prologue in the form of a dialogue between Wolsey (who does not appear again) and the Captain of the Guard. It has five acts and a Chorus, and it observes the unities: its action is continuous, and the place is the Tower of London. The first two acts are reasonably sober though prolix, but in Act III the *sacra rappresentazione* defeats classical tradition without a struggle. Baffled by More's constancy, Satan visits him in the shape of Bishop John Fisher and urges him to recant, but after some debate More recognizes the deception. St. George, England's patron, appears and beats Satan in a scene typical of popular comedy, then drives him back to hell, which opens to receive him in a spectacular burst of flames. St. Michael and attendant angels bring the real Fisher from his dungeon, garb him in a cardinal's robe sent expressly through their agency by the Pope,[10] and set in More's hands a golden wand of office. The act ends as the Chorus deplores the fate of England. In Act IV Henry VIII is told of the visitations but refuses to believe in them, and when Fisher appears in

---

9. *Enciclopedia dello Spettacolo*, art. "Gesuiti, teatro dei," Vol. V (Rome, 1958); art. "Scammacca," Vol. VIII (1961). Luigi Natoli, *H. Scammacca e le sue tragedie* (Palermo, 1885).

10. Fisher was created a cardinal by Paul III on 21 May 1535, two weeks after he had denied the supremacy of Henry. He was beheaded 22 June.

his cardinal's robes, Henry orders his death. In Act V More is led to his execution, which, with the vision that accompanies it, is described by the classical Messenger. Then angels appear to his sorrowing daughter, assure her that her father is in heaven, and promise to bear his body and Fisher's to her house to be preserved there until England is purged of heresy and they can be interred in a reconsecrated church.[11]

Henry VIII is represented as the conventional tyrant, yet the play has implications that are necessarily absent from Scammacca's tragedies about the saints and martyrs of the early Church, like St. Alessio or St. Lucia. In those there is a conflict between the individual Christian and a pagan ruler; in *Tommaso Moro*, from Act III on, Fisher and More typify the cleric and the layman, utterly devoted, each in his own sphere, to upholding the authority of a divinely established Church against a Christian but heretical King who is supported by Parliament and the local clergy. Thomas à Becket was part of the ecclesiastical hierarchy of England; Thomas More and John Fisher stand alone against the power of the English Church and, as well, of the English State. "Two columns," sings the Chorus in Act IV, "support the temple consecrated to God. The others do not even support their own state. They have been thrown to the ground by him who has shaken all foundations. While he seizes sacred honor to which he was not born, he makes himself unworthy of his own."[12]

Unfortunately, suffering from an inability to create character, Scammacca makes Fisher and More equally pompous. He distorts two of the anecdotes recorded by Sander and Stapleton to illustrate More's wit, obviously feeling that humor is out of place in a chancellor and a martyr, though buffoonery is permitted in a saint. A third anecdote, in which More rebukes his wife's lack of business sense in urging him to buy an

---

11. The bodies were in fact interred in a chapel in the Tower of London. None of the dramatists discussed here could stomach the grisly reality of More's severed head preserved by his daughter.

12. P. 169:

> Due colonne mantengono
> Il tempio a Dio sacrato.
> L'altre nè pur sostengono
> In piè lor proprio stato.
> Gittate a terra vengono
> Da chi 'l tutto ha turbato.
> Questi mentre honor prendesi
> Sacro, al qual non è nato
> Del proprio indegno rendesi.

added twenty years of life on earth at the price of losing an eternity of bliss, is spun out into two pages of rhetoric.[13]

More's wife and daughter both figure as characters, though their names are changed to Giovanna and Maria.[14] Maria, unwed, before the dissolution of the convents had hoped to be a nun. Thus the Chorus (composed of soldiers of the guard) is enabled to hymn the praises of virginity in the final scene of Act II. Like a new Cassandra, Maria prophesies the coming ills of England, including the exile of the true faith, unique bride of God, who will be replaced by harlots, an image echoed by later writers. As More recalls in Act V the care with which he taught his daughter Greek, he adds a few lines that reveal Scammacca's own poetic aspirations.

> Next [he reminds her] love of the Tuscan idiom induced you to beg me to instruct you in it. Then in your best interests I told you that such a tongue was not for you, yet I added that my hopes were high that in the course of time someone inspired and aided by Christ to a sweet, fair style would restore as virgins dear to God the sacred Etruscan Muses, to the bitter despite of carnal, ignorant, and uncouth minds.[15]

II

It was nearly a century before More was chosen as a hero by another dramatist, but he was not forgotten during the interval. Hope was one

13. Nicholas Sander, *De origine ac progressu schismatis anglicani* (Cologne, 1585); references in this essay are to the translation by David Lewis, *Rise and Growth of the Anglican Schism* (London, 1877). References to Stapleton's life of More from *Tres Thomae* are based on Philip E. Hallett's translation, *Life and Illustrious Martyrdom of Sir Thomas More* (London, 1928). The first two anecdotes noted here tell of More shutting down shop when his books were removed (Sander, p. 123; Stapleton, p. 140; Scammacca, pp. 295–298) and his declaration of a change of mind when he intends merely to shave off his beard (Stapleton, pp. 177–178; Scammacca, pp. 205–208, 211–216). The third is based on Sander, p. 123; Stapleton, p. 177; Scammacca, pp. 225–227.

14. "Jane" was the name of More's first wife. The name "Maria" may have been chosen in compliment to Margaret Roper's daughter Mary, also a Greek scholar, whose sons, Charles and Philip Bassett, were associated with Edmund Campion, and so of interest to a Jesuit writer. All the Italian dramatists present More's daughter as unmarried.

15. Pp. 275–276:

> Poi del Tosco idioma amor ti spinse
> A pregarme, ch'io ti facessi istrutta.
> Io per lo tuo profitto allhor ti dissi,
> Che per te non facea sì fatta lingua,
> Ma gran speranza haveva, al detto aggiunsi
> Che 'n processo di tempo alcun da Christo

of the principal themes of *La Regina di Scozia*, and Rome's optimistic plans for the conversion of Protestant England seldom flagged during the seventeenth century. James I did not, as Della Valle had predicted, invade England with the help of Spain to dethrone the wicked daughter of a wicked mother. When James legally inherited the kingdom, he was more tolerant of Catholics than his Protestant subjects approved, and his Queen had Catholic inclinations. The beheading of Charles I was greeted in Italy with consternation,[16] and Cromwell's rule was discouraging, but Charles II was known to be at least a crypto-Catholic, and both his wife and an influential mistress, the Duchess of Portsmouth, belonged to the Roman Church. Then, possibly as early as 1669, Charles's brother and heir, James, Duke of York, was received into the Roman communion, and in 1673 he married Maria d'Este of Modena, who was not only a Catholic but an Italian with close connections to Rome. Pope Clement X himself wrote urging the bride to accept a distasteful marriage so that she might foster the conversion of England. When her husband ascended the throne as James II, the long-awaited triumph over heresy seemed assured. James's subsequent exile in 1688 came as a shocking disappointment, which may be reflected in the second tragedy about the English schism.

A life of Thomas More by Domenico Regi, based on Stapleton, had appeared in 1675 and was reprinted in 1681, showing the continued interest in More during this period and anticipating a drama by Jacopo Rossi. Both editions of Rossi's *Tommaso Moro* (Lucca and Bologna) are undated, but the play was almost certainly written after 1689, probably after 1690, and performed at the seminary in Lucca. The author defined it as an *opera scenica*, and though it is in prose, its style and structure are modeled on the dominant theatrical form of that period, the opera *libretto*. Probably it was performed with some sort of musical accompaniment at appropriately dramatic moments and at the end of each of the three acts. There is a good deal of comic relief, also typical of contemporary opera (Lucca was a very musical city), in the quarrels and

----

Spirato aitato al sermon dolce e bello
Le Muse etrusche e dolci a rio dispetto
De' carnali ignoranti e rozzi ingegni
Vergini care a Dio tornar devesse.

16. A play on the subject, *Cromuele*, was written by the Duke of Modena's secretary and councillor, Girolamo Graziani, in 1671, two years before Mary of Modena's marriage to the future James II.

reconciliations of two court pages (Rosello and Ligustrino) and in the character of More's servant (Scarabotto), a figure from the *commedia dell'arte*.

In his preface Rossi mentions as his source only Sander's *De origine*, but like Scammacca he has drawn on Stapleton as well, probably through the intermediary of Regi's work. Stapleton had remarked that More left Henry's court when Lust began to rule there in place of Virtue (p. 78), and this possibly suggested Scammacca's image of the exile of the true faith. Rossi treats the metaphor more daringly and introduces two female characters, Intemperance and Religion, for whose names, he tells the readers, those of Anne Boleyn and Catherine may be substituted. The play opens with Henry violently dismissing Religion from the Council Chamber where he sits among his ministers, and repudiating her as spouse, though she warns him that with her will depart divine Grace, leaving behind impiety, perfidy, ingratitude, the vengeance of heaven, and the furies of the abyss. She is replaced by Signora Intemperanza, escorted by Thomas Cromwell, who takes the vacated throne and presides with Henry over the Council, which accedes to his demands. Much of the framework of the play dramatizes episodes from Stapleton, and the *libretto* form gives Rossi a freedom from the unities of time and place that he uses to advantage. The first act moves from the Council Chamber to More's house, where his daughter Margaret displays her learning and addresses the King in Latin, in the eloquent words of Maecenas promising Augustus attention and integrity in his ministry (I.ix). In Act II More in prison plans the *Letter of Consolation*, refutes Cromwell's charge that he has written against the King, darkens his cell when his books and papers are taken from him, and resists the pleas of his wife and daughter to sign an act of submission. The third act turns on More's ambiguous message to the King that he has changed his mind (Stapleton, pp. 177–178), which he finally reveals to be a decision to have his beard shaved off, the occasion for a comic scene between the barber and Scarabotto.

Particularly important in Rossi's play is the living tradition in Italy on which he draws. The Thomas volume of Scammacca's tragedies had been dedicated to Don Antonio Bicchett, canon and treasurer of the cathedral of Agrigento and vicar general of the Bishop, a descendant of members of the Becket family who had fled to Sicily to escape the persecution of Henry II. Even if the Venetian ancestry attributed to him by Domenico Regi is mythical, Thomas More had from his youth shown a strong interest in Italy, like most learned men of his generation. He translated into English the life of Pico della Mirandola, and had many Italian friends, among them Erasmus' correspondent, Andrea Ammonio of Lucca. Though more than a century had passed since More's death, another more famous friendship, still fresh in memory, is celebrated in this play. Antonio Buonvisi,[17] to whom More had written an affectionate and grateful letter from prison just before his death, was also a native of Lucca, as was Jacopo Rossi. The Buonvisi family, members of the silk guild, merchants and bankers with a patent of nobility in the Tuscan tradition, owned establishments in Lyons, Louvain, Bruges, and Antwerp, and so possessed an important financial empire. They had made loans to the Emperor himself, and the rulers of half of Europe were their debtors during almost two centuries. Antonio's father, Benedetto, had established himself in London as a banker and merchant of wool and jewels by 1474, and had close ties with the Curia and with the English ambassador in Rome. Antonio was born in Lucca in 1487, opened a bank in Rome in 1502, and joined the family business in London in 1505. More speaks in his letter of having received kindnesses from the Buonvisi family for more than forty years, indeed of being a protégé (*alumnus*) of their house, which may imply that they had made loans to finance his early career. In 1533 Antonio was godfather to John More's second son, Austin. Henry VIII owed money to the Buonvisi bank, and Antonio enjoyed his protection even when England became a dangerous place for Catholics and foreigners. After Henry's death, however, unable to count on continued favors from Edward VI, Antonio went in 1548 to Louvain, where he had become a partner in that branch of the family firms a year earlier. He showed great generosity to English Catholics in exile, and, when he died, left a gold ring to Nicholas Harpsfield, author of a life of More, who had gone to Louvain in 1550 and mentions having heard from Buonvisi many anecdotes about More and Cromwell.[18]

17. For his career in England, see the *DNB*, art. "Bonvisi" (the spelling of the name varies, and both Rossi and Bianchi use the ancestral form, "Buonviso"). For members of the Buonvisi family mentioned in this essay, see the *Dizionario Biografico degli Italiani*, Vol. XV (Rome, 1972).

18. Antonio Buonvisi (1487–1558) was the eldest of four brothers: Martino (1489–1538) remained in Lucca; Ludovico (1494–1550) was head of the family's Lyons branch and was associated with firms in Palermo and Naples; Vincenzo (1500–73?), who settled early in Lyons, where he remained for forty years, was interested in letters. All four shared the family palazzo in

Rossi makes Antonio Buonvisi the co-hero of the play, and his friendship with More is as fervent as the terms of the farewell letter might seem to indicate. Thus, the drama takes its place in the long tradition, classical as well as Renaissance, of the theme of faithful friends, contrasted on the comic level with the court friendship of the pages, united only in mischief, alternating blows and embraces. Buonvisi is the good angel of the More household, relieving the needs of the family when their goods are confiscated, smuggling food to More in prison, and even making unsuccessful plans for his escape.

Buonvisi comes to the aid of Religion, too, in her distress, provides her with money, and when she fears that she may have to flee to the wild caves of Ireland offers her a more civilized refuge.[19] His role in the play is symbolic as well as historical; just as Catherine and Anne Boleyn are presented as Religion and Intemperance, so More and Buonvisi typify two aspects of the Catholic layman, the contemplative and the active. Their first spiritual link is forged when More gives Buonvisi the ring in which his mother before his birth had seen a token of his future glory (I.xv; cf. Stapleton, p. 1), and their roles are defined in the following scene. Overhearing Buonvisi swear not to survive More, Religion appears and bids them both live and die in her service. "You, Thomas, shed for me the blood in your veins," she commands. "You, Buonviso, open for me veins of precious metals; of two different enterprises the reward shall be one, and for two different martyrdoms there shall be one crown." The scene closes in a characteristically operatic duet, not sung but undoubtedly spoken to music, by the two friends.

M.   No more conflicts.
B.   No more arguments.
M.   We are discordantly in concord.
B.   We are diversely united.

Lucca, and Ludovico was famous for his hospitality there during visits to his native city, and at the Villa Forci where he entertained men of letters as well as Pope and Emperor. It is probable that the first news of More's death reached Europe through the Buonvisi connection; the first translation of the *Utopia* was by Ortensio Lando, Vincenzo's protégé and Ludovico's guest. Louvain became an important center for English Catholic exiles after Antonio moved there.

19. This somewhat ungracious reference to the last British stronghold of the Catholic faith may be connected with James II's occupation of Ireland, 1689–90, after his flight from England, which also gives topical significance to the exile of Religion. Revived interest in More as a result of the deposition of James may account for the composition of two oratorios, both entitled *Tommaso Moro*: one is by Dottor Giambattista Neri (1688), the other by Giammaria Piantini, with music by Vincenzo Maria Orlandi (1696).

M.   To perform noble exploits.
B.   To carry out great works.
M.   In the cause of Religion.
B.   In defense of Piety.
M.   Open, oh my veins;
B.   Open, oh my coffers;
M.   Pour forth blood.
B.   Pour forth gold.
M.   What will you do with the gold you lavish?
B.   What will you do with the blood you shed?
M.   I shall dye myself a scarlet robe in heaven.
B.   I shall fashion for myself in heaven a diadem.[20]

How Buonvisi carries out his pledge he reveals in a later scene. He pays for the passage to Antwerp of Catholic exiles and gives them a letter of exchange on his firm there. He provides for dispossessed monks and sends a group of nuns to Calais, where his correspondent will find them a convent. Any victims of persecution who wish to go to Rome he assures of travel expenses; his house in Lucca will always provide rooms, food, and a warm welcome for English refugees (II.xiv). It is a vivid sketch, undoubtedly quite historical, of the resources that the Buonvisi connection could offer Catholic exiles.

In Act III his efforts to save More fail; Margaret brings him news of the execution with the famous farewell letter, in a version very close to the original, which he reads aloud (III.xxii).[21] While he sits alone

20.   Rel.   Voi,Tommaso, spargete per me dalle vene il sangue. Voi, Buonviso, aprite per me
                vene di preziosi metalli: di due diverse imprese una sarà la mercede, e di due
                diversi martirij sarà un'istessa corona.
       M.   Non più gare.
       B.   Non più contrasti.
       M.   Siamo discordemente concordi.
       B.   Siamo differentemente uniti.
       M.   In far nobili imprese.
       B.   In eseguire opre grandi.
       M.   Per causa della Religione.
       B.   Per difesa della Pietà.
       M.   Apritevi, mie vene;
       B.   Apritevi miei scrigni;
       M.   Spargete sangue.
       B.   Spargete oro.
       M.   Che farete voi con l'oro sparso?
       B.   Che farete voi con sparger sangue?
       M.   Mi tingerò in Cielo una porpora.
       B.   Mi formerò in Cielo un diadema.
                            (I.xix)
21.   See Wheeler, pp. 21–22.

mourning his dead friend, he falls asleep and in a vision beholds More in one of the *nuvolate* scenes so beloved by baroque stage designers. More points out to him the seat in heaven beside his own that eventually Antonio will occupy, urges him to continue his works of charity toward the persecuted, and assures him that heaven will bless his native city and his nephews. Then, in an image-filled prophecy, he foretells the future glories of the house of Buonvisi, particularly in the spiritual sphere:

Succeeding generations of your family will have their locks adorned with mitres, their brows and garments will blaze with the sacred scarlet [as cardinals], and their hearts will burn even more fiercely to serve religion. A Star of your house, sent as the harbinger of an Innocent Sun of the Vatican, will put to flight the sons of darkness who adore the Moon, and will restore to Hungary, formerly buried in the night of perfidy, the pure daylight of Faith. (III.xxvi)[22]

And in a finale of harmonious stichomythia the friends agree that earthly wealth and glory are smoke and shadow; virtue should long only for the eternal joys of heaven—a tactful conclusion, as the Buonvisi commercial empire had dissolved by the end of the seventeenth century.

Like most prophecies written after the event, these predictions were all verified. In succeeding generations of the family, three cardinals were created, Buonviso (1561–1603), a member of a collateral branch of the house, and two direct descendants, Girolamo (1607–77), the great-grandson of Antonio's brother Ludovico, and his nephew Francesco (1626–1700). Francesco was appointed Bishop of Thessalonia in 1670 and from 1675 to 1689 was the papal nuncio to Vienna, commissioned by Innocent XI (the Innocent Sun of Rossi's eulogy), who raised him to the cardinalate in 1681. He was present at the liberation of Vienna in 1683, and contributed money and advice for the defeat of the Turks under their crescent flag at Grau (1683), Budapest (1686), and Belgrade (1688).[23] In 1689 he returned to Italy, and the following year was made Bishop of Lucca, an office that his uncle Girolamo had also held. It is

22. "Haveranno i vostri posteri fregiato il crine di Mitre, ardente di Sacra Porpora la fronte e la veste, ma più infiammato il cuore di operare a beneficio della Religione. Una Stella di vostra Casa inviata per foriera di un Sole Innocente del Vaticano, fugherà i figliuoli delle tenebre adoratori della Luna, e all'Ungheria prima sepolta nella notte della perfidia, renderà il giorno purissimo della Fede."

23. Anna Maria Trivellini, *Il Cardinale Francesco Buonvisi nunzio a Vienna (1675–1689)* (Florence, 1958). An unbiased account of Cardinal Francesco's career and character when he was a candidate for the papacy is given in Count Scipio Pannochieschi d'Elci's *The Present State of the Court of Rome* (London, 1721), pp. 72–78.

probable that Rossi's play was written after this event,[24] and Cardinal Francesco may have been in the audience to hear this tribute to himself and his ancestor. He had earlier provided another link between his family and England, for he had attempted, unsuccessfully, to persuade Charles II to check the growing power of France by building up the English navy.

Fantastic as it is, and despite the surface frivolity inseparable from its operatic models, Rossi's play is surprisingly firmly rooted in actual facts, past and contemporary, foreign and local.

III

The third author under consideration here, Giovanni Antonio Bianchi, published his *Tommaso Moro* in 1724. Bianchi was born in Lucca in 1686, entered the Franciscan order of Minori Osservanti in 1703, and became an expert in canon law. He was employed by Clement XII to defend the claims of the Bishop of Naples against a rebellious movement led by the Duke of Gravina and supported by many of the minor clergy who demanded reforms. (In Piedmont, too, certain corrupt cardinals were challenged to surrender their usurped privileges, and they appealed to the Pope for support.) There is a close relation between Bianchi's polemical writings and some of his tragedies, particularly *Tommaso Moro*. Scammacca and Rossi had given More a special and elevated significance by associating with their hero a principal character—Fisher and Buonvisi, respectively. Bianchi gives a new and political interpretation to the familiar story by setting a powerful figure in opposition to More in the conflict between Church and State. The dominant figure in the play is not More but Thomas Cromwell—calculating, ambitious, hypocritical—who pretends friendship for More while maneuvering the vacillating Henry into ordering his death. The unjust man is opposed to the one just man. The tragedy is in prose, but its form is neo-classical, in five acts, observing the three unities; the place is an antechamber in the royal palace, and the action takes place within not more than three hours. Buonvisi plays a minor role as More's confidant, balanced by Cromwell's unheeded attendant, Odoardo, who is apparently older and wiser than Cromwell, whereas Buonvisi, actu-

---

24. Rossi's only other recorded play, *La Grazia*, was performed at the seminary in Lucca in 1690 and published in 1692.

ally nearly fifty at the time, is spoken of as a young man, "un giovane." Buonvisi offers to provide for More's family, but there is no mention of his benevolence to refugees.

The English implications had evidently become unimportant. The Jacobite rebellion of 1715 had been crushed, George I was firmly settled on the throne, and hopes for the conversion of the heretical island were no longer tenable. Bianchi is concerned only with the relation between the people, the Parliament, and the monarch on one hand, and the Church on the other. In one impassioned debate after another either More or his equally eloquent daughter defends the thesis that there can be no diversity of opinion in religion, that laymen can have no voice in religious matters, that Parliament has no real responsibility because it expresses only the will of the King (II.iii), and that submission to Rome is a divine not a human law (II.iv). More reminds Henry that "it is difficult for subjects to obey the prince's laws when the prince does not obey divine laws," a barely veiled warning that Rome may relieve subjects from their duty of allegiance with resultant danger to the King's life. The implications for the situation in Naples and Piedmont are clear, but Bianchi discreetly couches his admonition to the Italian sovereigns in a foreign idiom. Henry realizes too late that Cromwell is a traitor, and his credulity is an example to be shunned, for it is the monarch's fault if his servants are wicked (V.iii).

The tragedy, then, has contemporary significance, but for Italy rather than for England, and although Bianchi pays tribute in his preface to the many celebrated writers who have treated the subject, which he protests is so recent that it hardly needs explanation, he follows tradition less faithfully than either Scammacca or Rossi. He uses some of the anecdotes made familiar by Sander, Stapleton, and Domenico Regi, but he has no scruple about altering the episode of the "change of purpose," for instance. His More promises to yield to all the requests of the King with but one reservation. Henry rejoices, only to learn that More means he will offer the King his life but retain his own mind (II.vi; III.v). Here the use of the word "animo" rather than "anima" is symptomatic of the less fervid religious temperature of Bianchi's drama.

Rossi's portrayal of Henry VIII, based on Stapleton's account (p. 212), had been sympathetic. Sincerely attached to More, he is himself a victim of the wiles of Intemperance, and in a fit of remorse, after the execution, bids his guards take her to prison and have her strangled.

Bianchi goes even farther. More's execution is ordered by Cromwell with covert haste, and when Henry, whose outbursts of savage rage are always followed by a relenting mood, orders a reprieve, it is too late (V.i). Turning his anger on Cromwell, Henry orders his arrest and resolves to shed his own royal blood on More's tomb (V.iii), since with him, he laments, have perished the liberty, faith, innocence, and glory of his realm.[25] But he delays to give Margaret permission to receive her father's body for burial, and concedes that tears rather than blood shall be his tribute.

My tears and grief shall be the most illustrious ornament to adorn through coming centuries the tomb of More, and when my lamentations are known in future ages men will say that since the King's early virtue was buried in More's urn with the pristine Religion of the realm, Henry here had cause for weeping, because here Henry lost all.[26]

Bianchi's Margaret is far removed from Scammacca's devout virgin. A virago whose ferocious constancy ("feroce costanza") shocks her gentle stepmother, she provokes Henry, whom she outblusters, into ordering her arrest (III.iv). She seems to thirst for her father's beheading and dismemberment, and, when he appears to yield, swears she will cleanse the stain on his honor with her own blood. Her strongest motive is love of her country rather than of religion, and she invokes the name of *Patria* to justify her most violent outbursts. Indeed the whole play lacks the religious ardor of the preceding dramas. No longer do Religion and Intemperance delight the spectator in palpable form and, doubtless, imaginative costumes. Bianchi evidently was familiar with Rossi's work and speaks of the banishment of Religion, accompanied by More, from the royal palace and from the realm (II.i; IV.vii). But this is now little more than a figure of speech, and More dies a martyr not to the Catholic religion, despite his protestations, but only to the authority of the Pope; not to Christ but to Rome's interpretation of Peter.[27] Scammacca's

---

25. This may be an echo of Sander's comment that when the executioner beheaded More, "he struck off the head of justice, of truth and of goodness" (p. 126).

26. "Le mie lagrime, e 'l mio cordoglio saranno il fregio più illustre, che renderanno adorna per tutti i Secoli la tomba del Moro; e risapendosi nell'età futuro il mio pianto, dirassi che, rimanendo sepolta nell'urna del Moro colla prisca Religione del Regno la virtù primera del Re, Arrigo qui ebbe ragione di piangere, perchè qui Arrigo perdette il tutto" (V.v).

27. Stapleton says (pp. 205, 211) that More died for the primacy of the Pope, but gives a less legalistic tenor to his motive.

More rejoices that Fisher has celebrated mass in his cell and has given him communion; Rossi's More is immediately beatified; and Bianchi's More argues that twenty years of life are not worth his honor, or indeed—but this is almost a casual afterthought—his eternal happiness. He dies after the fourth act, and there is no triumphant vision in Act V, where Cromwell, Henry, and Margaret share the stage. For in Naples and Piedmont, to which Bianchi's play is directed, there was no question of schism, only of abuses of ecclesiastical privileges, privileges that Bianchi, like his mouthpiece More, was determined to defend against the encroachments of the modern state. Whereas Scammacca's More represented the layman as one of the twin pillars of established religion, and Rossi's personage typified the layman's intellectual and spiritual life, Bianchi's Tommaso is the lay lawyer, properly instructed in the rights of the Church, unshaken by threats or specious arguments against a divinely ordained institution, a man who, by his constancy and conspicuous example, will draw others to follow him.

IV

Silvio Pellico's *Tommaso Moro*, written in 1833, must be considered only as an epilogue to the series. During the century and more that had elapsed since Bianchi's tragedy, the tradition had faded, and Sander, Stapleton, and Regi were forgotten. When Pellico was asked by a lady whether he considered More's death *tragediabile*—a subject suitable for tragedy—he answered yes, but he evidently was not aware that other authors had used it. He says in his preface that he has read a recent life of More, probably Sir James Mackintosh's, published in 1831, the theme of which was the preeminent tyranny of an apostate King opposed to the preeminent rectitude of a faithful Catholic. While he was composing the play, he also read a novel by the Princesse de Craon, *Thomas Morus, Lord Chancelier du royaume d'Angleterre au XVIe siècle* (1832). An English Protestant historian, then, and a French novelist were his sources.

Pellico makes More the dominant figure of his play, in direct conflict with Henry. More has no confidant, and Cromwell is a minor figure, spiteful and conniving. The tragedy is written in the Italian romantic-historical style that Pellico himself had initiated in 1815 with his *Francesca da Rimini*, so much admired by Byron and Stendhal. It is full of local color, with crowds of citizens and soldiers, and an effective trial scene in Act IV, where Cromwell moves among the judges, subverting them. One of the witnesses is the historical figure Riccardo (Richard Rich), prepared to bear false testimony. Unlike its predecessors, the play ends with the flash of the headsman's axe.

More was a particularly appropriate and congenial hero to Pellico because the dramatist himself had been condemned to death for devotion to an ideal, and his commuted sentence had kept him in prison for twenty years. He was not released until 1830, and *Tommaso Moro* was written the same year that saw the publication of his memoirs, *Le mie prigioni*, which made him famous throughout Europe and America. The same spirit of charity and forbearance pervades both works. His More acknowledges that the Roman Church in England needed reforms, and that no social progress can be made without suffering; but he protests the policy of continued reprisals: "Happy calm will succeed the tempestuous reign of Henry VIII. . . . Freed from the Roman yoke, England's robust, lofty intellect will unfold with new, surprising power; she will become a light for other nations and enjoy glorious centuries of wisdom and strength."[28] Such a claim would have angered the earlier playwrights who saw in England a corrupt population and a wicked government, but by Pellico's day the English monarchy and the English constitution had become the envy of enlightened political philosophers throughout Europe. Consequently, Pellico's More answers with mingled sympathy and criticism: "Henry VIII must have envisaged a noble outcome. But his methods have failed. So strong is this fecund isle in the spirit of courage, liberty, and wisdom that despite wretched discord, despite tyrannical laws and bloodshed, perhaps it will raise its lofty head again, I hope, ere long."[29] He begs Henry to show tolerance, to

28.   D'Arrigo ottavo al tempestoso regno
        Succederà felice calma; ed opra
        Di tal regno sarà. Dal roman giogo
        Liberata Inghilterra, il suo robusto
        Alto intelletto spiegherà con nuova
        Sorprendente possanza, e lume all'altre
        Nazioni farassi e gloriosi
        Secoli avrà di senno e di fortezza.
                                        (III.v)
29.   E successo dovea nobil proporsi
        Arrigo ottavo. Ma fallito ha il modo.
        Tanto in questa feconda isola è spirto
        Di gagliardia, di libertà e di senno,

abandon persecution, to permit freedom of worship. His sentiments are far removed from Tudor reality.

The whole play, melancholy rather than tragic in tone, is imbued with a spirit of Christian forgiveness. Anne Boleyn, in typically romantic fashion, repents her guilty past and tries to soften Henry's heart toward those who have offended her. Compassionately she laments the fate of the Maid of Kent and pleads for Fisher, for More, and for his family. The shadow of her own approaching fate hangs over her. Margaret, timorous in her love, implores her father to yield to the King. He cannot, and dies not as a martyr to Rome but as a witness to the cause of human and divine love. He is Pellico's mouthpiece, but his message was alien to the rising spirit of the *Risorgimento*. The play was performed in 1833 to an unenthusiastic audience and remained unpublished until it appeared as part of Pellico's *Opere* (1856–60).[30]

The rift between the Church and Italian nationalism widened as the nineteenth century proceeded, and the new writers became increasingly anticlerical. For nearly three hundred years dramatists had been able to relate the story of More's conscientious resistance and his death to the prerogatives of Church and State in Italy as well as in England. Only when persecution became overtly political, as it had already done in Pellico's time, did the figure of the English martyr recede. The cause for which he had given his life lost its urgency, and the Italian stage looked elsewhere for its heroes.

Che di discordie scellerate ad onta,
E di leggi tiranniche e d'eccidi
Rialzerà forse tra breve, io spero,
L'alterissima testa.
(III.v)

30. A prose version of the play, purged of its female characters, was published in Milan in 1879 in the Novissima collana di rappresentazioni teatrali inedite per seminari, no. 92. See Salvioli, p. 210.

VI. Woman as Wonder: A Generic Figure in Italian and Shakespearean Comedy

Louise George Clubb · *Professor of Italian and Comparative Literature, University of California, Berkeley*

The method inherited from the old positivists of studying the Continental background of Elizabethan and Jacobean drama by tracing units of specific content to ultimate sources has constructed a Shakespeare conversant with learning of many kinds and ages. Recent refinements in the study of genre promise at last to relate him also to leading movements in the theater of his own time. Evidence that Shakespeare knew something of Italian drama, literary and improvised, has long lain about casually acknowledged in the positivistic manner as paired analogies (*Twelfth Night* with *Gl'ingannati*, *The Tempest* with Arcadian scenarios, and so on); it has not been organized into needed conclusions about kind, principles, commonplaces, movable units, and recurrent patterns, despite many exhortations such as Robert C. Melzi's to seek Shakespeare's frame of reference for *Twelfth Night* not only in *Ingannati* but in "the *Ingannati* family." [1] To search so is to find that Shakespeare often seems to be playing the game developed in Italian drama, with the customary pieces and principles but not by the usual rules, and always with original outcomes. A small portion of a *rapport*, probably irrecoverable in toto even by detailed reconstructions of the historical context in which fashions crossed the Channel, may be glimpsed by scrutinizing some generic features of *All's Well That Ends Well* and *Measure for Measure*, the comedies that G. K. Hunter calls "obvious twins" by virtue of the centrality to both of young women with divine missions and of the emphasis on forgiveness that allies them with the symbolic romances of Shakespeare's last period. [2]

The perception that the vital principles of *All's Well* and of *Measure for Measure* are to be found in ideas about the genre of tragicomedy and the direct linking of both plays with Guarini by Arthur Kirsch and by

---

1. "From Lelia to Viola," *Renaissance Drama*, 9 (1966), 69.
2. "Introduction" to the Arden edition of *All's Well That Ends Well* (London, 1959), pp. xxiii–xxiv and liv–lv. My quotations are from this edition.

J. W. Lever, respectively,[3] properly direct attention to Italian drama, for which tragicomedy was an incendiary critical issue, but they seal off Shakespeare from pertinent forces in the movement of which Guarini was only a part. Kirsch finds the germ of the providential plotting and the idea of tragicomedy behind *All's Well* in *Il pastor fido*, as Lever finds the formal cause of *Measure for Measure* in the *Compendio*, but while Guarini's practice and theory would bestow authority on the *tragicommedia pastorale* for the future, behind both lay decades of Italian tinkering with theatrical forms of representing ideas such as providence and of mixing tragedy with comedy. The hybrids produced earlier were various, including Giraldi Cinthio's *tragedia di fin lieto*. The most significant for comparison with Shakespearean comedy in general—and an important contributor to the development of the pastoral tragicomedy as finally established by Guarini—was the *commedia grave* of the stamp fostered by Bernardino Pino and praised by Tasso, exponents of which claimed "gravità" of form in the disposition, complexity, and thematic unity of their *intrecci,* and "gravità" of content in the morality, tragic emotion, fear, and "maraviglia" they mixed with comic conventions.[4] It was by retaining the lineaments and language of comedy, especially low comic types and bawdry and the prohibition of bloodshed, that *commedia grave* differed from the tragicomic mixture in *tragedia di fin lieto*, and it was by the juxtaposition of extremes, high and low, serious and hilarious, and by its urban setting that it differed from Guarini's kind of tragicomedy, a studiedly mild third genre created by the fusion and tempering of the extremes of the two others. The concern for theme or controlling idea, which appeared in *commedia grave* before it reached a fuller development in pastoral tragicomedy, signals the expansion of the Donatian *imitatio vitae, imago veritatis,* an expansion long aimed at by Italian comic playwrights so as to include more of the inner reality of emotion and the outer cosmic reality of forces beyond human sight or comprehension, encircling human life in benign surveillance. The enlarged range of

3. *Jacobean Dramatic Perspectives* (Charlottesville, Va., 1972), pp. 7–15 and 52–64; "Introduction" to the Arden edition of *Measure for Measure* (London, 1965; rpt., 1966), pp. lix–lxiii. My quotations are from Lever's edition.

4. For *commedia grave* and related pastoral, see L. G. Clubb, "Italian Comedy and *The Comedy of Errors*," *Comparative Literature*, 19 (Summer 1967), 240–251; "The Making of the Pastoral Play," *Petrarch to Pirandello*, ed. J. A. Molinaro (Toronto, 1973), pp. 45–72; "La mimesi della realtà invisibile nel dramma pastorale italiano e inglese del tardo Rinascimento," *Misure Critiche*, 4 (March 1974), 65–92.

comic vision also accommodated timely instruction in a new sensibility and in the spirit of civil and religious obedience to authority deemed necessary to the revitalization of the Roman Church.[5]

From among the Counter-Reformation *commedie gravi* there may be isolated for present purposes a number of works in which the play of abstraction is especially strong and the major theme or idea is invested in a feminine figure developed from the generic commonplace of the *innamorata*. While I think that Shakespeare used fashionable developments in both *commedia grave* and pastoral plays from the beginning of his career, the particular type of *commedia grave* in which the figure of the woman functions as vehicle for idea has a unique kinship with the "twin" comedies of his middle period.[6]

The figure is to be distinguished from the merely enterprising *innamorata* whose energy and charm arouse a wonder belonging to "ordinary" life rather than to any transcendent truth; the Shakespearean variations on this generic character are Viola, Julia, and Rosalind. The more spiritually specialized version of the *innamorata*, to whom Helena and Isabella bear a family resemblance, directs the spectator's attention to a wonder beyond the plot or fable. The figure is distinguished by a remarkable intrinsic worth, established by her effect on other characters and by structurally disposed contrasts with them as foils. She functions as an example of virtue for imitation and admiration, and, now more now less, she is associated with an extra-fabular reality illustrated not by an obvious allegory but as an image of a truth not physically visible but naturally related to the prima facie story. At

5. The move toward abstraction in Italian theater of this period has recently received attention, long overdue, with specific reference to the drama as a vehicle of Counter-Reformation social propaganda, e.g., Giulio Ferroni's valuable essays on Annibal Caro and Raffaello Borghini in his "*Mutazione*" e "*Riscontro*" nel teatro di Machiavelli e altri saggi sulla commedia del Cinquecento (Rome, 1972), and Guido Baldi, "Le commedie di Sforza Oddi e l'ideologia della Controriforma," *Lettere Italiane*, 23 (January-March 1971), 43–62. The depressing images of persuasion to conformity and passivity that emerge would seem to be the price paid on the side of content for the gains in dramatic form achieved when the concomitant trend toward religious propaganda began developing means to free comedy from the narrowly realistic interpretation of the principle of *imitatio vitae* and *imago veritatis*.

6. The means by which Shakespeare might have known the commonplaces of fashionable Italian drama were many: *commedia dell'arte* troupes in England or reported on from abroad, Italians at court or elsewhere in England, English travelers, pro-Italian men of fashion or university scholars, and printed editions from Italy or even from John Wolfe's London press. Printed plays offer the most nearly complete single view of the Italian theater, as the regular drama influenced and was influenced by the *commedia dell'arte*, and it is therefore from well-known works in print that I shall draw examples of the genre under discussion.

her full development the figure is known by a hush that falls about her, a sense of her being a thing enskied and sainted.

Antecedent to the figure is the dramatized topos of love in action, but the distance from love's wonder to woman's, from rueful amazement to respectful admiration, may be measured by the difference between the relation of love's power to woman's in Cardinal Bibbiena's *La Calandria* (1513), cornerstone of Italian literary comedy in general, and that in Alessandro Piccolomini's *L'amor costante* (written in 1531, perhaps performed in 1536),[7] which points forward to *commedia grave* in particular. In *Calandria* the transvestite Santilla is a mechanical figure. Whatever wonder at feminine behavior the comedy proffers is reserved for Fulvia the *malmaritata*, also briefly transvestite and driven thereto by her passionate pursuit of Santilla's twin brother. Love's galvanic effect on her is repeatedly observed as a marvel, but in the same state of moral suspension as that obtaining in the *Decameron* stories of which *Calandria* is a parade of quotations. Fulvia's wonder at her own bravery—"There is nothing, certainly, that Love may not force one to. I, who would hardly leave my room without company, now, moved by love, leave my house alone, dressed as a man" (III.vii)[8] —confirmed by the servants Samia (III.vi) and Fessenio (III.xi), remains comment on a mood, neither statement of theme nor didactic injunction. The event that occasions the musings is not edifying, an adultery to be concealed at the end, celebrating at most a triumph of wit over stupidity in the execution of a fervid but somewhat one-sided and joyless affair which promises only to become more so in the future.

Lucrezia of *Amor costante*, on the other hand, appears onstage only once (V.iv) but embodies a theme that has taken on moral connotations. Love is given structural status by the prologue: "we shall teach you with our comedy how a constant love (whence the comedy takes its name) always wins through and how manifestly mistaken it is to give up at setbacks in love: for that most compassionate god called Love never deserts anyone who serves him with perseverance";[9] and, as illustrated

7. Florindo Cerreta, *Alessandro Piccolomini, letterato e filosofo senese del Cinquecento* (Siena, 1960), p. 14.

8. "Nulla è, certo, che Amore altri a fare non costringa. Io, che già senza compagnia a gran pena di camera uscita non sarei, or, da amor spinta, vestita da uomo fuor di casa me ne vo sola" (Nino Borsellino, ed., *Commedie del Cinquecento*, II [Milan, 1967], 63).

9. Quotations from *Amor costante* in this and the following paragraph are from Borsellino, *Commedie*, I (Milan, 1962). Prologue: "vi ammaestraremo, con la nostra comedia, quanto un amor

by Ferrante and Lucrezia, separated by pirates after their secret marriage and elopement, each for seven years left in doubt of the other's survival, emphasis has shifted from love's power over nature to the virtue displayed by noble natures in love. Lucrezia's virtue in general is underscored in references to her "holiness and wonderful goodness" (II.iii), but it is ancillary to the particular virtue of constancy spelled out again in Corsetto's reaction to the lovers' trials and reconciliation: "Oh most happy pair of lovers! oh constant love! oh most beautiful coincidence worthy to be the subject of a most excellent comedy" (II.iii).

Other characters contribute variously to the theme: some voice their low opinion of woman's constancy (II.v), the *serva* Agnoletta exhibits her unsentimental sexual greed in direct contrast to the idealizing devotion of Margarita to Giannino, who in turn is indifferent to Margarita, but thinks himself a unique exemplar of constant love for Lucrezia (I.ix). When Lucrezia is proved to be his sister, Giannino easily turns to Margarita, whom Agnoletta thereupon apostrophizes as the true exemplar: "now your constant love will be an example to all the world. Learn, ladies, from her to be constant in your thoughts" (V.ix). Ferrante also vies with Lucrezia in a display of constancy, but she crowns the thematic spectacle. Fra Cherubino likens them both to Christian martyrs, describing how they contend for the first draught of the supposed poison they are forced to take ("I don't believe that any martyr ever went to death with so much constancy and fervor as those two," V.iii), but it is Lucrezia who snatches and tries to drink it all. Her refusal under pressure to marry, her devotion to a secret husband never enjoyed and presumed dead, make her seem nun-like, a saint (III.vii), until she is discovered in bed with Ferrante. Her accuser, Guglielmo, rejects her explanation but declares, "If it is so, there was never a woman more chaste than you nor a love more constant" (V.iv). The truth established, she emerges hallowed by that encomium, a vowed saint in the religion of love. The love in question has no philosophical or

costante (donde piglia il nome la comedia) abbia sempre buon fine e quanto manifesto error sia abbandonarsi nelle aversità amorose: perché quel pietosissimo dio che si chiama Amore non abbandona mai chi con fermezza lo serve" (p. 307); II.iii: "santimonia e bontà maravigliosa," "Oh felicissima coppia d'amanti! oh amor costante! oh bellissimo caso da farci sopra una comedia eccellentissima!" (pp. 348, 349); V.ix: "ora il tuo amor costante sarà esempio a tutto il mondo. Imparate, donne, da costei a esser costanti nei pensier vostri" (p. 423); V.iii: "non credo che martire mai si conducesse a la morte con tanta costanzia e fervore con quanto hanno fatto l'uno e l'altro di costoro" (p. 412); V.iv: "Se gli è così, non fu mai donna più casta di te né amor più costante" (p. 414).

theological overtones, but accords with cinquecento notions of domestic virtue, and is conceived as an ideal verity, of which Piccolomini's comedy undertakes to give a theatrical image.

In the later sixteenth century the pedagogical use of art encouraged by Counter-Reformation policy was bound to exploit the capacity inherent in the uniquely social art of drama to express the discrepancy between appearance and reality. In keeping with the universalist and neo-medieval trend in official Catholic thought, therefore, Italian drama began to shimmer with reflections of this discrepancy glimpsed as a contrast between human limitation and divine omniscience. Contemporary critical polemics over genres and over the interpretation of Aristotle's *Poetics* also contributed to dramatization of the contrast. Aristotle's comments on the form of *Oedipus the King* spurred experimenters in generic hybridization to adapt the principle of Sophocles' tragedy to comedy. The results make ironic peripeties teach quietistic trust in a divine plan, for to apply the structure of *Oedipus* to comedy in a Christian era was inevitably to make comedy of providence from tragedy of fate. The idea of fortune traditional to comedy and presented in the early cinquecento as an unforeseeable and all-powerful adversary or ally, with only an occasional passing reference to providence, was subjected in post-Tridentine comedy to an orthodox, though hardly searching, scrutiny and demoted to the only place it could properly claim in a Christian world, the place subordinate to "Him whose knowledge transcends all" firmly assigned it by Dante.[10] Overestimating fortune's power was seen by practical theologians to be dangerous not only to a right conception of providence but also to a proper belief in free will. Effects of the Inquisitional campaign against astrology and the other judiciary arts were commonly evident in prefaces to tragedy, where the author dissociated his personal faith from his characters' references to fate, chance, fortune, and stars, and from any implications of the supremacy of such forces, in opposition to the orthodox principles of the Unmoved Mover, divine providence, and free will.[11] Dramatists did not thereby turn into theologians bent on combating heresies of predestination or the inefficacy of good works, but, without

10. "Colui lo cui saver tutto trascende," *Inf.* VII. 73, *La divina commedia*, ed. G. Vandelli, 13th ed. rev. (Milan, 1929; rpt., 1946).

11. E.g., Francesco Bozza, *Fedra* (Venice, 1578), prologue; Ridolfo Campeggi, *Il Tancredi* (Bologna, 1614), dedication.

returning to the literal miracles and allegories of medieval drama, many responded to the widening of the theatrical spectrum to include abstract significance by expanding their dramaturgy to develop appropriate means of expression. Consciousness of the doctrinal implications of a comedy cliché like that of fortune led to the association of other conventional elements of the genre, notably the figure of the *innamorata*, with the wonders of providence and the cooperation with it of active virtue.

Elsewhere I have cited Raffaello Borghini's *La donna costante* (1578) as a theatrical metaphor of providential action.[12] Here I would re-elucidate Borghini's alliance of the theme of love with the transcendent idea of providence in the person of the title character, and his invocation of wonder through the design visible in the *intreccio*, the constant woman central to the plot and embodying throughout the divine permanence on which rests the providence that denies the supremacy of fortune. The abstracting tendency that Giulio Ferroni rightly sees in this comedy[13] is, in fact, the hallmark of Counter-Reformation theater, which, while it did not in Italy culminate in a Calderón, nevertheless produced the experimental models for putting ideas onstage as a symbolic process, distinct from the more direct allegories of medieval drama. The justice of Ferroni's view of Borghini as a jobber of merely serviceable abstraction confirming a fixed order and repressive social norms need not impede extending the aim of the abstracting tendency and the sphere of the fixed order to include theological doctrines from which the would-be monolithic society took its sanctions. When Borghini added the operations of divine providence to his objects of imitation, he did not do so alone. He was simply an exponent of an engaged dramaturgy that is historically relevant also to Shakespeare. Shakespeare's abstractions have been called allegorical and liturgical in consonance with the prevailing tenets of the state religion under Elizabeth and James,[14] but he possessed along with the inwardness lacking in

---

12. "Italian Comedy," p. 250. My references are to the second edition, Florence, 1582.

13. "Non si tratta di un'astratezza congelata e contraddittoria, segno di un rifugio nell'introversione e nell' 'idea' come salvezza dall'attacco di una realtà ostile e nemica. Il Borghini non è un artista dell'introversione (la sua scarsa intelligenza critica glielo avrebbe in ogni caso vietato), è invece un artigiano di un'astrazione tendente all'esterno, alla formulazione di norme sociali, alla organizzazione repressiva della realtà entro un circolo di dati vagliati e riconosciuti socialmente, nell'aspirazione alla conferma di un finale 'ordine' immobile e senza alternative (Ferroni, "Mutazione" e "Riscontro," p. 260).

14. Some of the best-known statements of such views are found in G. Wilson Knight, *The Wheel*

Borghini a genius, sometimes troubling to critics, for representing an experience simultaneously as an unforgettably individual datum and as a universal truth, verifiable by the workings of the spectator's own consciousness and even partially capable of abstraction from the context and of summation as a *sententia*.

The figure of wonder in *La donna costante*, a mosaic of dramatic commonplaces and novella situations (among which that of Romeo and Juliet is eminent), turgid with pathos and heroism, is the transvestite Elfenice, whose name seals her extreme proof of constancy in avoiding a second marriage by allowing herself to be buried for dead, a phoenix in the uniqueness of her virtue and in her resurrection. Her love for Aristide, banished slayer of her cousin, is paralleled by the love between her brother and Aristide's sister, who engage in a secondary display of self-sacrificing constancy. As in *Amor costante*, auxiliary characters are used to enhance the wonder of the heroine's persevering fidelity with negative comments confuted by the facts (I.i) or with positive ones supported by them (I.iii).

The topos of fortune is put through standard comic permutations with an unwonted insistence—from the glutton's parodic garble on the reverses of fortune (I.i); through a *servo*'s conclusion that fortune is powerful despite the (Counter-Reformation?) sages (II.i), a *serva*'s comic lament on fortune (III.x), the hero's recital of classical examples of fortune's shifts (IV.iv), his friend's brooding on the subject (IV.iv; IV.vi), and the heroine's discourse (III.i) and solo aria "O Fortuna crudele" (IV.viii); to the fourth and fifth *intermedi* representing the triumph and the downfall of Rome—to illustrate "How fortune goes changing its style" (fifth *intermedio*).[15] By such elaboration fortune is set up to be duly knocked down, and it is Elfenice who emerges as the embodiment of the subduing power. Throughout the apparent reign of fickle fortune, Elfenice's eleven-year-long constancy is unswerving; like the miraculous bird she is named for, she seems to surmount even death. The fifth-act reversal shows all the musings on fortune to have been mistaken: the capricious play of chance is not allowed responsibility for

---

of *Fire* (London, 1930) and *The Sovereign Flower* (London, 1958); Roy W. Battenhouse, "*Measure for Measure* and the Christian Doctrine of the Atonement," *PMLA*, 61 (1946), 1029–59; Nevill Coghill, "Comic Form in *Measure for Measure*," *Shakespeare Survey*, 8 (1955), 14–27.

   15. "Come fortuna va cangiando stile."

the happy peripety. Nor is fortune's defeat just another novellistic triumph of love. Elfenice thanks the "Mover of Heaven" (V.xiv) in the formulaic phrase by which sovereignty of providence over chance and fate was recognized in scholastically worded prefaces to tragedy. After this endorsement of providence by a title character whose constancy works miracles, there follows a final *intermedio* in which a Neoplatonic identification of love with the action of the "Sommo Motor" is made: love is announced as first cause of all good sent by the Prime Mover, and pagan gods descend from heaven in a spectacle of love's universal triumph. This decorative Neoplatonizing would find more scope in the pastoral drama, but here it shows the degree to which in serious comedy love as wonder, illustrated in the action of a singular woman, could be associated with idea and with Christian doctrine as the generic figure becomes more abstract. Love is promoted to the rank of grace and providence, and the commonplace of feigned death and burial is used as more than an example of cleverness, as a wonder of steadfastness signifying the right human action that cooperates through love in the stability of the Unmoved Mover, who is the source of love and of the providence that controls the mutability of fortune.

The woman who carries more than her own spiritual weight appears with a difference in Giambattista Della Porta's *Gli duoi fratelli rivali* (written in the 1590s, possibly earlier).[16] The nucleus of the plot is an analogue of *Much Ado about Nothing*, and the heroine, Carizia, is not called on to perform miracles of constancy but to be the occasion and victim of the principal psychological action, the conflict of two brothers who love her, one maligning and the other repudiating her, causing her apparent death. The character of incarnate marvel is first established for her by conventional hyperbolic compliment and by the familiar device of using a paler image as foil in Don Ignazio's description of Carizia and her sister as angels, the former incomparably superior, nature's very model of beauty in all its works (I.i).[17] At next sight Don Ignazio hails Carizia with a Petrarchan commonplace identifying her with the source

16. The first edition, *Gli duoi fratelli rivali* (Venice, 1601), is followed in Giambattista Della Porta, *Le commedie*, ed. Vincenzo Spampanato, II (Bari, 1911), from which my quotations are taken.

17. ". . . la maggiore avea non so che di reale e di maraviglioso. Parea che la natura avesse fatto l'estremo suo forzo in lei per serbarla per modello de tutte l'altre opere sue, per non errar più mai" (pp. 202–203).

of light and life, as they engage in the related dramatic commonplace of the window (or balcony) scene (II.ii, iii).[18] Her responses are exemplary Counter-Reformation displays of chastity, generous love, concern for family honor, filial duty, and ceremonial tact, expressed in words and gestures drawing further on the repertory of comic conventions to add moral perfection to superhuman beauty.

It is by association with Christian ideas, however, that Carizia becomes something more than a model young lady. The commonplace of fortune appears in this comedy not only in the usual exclamations but also in expanded discussions of how to bend it to one's ends, assigned conspicuously to the "wrong" side, to Don Flaminio and his servant Panimbolo, who, although less wicked than Don John and his henchmen in *Much Ado*, are cast as the villains of the piece. In contrast to Don Ignazio and Simbolo, Don Flaminio and Panimbolo swear by self-interest, have dishonorable intentions toward Carizia, attempt to justify using bad means for their ends, and entertain Machiavellian opinions of fortune (II.ix; III.i). Their views are shown to be as incorrect by orthodox standards as their machinations are morally wrong. The local shifts of fortune lead to a catastrophe, but the general motion and happy peripety that make all right are attributed explicitly to providence. The existence of fortune is not denied, but its place is defined as subordinate to providence and its power is limited downward as well, in that while it can influence human impulse, it cannot overcome the freedom to act virtuously. The character in whom the ideas of free will and providence are reposed is not Ignazio, who only by his matrimonial intentions and

18. Ignazio's outburst at Carizia's appearance from above—"Giá fuggono le tenebre dell'aria, ecco l'aurora che precede la chiarezza del mio bel sole, giá spuntano i raggi intorno" (II.ii, p. 202)—has antecedents in other *commedie gravi*, e.g., Pino's *Gli ingiusti sdegni* (Rome, 1553), in which the window scene between Licinio and Delia (I.v) includes this and other commonplaces of speech and gesture used in Della Porta's scene and in *commedie erudite* from the first half of the century (such as Ercole Bentivoglio's *Il geloso* [Venice, 1544], in which Fausto complains that Livia does *not* appear and apostrophizes her house as the dwelling of the sun [II.i]). The association of the lady with the sun, and her abode and place of appearance with the east, was a well-established lyric trope; the Neapolitan poetaster in Cristoforo Castelletti's *commedia grave*, *Le stravaganze d'amore* (Venice, 1584), gives as a sample of Tuscan love poetry, "la vostra fenestra è il mio Oriente, e'l lume de l'occhi vostri è il mio Parnaso" (III.v). The lady as sunlight and dawn was part of the Petrarchan tradition. In *Le rime di Francesco Petrarca*, ed. Giosuè Carducci and Severino Ferrari (1899; rpt., Florence, 1943), commenting on Sonnet 219, Carducci notes Latin antecedents and Renaissance variations (p. 313). In comedy the conceit was adapted to the physical place and to plot conventions governing lovers' encounters, so that it became a movable part of the genre. Romeo's "what light through yonder window breaks?/ It is the east, and Juliet is the sun!" (II.ii) testifies to the international dissemination of the commonplace and the heights to which it could be carried.

relative silence on the subject of fortune reveals himself as the "good" brother, but Carizia, in whom the exercise of positive, non-Machiavellian *virtù* is linked in orthodox paradox with the idea of providence. The connection is established in a scene of parental rejoicing at the engagement that will restore the family's prosperity. The mother associates Carizia's virtue with a providential plan and recounts how an impulse from heaven made the usually retiring girl insist on attending the festival where Ignazio first saw her.

> Eufranone. Who can penetrate the hidden secrets of God?
> Polisena.   Oh God, have you ever failed anyone who put all his hopes in you? She has always placed her trust in you, and you have answered her prayers, rewarded her goodness and the extraordinary obedience she pays to her father and mother. (II.vii)[19]

This trust in providence that places the parents also on the right side is not yet to be fulfilled, there being another ordeal ahead when Flaminio's deceit results in Carizia's supposed death. As she rises again, miraculously produced by her mother just as the brothers are about to kill each other and even the desperate Ignazio abandons hope and blames all on fortune, Polisena hammers home the orthodox lesson: this is not merely another caprice of mutable fortune, nor even an accomplishment of unaided human volition, but the conclusion of a complex plan of providence: "Give thanks to God, not to me his unworthy servant! He alone ordered in heaven that events so difficult and impossible to resolve be brought to so happy a conclusion" (V.iii). The free exercise of virtue and the work of providence are definitively brought together in a final didactic crescendo when Carizia formally forgives everyone, sealing the bloodless reconciliation that distinguishes *commedia grave* from the the tragicomic mixture in *tragedia di fin lieto*, and her father says: "Your goodness, oh daughter, has moved God to aid you; in the secrets of your fate He had ordered that everything be made peaceful for you, and therefore He who had made misfortune become good fortune and pains

---

19. This and the following quotations appear thus in the original: "*Eufranone*. Chi può penetrar gli occulti segreti di Dio? *Polisena*. O Iddio, che mai vien meno a chi pone in te solo le sue speranze? Ella si è sempre raccomandata a te, e tu li hai esaudite le sue preghiere, rimunerata la sua bontà e l'ubidienza estraordinaria che porta al suo padre e sua madre" (p. 234); V.iii: "Rendete le grazie a Dio, non a me indegna serva! Egli solo ha ordinato nel cielo che i fatti cosí difficili e impossibili ad accommodarsi siano ridotti a cosí lieto fine" (p. 296); V.iv: "La tua bontá, o figlia, ha commosso Iddio ad aiutarti: egli ne' secreti del tuo fato aveva ordinato che per te ogni cosa si fusse pacificato; e perciò di tutto si ringrazi Iddio che ha fatto che le disaventure diventino venture e le pene allegrezze" (p. 299).

become joys must be thanked for everything" (V.iv). Meanwhile, the brothers' uncle, Viceroy of Salerno, figure of civil authority and by definition upholder of Tridentine orthodoxy, declares that seeing Carizia convinces him that God has planned the whole thing.

The analogous *Much Ado* is Italianate in story and in the dramatic articulation that uses labyrinthine structure to reveal invisible reality in contrast to visible appearance, another form of the pattern by which a providential plan is revealed at the expense of fortune; but it was not until *All's Well* and *Measure for Measure* that Shakespeare employed the generic figure of the woman to suggest the working of grace, investing her with the fairy-tale luminousness that looks toward his late romances. Although Carizia's situation is that of Hero, and she shares more than one stage commonplace with Juliet, she belongs to the series of women, quivering with transcendent significance, that includes Elfenice, Helena, and Isabella and points forward to Imogen.

The necessarily multilateral approach to Shakespeare's Helena and Isabella via generic formulae must include Girolamo Bargagli's celebrated *La pellegrina*, written earlier than *Donna costante* or *Fratelli rivali*,[20] and recommended to English readers in 1598 by its inclusion among the listed sources in John Florio's *A Worlde of Wordes*. The title character, although not identified with providence, is a well-developed specimen of the woman as wonder and bears a strong generic resemblance to Helena.

In the story of Drusilla, who arrives in Pisa (from Spain in the first version, from France in the revision) disguised as a pilgrim seeking Lucrezio, to whom she has been secretly married for some three years, appear the most characteristic elements of *commedia grave*: juxtaposed extremes of laughter and tears, careful complexity, thematic unity, Counter-Reformation didacticism, and effects of surprise, irony, pathos, and heroism calculated to arouse wonder. The plot combines a great variety of recognized narrative and dramatic sources, examined by Cerreta, to which Boccaccio's tale of Giletta of Narbonne (*Decameron*, III.9) should be added as analogous in such details as the combination of the lady's pilgrim disguise, inherited medical knowledge, choice

20. *La pellegrina* was written in 1567–68 and was first printed in a version revised by Scipione Bargagli (Siena, 1589). It is in this version that the play has been known, but the original version has recently been published from the authorial MS by Florindo Cerreta (Florence, 1971). I shall quote from Cerreta's edition, the speeches in question being substantially the same in both versions.

of two chaperones (male and female), her status as married virgin, and her sense of rejection (in Drusilla's case unfounded). Examining the construction of *Pellegrina* with an eye rather to the flourishing dramatic practice of shuffling commonplaces and formulae than to the specific provenance of each plot datum, however, reveals that greater weight (more than even Cerreta, an authority on *Intronati* drama, allows) should be attached to the influence of *Amor costante*, distinguished precursor in the *Intronati* tradition to which *Pellegrina* belongs and the model for the representation of a heroine of constancy through an intrigue plot turning on a theme illustrated by comparisons and contrasts of actions and characters. As in *Amor costante*, there is the danger that one of the lovers will be contracted to someone else, in this case Lucrezio to Lepida, who is already pregnant by her secret husband, Terenzio, and feigning madness to avoid the new match. Also as in *Amor costante*, the secondary example of constancy, Lepida again, is pursued by still another suitor and is attended by an affectionate servant, a nurse, whose easygoing sexual and moral standards are a foil to the girl's ideal of constancy. Like Piccolomini's Lucrezia, the nun-like Drusilla lacks the symbolic bond with the stable power of heavenly providence and love controlling mutable fortune that Elfenice of *Donna costante* will exhibit a decade later. Whereas Lucrezia is only a saint of constancy, however, the more active and articulate Drusilla is elevated to a broader patronage, dispensing wisdom, blessings, and scrupulous example. Her refusal to be bedded or even kissed after her secret wedding or to enjoy its privileges until it is publicly sanctioned (I.iv) distinguishes her from other participants in the dramatic commonplace of clandestine marriage, including the secondary heroine Lepida, whose pregnancy enhances by contrast the saintly Counter-Reformation rigor of Drusilla's chaste and law-abiding self-denial. It is explicitly pointed out that such marriages as Lepida's have been forbidden by the Council of Trent (V.iv),[21] but in comedy this stock device continued to meet with indulgence, so that Drusilla's strict observance of the Tridentine spirit and letter appears the more wonderful. Her further practices of self-denial are more pleasing to modern taste. On learning of Lucrezio's new engagement, without realizing that he thinks her dead, Drusilla plans to go away quietly instead of urging her prior legal claim, even while

21. Cerreta notes that the conciliar decree "de clandestinis matrimoniis" went into effect on 1 May 1564 (*La pellegrina*, p. 193, n. 117).

admitting that she would rather have Lucrezio "ungrateful and unfaithful than another, loyal" (II.i).[22] She decides to stay because Lepida's madness throws the engagement in doubt and because there is need for her own medical knowledge, which she says she always uses for the good of others (II.vii). Though he does not penetrate her disguise, Lucrezio is struck almost dumb by her noble aspect, not because of a subconscious memory but as further evidence of Drusilla's intimidating superiority. Her landlady, Violante,[23] an aging prostitute and additional foil to the figure of ideal constancy, is at first not sympathetic to the "donna tanto mirabile," but even her irritation at Drusilla's inviolability is expressed by a classification of the pilgrim as something different from the rest of mankind (II.iii). Seen from any angle, Drusilla is a thing apart, all impressions of her testifying to a combination of enterprise with moral and intellectual superiority not originating in the individual sources of the play but developing in the *commedia grave* figure of the woman as an embodiment of spiritual values.

Bargagli does not incorporate doctrinal issues in his comedy, but he disposes the denouement so as to define Drusilla's pilgrimage of love as more than a holy simile, as in itself holy, by emphasizing her efficacy as benefactress and conscience to all the other characters and as resurrected saint to Lucrezio. Although only indirectly concerned in it, she presides over the climactic recognition scene of the Lepida-Terenzio plot. Lepida's father, Cassandro, still adamant even after Terenzio is proved to be a good matrimonial catch, demands punishment for the seduction: "Only one who has suffered an offense can know how sweet vengeance can be and how ardently desired" (V.iv). Terenzio pleads, as does his brother, but the final plea and the one that moves Cassandro is Drusilla's: "There is nothing in which man makes himself more like

22. These quotations occur in this and the following paragraph. II.i: "ingrato ed infedele che un altro leale" (p. 109); II.iii: "woman so wonderful" (p. 115); V.iv: "Non sa quanto dolce cosa sia la vendetta né quanto ardentemente si desideri se non chi ha ricevuta l'offesa" (p. 196), "Non è cosa nella quale l'uomo si faccia più simile a Dio che nel perdonare" (p. 197); V.vi: "my divine Drusilla" (p. 205), "ora è finito il pellegrinaggio, ora è ottenuta la grazia, ora sono adempiuti i voti" (p. 207).

23. Although my purpose is to suggest generic similarities rather than specific debts, it is tempting to speculate on the First Folio stage direction to the scene in *All's Well* in which Helena as a pilgrim meets her landlady, the widow, and the daughter Diana, accompanied by "Violenta, and Mariana" (III.v). Violante, a name not uncommon but not associated with landladies except in *Pellegrina*, was metathasized in French translation and taken over twice by Painter in Tales 37 and 42 of *The Palace of Pleasure*, though not in his tale of Giletta, 38, Shakespeare's source. The introduction of the name by Shakespeare or by the scribe of the Folio copy into a situation generically similar to that in *Pellegrina* is, at any rate, a teasing coincidence.

God than in forgiving" (V.iv). The following and final scenes are reserved entirely for Drusilla and the fulfillment of her heart's desire,
dragged out for dramatic effect and emotional impact by her soliloquy
and the scene of reconciliation with Lucrezio, who speaks of his supposedly dead wife as a saint and greets her on recognition as "Drusilla
mia divina" (V.vi). In this exalted mood Bargagli chooses to end,
assigning the *envoi* not to a comic character, as is more common, but to
Drusilla herself, in the manner of some of the grave late cinquecento
comedies and of Shakespeare in *All's Well, Measure for Measure*, and
the romances that are concluded by serious characters. Drusilla reas-
serts the thematic unity of her story, ending on a metaphor: "now the
pilgrimage is ended, now the grace obtained, now the vows fulfilled!"
(V.vi). Placed as finishing touch to a portrayal of the *innamorata* as an
emblem of Counter-Reformation virtue, however, the metaphor is no
simple expression of the quest, reward, and promises of love through
the vocabulary of religion. Heaven has not been demoted to a vehicle
for an amatory or at best temporal tenor. A pilgrimage of love that
culminates in conventional tableaux of reconciliation made to radiate
suggestions of ritual Christian forgiveness and miraculous resurrection
offers a theatrical image integrating the secular and the religious.

   To estimate precisely the extent of the vogue of this variety of
commedia grave, the use in it of the woman to arouse moral and
religious wonder, and the range of commonplaces employed for didactic and symbolic ends constituting the particular tragicomic mixture in
which Shakespeare might have found a starting place for his more
intellectual and symbolic casting of the formulae, would require a
survey of many other literary comedies, in which two of Sforza Oddi's
would also have to be included.[24] Erminia of *Prigione d'amore* (written
ca. 1570), who substitutes herself for her brother and undergoes apparent execution in prison, is a primary illustration of the Counter-
Reformation injunction to quietism and trust in the powers that be, here
the Duke of Ferrara, never present onstage but by reference and by effect
on the action associated with the idea of providence, an example of the
unitary civil and religious concept of power in post-Tridentine Italy. By
means of a denouement in which the commonplace of supposed death

---

   24. *Prigione d'amore* (Florence, 1590; colophon 1589); *I morti vivi* (Perugia, 1576). Baldi
analyzes the civil aspect of Oddi's three comedies as a "modello di comportamento conformistico,
bassato sulla passività e la rinuncia" ("Le commedie di Sforza Oddi," p. 45).

takes the form of execution in a prison less grotesque than that of
Measure for Measure but likewise frequented by clowns, the characters
of *Prigione d'amore* learn and teach the lesson of submission to divine
and ducal laws in their hierarchical relationship, and realize that the
conflict of love and law is a false appearance, the reality being the benign
providence of a paternalistic government. More directly concerned with
providence is Oddi's *I morti vivi* (written after 1571), in which the
Greek romance of Clitophon and Leucippe (also used by Annibal Caro
in *Gli straccioni*) is refashioned to create a pattern of miraculous
resurrections, with the baptized Egyptian heroine, Alessandra, func-
tioning centrally as visible proof of God's miraculous providence and as
example of the virtues of faith, hope, and charity, which she illustrates
by resignation on the one hand, perseverance on the other, and forgiveness to crown all. The diction throughout is weighted with allusions to
heaven's will, providence, and miracles, and the characters exist in a
state of collective wonder, especially with regard to Alessandra. Oddi
alters his source by eliminating adultery, bringing the dead to life in a
general reconciliation of families illuminated by Counter-Reformation
zeal (a vow to make a pilgrimage to Loreto is part of the final rejoicing);
and in the baptism of Alessandra and her father, Abraim, born again of
water and the Holy Ghost, he attaches an original and ponderous
Christian symbolism to the commonplace of the return from death that
he employs as organizing theme.

Although Shakespeare's strong reliance on the tale of Giletta of
Narbonne makes the action of *All's Well That Ends Well* a *con-
taminatio* less eclectic than some of his other comic plots, the result
nevertheless is more like *commedia erudita* than like any other form of
dramatized novella, more like *commedia grave* than any other species
of *commedia erudita*, and more like the kind than like any particular
example of it. While Helena inevitably has something in common with
Giletta and with the heroine of Bernardo Accolti's fifteenth-century
dramatization, *La Virginia*, she is by quality and function distant from
them—and also from such Shakespearean *innamorate* as Rosalind and Viola—much as Elfenice, Drusilla, and their kind are distant
from the many enterprising Italian heroines whose significance stops
short of transcendent symbolism. The plane of meaning on which
Helena rather uncomfortably moves is the one less consistently attained
by the feminine *exempla* and idea-carriers, and Shakespeare's modifica-

tions of the novella bring the story closer to the dramatic genre in which they appear. Shakespeare magnifies Helena's intrinsic worth by enlarging on the wisdom, character, and beauty found in his source and by eliminating the external supports of relatives and wealth, so that Helena's native merit stands alone. He increases her power to arouse admiration by inventing the dowager Countess, who calls Helena "the most virtuous gentlewoman that ever nature had praise for creating" (IV.v.9–10), and by introducing, in contrast to Bertram, young nobles very willing to marry her. The use of the Clown, cynical about goodness in women (I.iii.79 ff.), and of Parolles as foils to Helena's goodness and benign influence on Bertram also heightens her value and reflects the practice of Italian comic dramaturgy. In keeping with the theme of industry and perseverance proclaimed for the Third Day of the *Decameron*, Giletta is fixed unswervingly on her goal, but Helena, rejected by Bertram, at first decides to go away and spend her life in pilgrimage rather than block his return to Rossillion. It is not perseverance or ingenuity that Shakespeare is offering for our admiration at this juncture but the spirit of sacrifice common to the Drusillas, Erminias, and Alessandras. Like Drusilla, Helena resumes the initiative when circumstances change, and with a still more altruistic incentive to add to that of self-interest, in that Bertram is falling into bad ways and needs the help he spurns. The form her help takes, the substitution of herself for Diana in a dark bedroom, that gnawed bone of Shakespearean controversy, was essential to the story and had been a stage commonplace in Italy for almost a century.[25] Distasteful or not, this action is the principal occasion for the figure of Helena to take on, in addition to the meanings she shares with Giletta and Drusilla, an identification with providence most recently and convincingly argued in Arthur Kirsch's analysis of the providential pattern in *All's Well*.[26] The dramatic conventions expressing the plan and Helena's role in it correspond more directly to the kind of *commedia grave* in which Counter-Reformation orthodoxy is taught or Sophoclean peripety is adapted to comedy and made to function as metaphor for providence than to the Guarinian

25. A list of instances would be a catalogue of some hundreds of Italian comedies. In Marcantonio Raimondi's *L'erotodynastia, over Potenza d'amore*, performed in 1614 (Venice, 1626), obviously too late to be a direct source of *All's Well* and offered as an example of the frequency with which the commonplaces and their details repeat each other, a landlady named Diana arranges for a girl to sleep with her future husband in Diana's house and in place of Diana herself (IV.iv).

26. *Jacobean Dramatic Perspectives*, pp. 59–60.

pastoral drama, incorporating the same idea and structural pattern, with which Kirsch links *All's Well*. Shakespeare's knowledge of this species of grave comedy and his creative awareness of its potential are apparent in his investment of idea in the figure of the woman, leading to a concluding secular miracle that gives off secondary religious "vibrations" for an audience attuned to everyday Christian interpretations of life.

The brief acknowledgments of divine auspices in the source novella are expanded in Helena's urging:

> It is not so with Him that all things knows
> As 'tis with us that square our guess by shows;
> But most it is presumption in us when
> The help of heaven we count the act of men.
> Dear sir, to my endeavours give consent;
> Of heaven, not me, make an experiment.
>   (II.i.148–153)

This statement has been contrasted with her earlier:

> Our remedies oft in ourselves do lie,
> Which we ascribe to heaven; the fated sky
> Gives us free scope; only doth backward pull
> Our slow designs when we ourselves are dull.
>   (I.i.212–215)*

The contrast has been used to support the conclusion that Helena moves from an unjustified sense of self-sufficiency expressed in her first appearance to a reliance on God's power and providence. Arguing that Helena's method of cure was the Paracelsian chemical system, based on the theory of contraries, which challenged the orthodox Galenic herbal system, based on the theory of humours and endorsed by the College of Physicians, Richard K. Stensgaard relates the Paracelsian reformers' sense of divine intervention in opposition to the Galenists' "pagan atheistic" naturalism to the theological controversy then alive over the roles of supernatural versus natural agencies in curing the plague. He concludes that Helena, like the reformers, comes to know the error of the doctrine of human self-sufficiency.[27] Stensgaard's presentation of the medical issues illuminates Helena's principles as physician (and Shakespeare's interest in the controversy), but it does not follow that her

27. "*All's Well That Ends Well* and the Galenico-Paracelsian Controversy," *Renaissance Quarterly*, 25 (1972), 173–188.

views of human action and of providence are mutually exclusive. In the speech last quoted, Helena does not oppose self-sufficiency to dependence on God, but free will to astral influences. Limiting the power of the stars to influences and tendencies, she assigns the responsibility for actions to free will. This is like Aquinas' or Dante's pronouncements on the same subject, and also like those of neo-medieval Counter-Reformation orthodoxy in its campaign against the judiciary arts of astrology and fortune-telling.[28] The context in which Helena makes this statement is that of her domestic and social situation, of her love for Bertram and its seeming impossibility, of her determination to do for herself what she can. Her expression of faith in a power above herself, however, refers not to fate or the stars but to divine providence, to which fortune is subordinate and which is the only kind of destiny admitted to a Christian universe, a kind which, on the broadest basis of Renaissance Christianity, Catholic or Protestant, guaranteed freedom to choose the good.[29] The bed trick demands initiative action—not to say acting— like Giletta's, but Helena sees it additionally as cooperation with providence, assuring the Widow:

> Doubt not but heaven
> Hath brought me up to be your daughter's dower,
> As it hath fated her to be my motive
> And helper to a husband.
>
> (IV.iv.18–21)

Helena's actions and her awareness of their meaning do not chart a conversion—that is left for Bertram—but they metaphorically clarify the relation of invisible forces: providence encircles all, permitting some scope to fortune and the stars, but protecting free will and guiding human affairs to a good end, most happily reached when human will participates in God's plan.

Shakespeare's annexing of a ritual religious dimension to his secular drama surpasses in integrity any Italian representation of spiritual

---

28. *La divina commedia*, Purg. XVI.73–84, and notes. Della Porta's defensive attempt to prove his orthodoxy in this regard is a comparable statement (*De humana physiognomonia libri IIII* [Vico Equense, 1586], dedication).

29. Roland Mushat Frye, *Shakespeare and Christian Doctrine* (Princeton, 1963), quotes Calvin's affirmation of the anti-astrological commonplace (p. 160) and relates it to *All's Well* (p. 162). In connection with *Hamlet* he cites Calvin's pronouncement that "chances as well of prosperity as of adversity the reason of the flesh doth ascribe to fortune," while the Christian mind "will firmly believe that all chances are governed by the secret counsel of God" (p. 232).

reality in comedy, and his doing so realizes the potential and transforms the commonplaces of an Italian genre. Even Helena's spreading word of her own death at Saint Jaques le Grand so that her reappearance seems a miraculous resurrection, the very common commonplace of Italian comedy that Shakespeare added to the novella, had a particular affinity for and relevance to the figure of the woman as wonder. It is no accident that every Italian heroine of *commedia grave* named above, whatever else she may lack, goes through the formulaic action of apparent death.

Shakespeare's treatment of the culminating act of forgiveness is also more elaborate and extra-fabular in applicability than in any *commedia grave*. By blackening Bertram's character beyond anything in his sources, Shakespeare creates a need of forgiveness, paralleling but intensifying a fact of reconciliation scenes in Italian comedy; whatever the effect on the psychological verisimilitude of the resolution, the alteration strengthens the symbolic charge of the finale, in which Helena's climactic appearance seems a benediction and miracle of grace to the remission of sin. Although her Italian generic analogues are even less suited than Helena herself to bear the mystical weight G. Wilson Knight attaches to the figure,[30] it is their centrality, exemplary goodness, and identification with conceptions of active virtue, forgiveness, and resignation to providence that indicate the species of tragicomedy to which Shakespeare adapted the tale of Giletta. His intensification of the sense of wonder, emphasizing in speeches like Lafew's (II.iii.1–6) the miraculous aspect of Helena's progress, and the movement Hunter senses in this play toward the late romances, especially in the actions of the "magical" heroine, place *All's Well* in an accelerated Shakespearean phase of a movement toward symbolic drama begun by fits and starts in the *commedia grave*.

In *Measure for Measure* the seriousness that Lever compares to the tone of Giraldi's *tragedia di fin lieto*, *Epitia*,[31] and the concerted attempt at tragicomedy he links with Guarini's theory of tragicomedy in the *Compendio* are still more clearly associated with the Italian generic structures I have proposed as antecedent and analogous to *All's Well*. "Measure," as Lever demonstrates it to be thematically at work in Shakespeare's play, is different from "measure," as Guarini made it a

---

30. *The Sovereign Flower*, pp. 100–102.
31. "Introduction" to the Arden edition of *Measure for Measure*, pp. xl–xli.

principle of constructing tragicomedy, dictating that mitigation of extremes, blending instead of juxtaposing, which produced *Il pastor fido*. The sharp contrasts, moral, tonal, structural, social, even ontological, in *Measure for Measure*, distinguish it from Guarini's version of tragicomedy, as the low comic elements and the eschewing of deaths—even deserved ones like that intended for Barnardine—distinguish it from Giraldi's tragedy with a happy ending. *Measure for Measure* does not correspond exactly to any Italian genre, nor to any English one, certainly not to "mongrel tragicomedy" as represented by *Promos and Cassandra*; but as the *commedia grave* in range and decorum is the genre closest to Shakespearean comedy, so the kind of *commedia grave* in which the figure of the woman is used to create wonder is the tragicomic mixture closest to *Measure for Measure*.

As in *All's Well*, Shakespeare's modifications move toward Italian stage commonplaces. Claudio and Juliet become privately plighted expectant parents, like Lepida and Terenzio in *Pellegrina*. The Marianna plot depends on the commonplace of substitution in a dark bedroom, ratifying as marriage the betrothal that constituted *de futuro* spousal. The interpolation of these unions (which in time add up to marriage but in some phase fall short of the fully sanctioned sacrament insisted on by a Drusilla) and Shakespeare's use of them as foils and as measuring marks on a thematic scale that runs from Mistress Overdone's prostitution and Angelo's blackmailing proposition to Isabella's proposal to become the Bride of Christ at the beginning and the Duke's "motion" that she become a Duchess at the end, are (like the structured alternation of appearances of Isabella and of characters from the underworld) part of the "systematized contrasts" Lever descries in the first half of Shakespeare's tragicomic structure.[32]

Isabella herself is the strongest argument for Shakespeare's acquaintance with the Italian genre and for his interest in testing further the dramatic capabilities of the feminine figure. Except in the preservation of her virginity made possible by Shakespeare's overthrowing his sources, Isabella performs few of the formulaic functions. She does not return from the dead (except by leaving the convent, where she would become dead to the world); she is neither agent nor emblem of providence. She is not even in love. By this last radical change Shakespeare

32. "Introduction," p. xliv.

takes a figure that was nun-like even in its unfledged state and more so in the post-Tridentine *innamorate* with their pious garb or vocabulary and their auras as of saints performing miracles, and he makes her a real nun (at least a novice),

> enskied and sainted
> By your renouncement, an immortal spirit,
> And to be talk'd with in sincerity,
> As with a saint.
>
> (I.iv.34–37)

The test she leaves her convent to face is not one of constancy in love or of power to unite love with goodness, charity, or faith in providence, but a stark trial of virtue and principle, unsupported by exalted passion.

The figure of the woman as wonder begins as a dramatic representation in which religion is only a metaphor: in *Amor costante* Lucrezia is votaress and saint in the religion of love. In late *commedie gravi*, religious law and ecclesiastical law are extra-fabular realities that also form the secular context in which the heroine may demonstrate the wonder of love's power and of her nature by conscious virtue and unconscious harmony with providence in her altarbound action. Identification of Isabella as the soul of man, elected to be the Bride of Christ in an allegory of the Divine Atonenent, is not requisite to recognizing that she is a vehicle for idea and that her personal, visible action may incarnate onstage in the realm of the particular and local a human possibility that has another existence in that of the general and the universal. Setting aside questions of whether Isabella can be likable to any audience, whether she must appear prudish and uncharitable in her zeal for salvation, or whether she is ignorant of the true nature of chastity, and confining the inquiry to the frame of reference composed of women who act as wonders in the kind of play that of all others this one resembles, we find that there remains one idea which Isabella consistently demonstrates through ordeals that involve her in a set of Italian stage commonplaces and that conclude in a final test which she passes by an act of forgiveness. From the moment Lucio begs her to leave her convent, Isabella has to make painful choices in order to do what she believes is right. Standing by Christian principles in conventional order of importance (duty to kin, chastity, charity), she acts out the principle of free will. The analogy with Lucrece by which Lever supports his view that Isabella's conception of chastity is tinged with pagan error[33] rests on the assumption that the issue is the same in both cases. The action for which Lucrece could be held responsible, however, was suicide. Isabella, on the contrary, is not threatened with rape. Although Angelo sophistically suggests that compliance would be but a "compell'd" sin (II.iv.57), Isabella sees that she has a choice. The drama requires that her will be free. As she is without the excuse of physical force in one test, so in the other she is deprived of any tie with Angelo to motivate a plea for mercy toward him. The Duke refuses to remove her just cause for hatred; by letting her think Angelo her brother's murderer, he makes her choice of Christian forgiveness harder and therefore more illustrative of the will's freedom. The double function of Helena in *All's Well*, as the human will to good working like a miracle within a providential plan and as emblem of providence itself, is divided in *Measure for Measure* between the Duke and Isabella: he identifying himself with providence and partaking in its omnipotence, confirmed by his status as civil authority; she lacking full knowledge but cooperating in a design that offers her a part to be freely improvised in a miracle of forgiveness which seems superhuman only because, as Drusilla says, it is the human action nearest the divine. Isabella cooperates with providence, as do Helena and the forgiving women of *commedie gravi*, but she is more forgiving than they need be. Having gone to some pains to underscore the freedom of her prayer for Angelo, Shakespeare puts only compassion and mercy in the balance against the good reasons for Angelo's death. The more difficult the exercise of free will for good, the greater the wonder; this aim, achieved, confirms the radical rightness of Shakespeare's removing from Isabella the principal motive of the *innamorata*.

The *commedia grave* characterized by the confluence of the exemplary heroine, generic mixture through contrast, and Counter-Reformation principles of active virtue and providence is a kind of romantic comedy in which the originally neoclassical structures of the Italian theater are developed into forms prophetic of the comedy of forgiveness defined by Robert G. Hunter and illustrated to different degrees by *All's Well* and *Measure for Measure*.[34] Italian attempts at symbolic drama were limited, however, and were dictated by the

33. *Ibid.*, pp. lxxx–lxxxi.
34. *Shakespeare and the Comedy of Forgiveness* (New York, 1965), pp. 106–131 and 204–226.

Counter-Reformation preoccupation with achieving doctrinal, civil, and social homogeneity. Shakespeare's variations were neither so limited nor so dictated, and he had the benefit of the tradition of English medieval and Tudor drama. But the latest Italian drama in his day, its neo-medieval abstraction, symbolic instead of allegorical, representing spiritual truths incidentally and pragmatically, was no secret outside of Italy. The sophistication of Shakespeare's technique, the commonplaces of form and substance he chose, and the generic mixtures he made suggest more than a glancing knowledge of the polished, stageworthy, contemporary drama that had already developed structures and instruments to accommodate a neo-medieval symbolizing impulse not unlike his own. The technical finish and formal capacity of these plays made their appeal to discerning dramatists—Christians, of course, but not theologians, Catholic or Protestant—and Shakespeare probably helped himself to what he liked with characteristic ease and discrimination.

VII. Mary, Queen of Scots, in France

W. L. Wiley · *Professor Emeritus of French, University of North Carolina at Chapel Hill*

The mysterious and ill-starred career of Mary Stuart—better known as Mary, Queen of Scots—has provoked the interest of many historians, poets, and dramatists in many lands. Her life on this earth has been rather thoroughly scrutinized by a host of biographers, from the moment of her birth early in December 1542 at Linlithgow Palace until her death on the executioner's block at Fotheringay Castle on 8 February 1587. It is not the purpose of this study, then, to reexamine in full detail the four and one-half decades of Mary's hectic sojourn on our planet. There will be little emphasis, for example, on her last sad years and her relations with Lord Darnley or the Earl of Bothwell or Queen Elizabeth. We shall be concerned primarily with happier moments in France, where as a little girl Mary charmed the court of Henri II, softened the rigors of scholars who taught her Latin and French, and attracted the attention of poets and artists who circulated in the ambience of Fontainebleau.

Mary Stuart was readily inclined toward things French because her mother, Marie de Lorraine, was a Guise and a sister of François duc de Guise, one of the mightiest warriors of a family of mighty warriors. James V of Scotland, Mary's father, had a definite penchant for French culture and wives since his first wife was Madeleine, the daughter of Francis I. Upon her death, James V, who did not enjoy being a widower, was permitted to marry Marie de Lorraine. The visits of the Scottish monarch to France, which was in the midst of an Italianized renaissance in the arts and architecture, caused him to bring French and Italian workmen back to Scotland to help civilize his own bleak domain. These sculptors and stonemasons left their mark in particular on such places as Falkland and Linlithgow. But the gay and debonair James V was no great leader of troops on the field of battle; he was defeated by the English and died on 14 December 1542, one week after the birth of his daughter, the future Mary, Queen of Scots. He never saw her, thus missing the gleam that must even then have been shining in her eyes.

Scotland was becoming more and more a land of religious dissension, with Protestantism pushing aside a weak Roman Catholic clergy. Henry VIII would have liked to have the baby Mary Stuart betrothed to his son, Edward, and was willing to go to war to bring about this union. But Mary was taken quietly by Cardinal Beaton to Stirling Castle and there, though an infant not many days old, she was crowned Queen of the Scots. Francis I dispatched troops to aid the Catholic party, but to no avail. The power of the somber John Knox was growing, and in the continuing war Cardinal Beaton was slain in 1546. In September 1547 the Duke of Somerset, with a force of English archers, defeated the Scots—which prompted Marie de Lorraine to snatch little Mary Stuart away from Stirling Castle to hide her on the Lake of Menteith. Marie de Lorraine's cries to France for help were finally answered: late in July 1548 a French fleet, after some clever and confusing maneuvers, picked up little Mary, Queen of Scots, with her retinue at Dumbarton and sailed a twisting course for France.

Mary Stuart, in the high-level planning that was a mixture of politics and religion, was destined for betrothal to the Dauphin François, the son of Henri II and Catherine de Médicis, who was to rule briefly over France as Francis II. At the Dumbarton embarkation Mary Stuart was welcomed aboard ship by the ambassador of Henri II, M. de Brézé, and also (according to one report) by one of France's finest lyric poets, Joachim du Bellay, who was at the time some twenty-four years of age.[1] It was a difficult passage down the North Sea across the Channel, made doubly risky by bad weather and lurking English vessels hidden in the fog. With good luck the convoy bearing the Scottish Queen, who was now more than five years old, reached the small French port of Roscoff on 13 August 1548. The whole province of Brittany had been alerted to the arrival of *la petite reine*, and her continuing voyage on to the city of Nantes was one of triumph. She was welcomed there by some one hundred fifty youngsters of her own age, dressed in white satin and standing militarily at attention.

1. The presence of Du Bellay on the expedition is suggested by Paule Henry-Bordeaux in her *Marie Stuart* (Paris, 1967), p. 27: "Un poète est là pour accueillir la reine. Près de M. de Brézé, ambassadeur d'Henri II, se tient Joachim du Bellay. Il accompagnera Marie Stuart. . . ." I have found no evidence in Henri Chamard's authoritative biography of Du Bellay of the poet's having been aboard Mary Stuart's escaping ship; nor have I found confirmation of his presence there in such a contemporary document as Brantôme's "Sur la Reyne d'Escosse." Much of this material in Pt. I is taken from Paule Henry-Bordeaux, *Marie Stuart*, and from A. Chéruel, *Marie Stuart et Catherine de Médicis* (Paris, 1858), pp. 13–28.

Mary Stuart and her future husband, who was to rule as Francis II, did not meet until 18 October 1548, at the old chateau of Carrières-Saint-Denis. It was apparently an amiable confrontation, although the frail François must have been overshadowed by Mary, who was a robust and vital child one year older than he. Her hair was between blonde and chestnut, and would be one of the particular features (along with her eyes) later described by court poets in their admiration of her. Everybody at court was delighted with the brightness of the small princess from Scotland, who smiled and gesticulated without timidity and talked a piquant mixture of Scottish and French. Brantôme said she was dressed horribly—in Scottish fashion[2] —but no one seemed to care, and her delightful mannerisms won over completely her father-in-law-to-be, Henri II. In the midst of her conquest of Fontainebleau and the doting homage of her Guise uncles, sickly François wandered around looking unfortunately like Catherine de Médicis and unable to blow his nose, a bodily function that even later he never really mastered. It was an ironic gesture of the Fates that Henri II, the strong man with the black beard and the best athlete of his realm, should have joined Catherine de Médicis in producing the pathetic Dauphin François.

At the court of Henri II, Mary Stuart was quick to absorb the training in French manners and culture that was lavished upon her along with a rather thorough bit of spoiling that she received from her grandmother, the duchesse de Guise. At any rate, Mary was given every sort of instruction considered appropriate for a royal princess. The keenness of her mind was noticed by the King's sister, Marguerite de France, who was herself well-versed in Greek and Latin, and who was to play a great part in the formal education of Mary Stuart. Thus, Mary had as tutor in Latin (even as did the Dauphin) one of France's best scholars, Jacques Amyot, whose translation of Plutarch still remains a notable accomplishment from the sixteenth century. She learned Latin very easily and became quite proficient in the language. She also loved music and dancing, which pleased Henri II. As for training in French poetry, she had the two greatest lyricists of the French Renaissance at her beck and call, Pierre de Ronsard and Joachim du Bellay. They were not able to make of her a master of French versification, but she did compose in

2. See Brantôme, *Oeuvres complètes*, ed. L. Lalanne (Paris, 1873), VII, 407, where he says that she appeared as "une vraye déesse" even in "la barbaresque mode . . . de son pays."

French. She seemed to love reading and contact with books—and, according to one rather typical French judgment, she had a "goût très sûr, le goût français." [3]

In 1553 when Mary Stuart was ten years of age and the Dauphin François nine, they made something of an official entry into the life of the French court as an engaged couple. Mary had learned her lessons well. They had included not only training in manners, music, languages, and the arts, but also a continuing indoctrination in Romanism under the guidance of her influential uncle, the cardinal de Lorraine. Ladies and gentlemen of the court praised her as a charming and precocious child. Though it would hardly be correct to call her a prodigy, she eclipsed the Dauphin by every measurement that might be applied—manners, intellect, or personality. Even if he had possessed more of the attributes of his father or of his grandfather *le grand Roi François Premier*, the nine-year-old Dauphin would still have been outclassed by his fiancée, Mary, Queen of Scots.

The next few years in the atmosphere of Fontainebleau were happy ones for the young Scottish princess. She could see the full blooming of the hunting lodge (Fontaine-belle-eau, "fountain of beautiful water") into a royal palace, shining with the frescoes of Primaticcio and Rosso, and reflecting the craftsmanship of Benvenuto Cellini. And she herself was to pose several times for the French Renaissance master of portraiture, François Clouet. [4]

During 1557 and 1558, however, the cities of Saint-Quentin and Calais were to fall before the armies of Spain and England, awaiting the strong arm of Mary's uncle, François duc de Guise, to effect their recovery. François duc de Guise (known as "Le Balafré" because of the saber scar proudly borne across his cheek) accomplished something of a military miracle in stopping the Spanish Imperials early enough in 1558 for a springtime wedding of Mary and François. The ceremonies of the royal union took place on 24 April 1558.

It was a soft morning in Paris on this date, with few clouds and a gentle breeze (instead of the cold rain that might have occurred), as the bells of Notre Dame pealed forth the announcement of the prospective

3. Paule Henry-Bordeaux, p. 40.
4. One of Clouet's most striking efforts hangs today in the Musée Carnavalet in Paris and shows the nineteen-year-old, widowed Mary in her white veils of mourning for her dead husband, Francis II.

regal binding of Scotland to France. Among the dignitaries on hand for the occasion was François duc de Guise, hero and savior of France— and uncle of the bride. Mary Stuart entered the resplendent cathedral of Notre Dame on the arm of Henri II, attired in a white gown sewn with diamonds and pearls. According to a later chronicler, she seemed like "une grande fleur sur laquelle la rosée brille encore."[5] The Dauphin appeared to be his usual pale and sickly self. Many deputies from Scotland were present, but not Marie de Lorraine, who could not leave Edinburgh, even for her daughter's wedding, because of political problems besetting her land. However, Mary Stuart wrote her mother on the night of her marriage to say, in a momentary spirit of illusion, that she was the happiest of women. She had already signed documents that, in the event she might die without an heir, would hand Scotland over to the French. It is probable that she had failed to read the fine print of the agreement, and thus made this impossible commitment unknowingly. Given the debilitated condition of the Dauphin, any immediate creation of an heir to the French throne was most unlikely.

Elizabeth, the daughter of Henry VIII and Anne Boleyn, was crowned Queen of England in January of 1559, despite any claims that might have been advanced by Mary. France, with her cities on the Channel secured by the Treaty of Cateau-Cambrésis, turned her attention toward her frontiers to the east. While John Knox and Protestantism were growing more potent in Scotland, Henri II was trying to stamp out the Huguenot heresy in France. In the midst of the political and religious jockeying, Henri II was killed by a broken lance while riding at the barrier in the jousts celebrating the marriage of his sister, Marguerite de France, to Philibert-Emmanuel de Savoie. This tragedy occurred on 10 July 1559 and took away the last strong monarch in the Valois dynasty; and it made Mary Stuart at the age of sixteen Queen of France. She was gracious and decorative, she dressed ravishingly, she played the lute, and she could ride a horse; but she was scarcely equipped for the job suddenly thurst upon her by the lance shaft of her fellow Scotsman, Montgommery, which lodged in the temple of the King of France.

It was almost incidental that the Dauphin François became Francis II at the age of fifteen, and that the religious formalities of his coronation were solemnized in the cathedral of Rheims on 18 September 1559. The

5. Paule Henry-Bordeaux, p. 45.

Queen Mother, Catherine de Médicis, took over the reins of government from her weakling son and faced up immediately to her enemies from Lorraine, the Guise family to whom Mary Stuart was bound by blood. Catherine was sufficiently astute to realize that the Guise contingent hoped to use the growing conflict between Catholic and Protestant in France as a weapon to overthrow the feeble Francis II and place one of their own house on the throne. The delicate and immature young King spent most of his time hunting in the country, avoiding Paris and its political manipulations around the somber Louvre. His young Queen became thin and nervously tense, and rumor had it that there had not been enough activity in the royal bed to remove her virginity. The Huguenots were becoming stronger in France, despite the hanging of some of their number from the parapets of the chateau of Amboise because of a suspected conspiracy to kidnap Francis II. Marie de Lorraine died on 14 June 1560, and the Catholic party was ejected from Scotland. Mary Stuart was distressed, but the French Romanists, buried in internal strife, could do nothing to help the Scottish situation. Francis II continued to chase the stag and died on 5 December 1560 of a brain abcess. Two days later Mary reached the age of eighteen.

There could scarcely have been a more distressing situation for the widowed Mary, Queen of Scots. She was in theory Queen of France and Queen of Scotland; in actuality she had little power over either domain. Queen Elizabeth and her Protestant supporters progressively diminished the influence of the Catholic Mary in her own land, and the Treaty of Edinburgh (5 July 1560) had already proclaimed that, despite the promises of Mary Stuart, the protectorate that France had long maintained over Scotland was ended. Further complications came from the fact that the Queen Mother, Catherine de Médicis, despised and distrusted her daughter-in-law, who had treated Catherine most aloofly as a "fille de marchand."[6] The Guise family, meanwhile, through the machinations of the cardinal de Lorraine, hoped to arrange a marriage between Mary Stuart and Don Carlos, the son of Philip II of Spain, at that time the most powerful monarch in Europe—and a Catholic. For different reasons, both Queen Elizabeth of England and Catherine de Médicis of France opposed this union.

Whatever the future might hold for her in Scotland and England, it

6. See Chéruel, p. 17, for information on this epithet.

was now necessary for Mary Stuart to leave France. Catherine de Médicis—who was still at the governmental controls even after her next son became King of France as Charles IX—no longer wanted her there. Therefore, Mary, nervous and fearful of what might be awaiting her across the Channel, left the French court. She arrived in Rheims on 26 March 1561 for a final visit with and a farewell to her Guise relatives. Then she proceeded along her lonely way north toward the Channel. It was a bleak journey in spite of the accompaniment of a retinue that she merited since she was twice a queen. At Saint Dizier she met her brother James Stuart (the French designated him "le Bâtard"), who was the choice of Queen Elizabeth for occupancy of the throne of Scotland.

Mary Stuart was yet to discover the full complexity of the political and religious situation in Scotland, which involved the continued disintegration of the Catholic powers and the ruthless decisions of Queen Elizabeth. Mary was cognizant, however, of Elizabeth's attitude toward her and feared arrest if her small fleet touched England. Her convoy weighed anchor out of Calais on 15 August 1561, with English ships in pursuit. Mary Stuart had been in France almost exactly thirteen years, most of which had been a happy time. She left her adopted land with the heaviest of hearts; on clearing Calais she sat aft on deck in her heavy robes of mourning and watched the coast of France disappear in the fog. In her tearful sorrow she decided to spend the whole night topside saying her last *adieux* to France. A young French gentleman, a chronicler of the lives of many ladies and gentlemen of the sixteenth century, was aboard Mary Stuart's galley and has left a record of the crossing. A little farther along in this account we shall listen to his story. For the moment it may be said simply that Mary Stuart's ship eventually reached Leith, and she arrived at Holyrood on 19 August 1561, terrified and alone.

II

As has been suggested earlier in this survey, the poets and scholars around the court of Henri II had grown to adore Mary, Queen of Scots, and to lavish praise upon her in their verses and dedicatory epistles. It is true that in their encomia they might well have hoped to gain favor for themselves and possibly an additional royal pension. But there seems to be a large element of sincerity in many of the poems that were written for Mary, some of them by the best versifiers of the period. If it had been earlier in the Renaissance she would certainly have had many *bla-sons*—that type of stanza that apostrophized a bosom, a nose, the eyes, or other anatomical attributes of a beautiful lady—composed in her name. Clément Marot, in the first part of the sixteenth century, used the *blason* to pay homage to damsels that he admired, but after 1550 the favored poetic forms for praising feminine charms were the sonnet and the ode. Ronsard, the Prince of Poets and leader of the Pléiade, used them both (as well as *discours, bergeries,* and other devices in verse) to give his salutations to Mary.

Ronsard, like everyone else at the court of Henri II, was greatly impressed by the beauty of Mary Stuart's eyes. In part of a *bergerie* published in 1565 he calls them twin suns moistened with the dew of tears as she thinks of her departure from France. Unfortunately, ignor-ing the facts of history and feminine antipathies, Ronsard also speaks of Queen Elizabeth and Mary Stuart as "two Venuses traversing the froth of the waves":

> Ie vy des Escossois la Royne sage & belle,
> Qui de corps & d'esprit resemble une immortelle:
> I'approchay de ses yeux, mais bien de deux Soleils,
> Deux Soleils de beauté qui n'ont point leurs pareils:
> Ie les vy larmoyer d'une claire rosée,
> Ie vy d'un beau crystal sa paupiere arrosée,
> Se souvenant de France, & du Sceptre laissé,
> Et de son premier feu comme un songe passé.
>   Qui voirroit en la mer ces deux Roynes fameuses
> En beauté, trauerser les vagues escumeuses,
> Certes on les dirot, à bien les regarder,
> Deux Venus qui voudroient au riuage aborder.[7]

Ronsard had previously linked Elizabeth and Mary Stuart in a "Dis-cours à très-illustre et très vertueuse Elizabeth, Royne d'Angleterre." Here he uses also the figure of "twin suns" as he praises the beauty of the two Queens:

7. See Pierre de Ronsard, *Oeuvres complètes,* Nouvelle édition revisée, augmentée et annotée par Paul Laumonier, 8 vols. (Paris, 1914–19). All quotations from Ronsard will be from this edition, which I have found more convenient to use than the later edition of Professors Laumonier, Raymond Lebègue, and Isidore Silver. The above excerpt is from III, 383–384.

> Alors ie dy, si ceste Royne Angloise
> Est en beauté pareille à L'Escossoise,
> On voit ensemble en lumiere pareils
> Dedans une Isle esclairer deux Soleils.[8]

In a slight variation of the theme, in "L'Hymne de Charles, cardinal de Lorraine" (first published in 1559), Ronsard says that the "pleasing eyes" of the Cardinal's niece would have merited a ten-year combat around the walls of Troy:

> Diray-ie ta niepce en beauté la plus belle
> Que le Ciel a fait naistre? & dont les yeux plaisans
> Meriteroyent encor' un combat de dix ans,
> Soit qu'elle fust dix ans par les Grecs demandée,
> Ou qu'elle fust dix ans par les Troyens gardée?
> Laquelle a pour mary du Roy le fils aisné,
> Et luy a pour doüaire un Royaume donné. . . .[9]

In this excerpt Ronsard indicates that he had heard of the agreement by which Mary Stuart had signed over the realm of Scotland to France— and also that the poem was composed before the death of Henri II. Ronsard's collection of *Poèmes*, first assembled in 1560, was later "dédié à très-illustre et vertueuse princesse Marie Stuart, Royne d'Escosse." In the first quatrain of a later sonnet at the head of the second book of this assembly, the poet once more remarks on the beauty of Mary's eyes, and then goes on to rebuke the French for not defending the faraway princess as knights of old would have done:

> Encores que la mer de bien loin nous separe,
> Si est-ce que l'esclair de vostre beau Soleil,
> De vostre oeil qui n'a point au monde de pareil
> Jamais loin de mon coeur par le temps ne s'egare.
> . . . vous n'avez, François,
> Ny osé regarder ny toucher le harnois
> Pour oster de seruage une Royne si belle.[10]

In a *discours* that forms a part of these same poems Ronsard laments the sailing of the ship that, in taking Mary's eyes away from France, took the Muses along with them:

8. *Ibid.*, III, 243.
9. *Ibid.*, IV, 243–244.
10. *Ibid.*, V, 3–4.

> Le iour que voistre voile aux Zephyrs se courba,
> Et de nos yeux pleurans les vostres desroba,
> Ce iour, la mesme voile emporta loin de France
> Les Muses qui souloyent y faire demeurance. . . .[11]

In continuing this *discours* the poet praises all elements of Mary's beauty almost as in a *blason*—brow, eyes, hair, lips, ivory bosom, etc. The eyes, naturally for Ronsard, are emphasized, the star-lit eyes that form two lodgings for love and turn the night into day. Then, again, her departure has taken away the Muses and thus silenced the writers of verse:

> Comment pourroyent chanter les bouches des Poëtes,
> Quand par vostre depart les Muses sont muettes? [12]

In a succeeding poem dedicated "A elle-mesme" ("To her"), published in 1567, Ronsard describes the sad and unadorned beauty of Mary as she walked through the "longues allées" of Fontainebleau before she left France; the rocks and the waters wept. In this same rather long poem it is pointed out that even in a portrait Mary's brown eyes gleam so brightly that they intrigue Charles IX in another portrait as he looks at her—all a bit complicated and *précieux*:

> On iugeroit qu'il contemple vos yeux
> Doux, beaux, courtois, plaisans, delicieux,
> Vn peu brunets, où la delicatesse
> Rit. . . .[13]

Ronsard continues with his homage in an *elégie* that was probably written before Mary Stuart left France in August of 1561. In it he says that there has never before been such a beautiful creature, combining as she does the whiteness of lilies with the redness of roses tinted by the blood of Adonis, along with eyes made for her by Cupid himself:

> Au milieu du Printemps entre les Liz nasquit
> Son corps, qui de blancheur les Liz mesmes veinquit,
> Et les Roses qui sont du sang d'Adonis teintes,
> Furent par sa couleur de leur vermeil depeintes:
> Amour de ses beaux traits luy composa les yeux. . . .[14]

11. *Ibid.*, V, 4.
12. *Ibid.*, V, 5.
13. *Ibid.*, V, 10. Ronsard might well have been referring to a shining portrait of Mary done while she was in France and now hanging in the National Gallery in London.
14. *Ibid.*, V, 16.

As this poem goes on, it becomes almost a pitiful lament: Ronsard regrets the departure of Mary and wishes that there were a Roland or Renault de Montauban in Scotland to defend her. In a following *elégie* Ronsard shows that he knows the history of Mary Stuart's childhood and the rigors of fortune that have left her like a sad turtledove, while taking her and her beautiful eyes away from her adopted land:

> En nous voulant priuer de ses beaux yeux,
> Yeux qui font honte aux estoiles des cieux. . . .[15]

In an *odelette*, "A la Royne d'Escosse, pour lors Royne de France" (which is slightly anticipatory since it was written in 1556), Ronsard lapses into a rather historical vein and speaks of the time (1537–39) when he was in Scotland as a page at the court of James V:

> O belle & plus que belle & agreable Aurore,
>   Qui auez delaissé vostre terre Escossoise
>   Pour venir habiter la region Françoise,
>   Qui de vostre clarté maintenant se decore:
> Si j'ay eu cest honneur d'auoir quitté la France
>   Voguant dessus la mer pour suiure vostre pere:
>   Si loin de mon pays, de freres & de mere,
>   I'ay dans le vostre vsé trois ans de mon enfance:
> Prenez ces vers en gré, Royne, que ie vous donne. . . .[16]

Ronsard goes along with political and national matters in "Chant de liesse," written for Henri II in 1559 but also involving Mary, Queen of Scots:

> Sire, tu as ainsi comme il me semble
> Seul plus d'honneur que tous les Rois ensemble:
> De ton vivant tu vois ainsi que toy
> Ton fils aisné en sa ieunesse Roy,
> Qui pour ta brus t'a donné la plus belle
> Royne qui viue, & fust-ce vne immortelle,
> Et qui peut estre aura dessus le chef
> Vne Couronne encores derechef,
> Pour ioindre ensemble à la terre Escossoise
> L'honneur voisin de la Couronne Angloise.[17]

It will be noted that here Ronsard in his optimism assumes that Francis II (yet to be) is already King of Scotland, through his marriage to Mary

15. *Ibid.*, V, 20.
16. *Ibid.*, VI, 306–307.
17. *Ibid.*, VI, 313.

Stuart, and that Mary one day will be queen of both England and Scotland. In his further revision of history to fit it around Mary Stuart, Ronsard says in a short poem, "A la Royne de France," which appeared in 1560 when Mary Stuart really was Queen of France, that England, Scotland, and France each wanted Mary as Queen. Therefore Jupiter, in order to calm "these three sisters," decreed that Mary should rule a portion of the year in each country:

> Que tu serois trois mois la Roine des Anglois,
> Et trois mois ensuyuant Roine des Escossois,
> Et six mois Roine apres de la terre Françoise.[18]

The Prince of Poets proved to be an inadequate forecaster of the sad career that awaited Mary. But his verses in praise of her beauty and charm (some of which have been omitted here to avoid too much repetition) have in them the ring of sincerity and the resonance of truth.

Joachim du Bellay, a friend of Ronsard and possibly the most gifted lyricist of the Pléiade, also paid his respects in verse to Mary, Queen of Scots. Despite the emotional quality of Du Bellay's poetry (he has been classified as a precursor of the Romantics), he was less rapturous in his homage to Mary than was Ronsard. This is something of a surprise, and a trifle paradoxical. It would seem quite logical that Du Bellay, the portrayer of his own loneliness in his collection of sonnets that he called *Les Regrets*, might have described more feelingly the progressive loneliness of a Scottish princess widowed at seventeen and living at the French court under the dominion of Catherine de Médicis. But it must be remembered that Du Bellay himself died in 1560, when the full tragedy of Mary Stuart's life had not yet developed. In any case, the standard biographer of Du Bellay, Henri Chamard, has said that Mary Stuart had a "particular affection" for Du Bellay and that he in turn was smitten by her charms.[19]

Du Bellay, who was a fine Latinist, rendered his official homage to Mary Stuart and the Dauphin François in a formal Latin poem composed well in advance of their wedding in April 1558: "In futuras nuptias Francisci Gall. Delphini, et Mariae Stuartae Scotorum Reginae." There was hardly any more warmth in this creation than in one

18. *Ibid.*, VI, 338.
19. See Henry Chamard, *Joachim du Bellay, 1522–1560* (Lille: Au Siège de l'Université, 1900), pp. 445–446: "A la Cour des Valois, Marie Stuart, dans la fraîcheur de son printemps, mettait l'éclat de son esprit et de sa grâce. Elle aimait les poètes et les poètes allaient vers elle. Du Bellay, qu'elle honorait d'une affection particulière, fut pris au charme. . . ."

of Ronsard's Pindaric odes—none of which, incidentally, he dedicated to Mary Stuart.

Du Bellay, like so many Frenchmen of the sixteenth century, thought of Scotland as a wild land, as is indicated in *Les Regrets*, CLXXXVI, where he tells the famous Scottish humanist George Buchanan that it is rather remarkable for the Muses to have allowed him to be born in "l'Ecosse sauvage."[20] Du Bellay undoubtedly believed that France had had a civilizing influence on Mary Stuart, and this attitude is suggested in his "Epithalame" for the nuptials in 1559 of Philibert-Emmanuel duc de Savoie and Marguerite de France, wherein it is said that Hymen has already taken possession "De la Nymphe Escoçoise/Pour la rendre Françoise."[21] It will be remembered that Mary Stuart and Francis II had been married earlier, in 1558. Du Bellay felt that France had done a great deal for Scotland, a point that is made in his "Ode sur la naissance du petit duc de Beaumont," in which great claims are made for Henri II's assistance to the Scots in resisting the English:

> Un grand Prince belliqueur,
> D'esprit, de force, et de coeur
> Indontable se descoeuvre,
> Ayant d'un secours humain
> Sauvé la gent Escoçoyse . . .[22]

Du Bellay's feeling that Mary Stuart is a part of the political picture is further intimated in sonnet CLXX of *Les Regrets*, also included, with the title of "Sonnet à la Royne d'Escosse," in a series of poems praising Henri II for the victory at Calais, published in 1558. Here Du Bellay ventures the opinion that Mary, Queen of Scots, had been given such "beautez d'esprit et beautez de face" in order to join through a marriage the forces of three great nations (France, England, and Scotland) against the pride and audacity of Spain. In the first tercet Du Bellay tells Mary what "les Destins" wish for her:

> Ilz veulent que par vous la France et l'Angleterre
> Changent en longue paix l'hereditaire guerre
> Qui a de pere en fils si longuement duré. . . .[23]

---

20. Joachim du Bellay, *Oeuvres poétiques, édition critique . . . par Henri Chamard*, 6 vols. (Paris, 1908–31). All references to Du Bellay's poetry will be from this edition. This sonnet is in II, 200.
21. *Ibid.*, V, 210.
22. *Ibid.*, V, 291.
23. *Ibid.*, II, 187–188 and VI, 35–36.

Du Bellay finally got around to paying more legitimate homage to the beauty and charms of Mary Stuart in some verses that formed a part of the celebration of the much-heralded marriage of Philibert-Emmanuel de Savoie and Marguerite de France, under the general title of *Entreprise du Roy-Daulphin pour le tournoy.* Among several *inscriptions* there is one for "La Royne-Daulphine" (or Mary Stuart):

> Toy qui as veu l'excellence de celle
> Qui rend le ciel sur l'Escosse envieux,
> Dy hardiment: Contentez vous, mes yeux,
> Vous ne verrez jamais chose plus belle.
>
> Celle qui est de ceste Isle Princesse,
> Qu'au temps passé lon nommoit Caledon,
> Se en sa main elle avoit un brandon,
> On la prendroit pour Venus la Deesse.
>
> Par une chaisne à sa langue attachee
> Hercule à soy les peuples attiroit:
> Mais ceste cy tire ceux qu'elle void
> Par une chaisne en ses beaux yeux cachee.[24]

Here Du Bellay speaks more warmly of the Princess of Caledonia, compares her to Venus except for the firebrand in her hand, and says that the "chain" of her eyes has drawing power similar to the chain Hercules had attached to his tongue. Possibly the most complete obeisance paid by Du Bellay to Mary, Queen of Scots, is in a sonnet, "A la Royne d'Escosse" (also a part of the above-mentioned *Entreprise*), where the poet compares Mary to a mirror in which is reflected all that is beautiful and admirable:

> Pour nous monstrer, ainsi qu'en un miroir,
> Tout ce qui est de grand et d'admirable,
> De precieux, de beau, de desirable,
> Le ciel vous feit en ce monde apparoir.
>
> Nature aussi nous voulant faire voir
> Tout ce qui est de plaisant et d'aymable,
> Sur vostre face, ainsi qu'en une table,
> Monstra son art et son plus grand sçavoir.

24. *Ibid.*, VI, 58. It is to be noted that in this *Inscription* and in the following sonnet Du Bellay has made good use of the ten-syllable line, with a caesura after the fourth syllable. The twelve-syllable alexandrine was never very popular in France during the sixteenth century.

> En vostre esprit le ciel s'est surmonté,
> Nature et l'art ont en vostre beauté
> Mis tout le beau dont la beauté s'assemble:
>
> Et les neuf Soeurs m'ont faict poëte aussi,
> Pour imiter, en vous louant ainsi,
> Le ciel, nature, et l'artifice ensemble.[25]

In this fine poem Du Bellay has praised not only Mary Stuart but also the idea of beauty as it is reflected in creative art. With the death of Henri II in the midst of the tourney of 1559, Du Bellay became somber and had little more to say about Mary. He hoped only that the malady of Protestantism which was invading her native Scotland would not pass over the ocean and "become French." [26]

Other poets and scholars, in Latin and in French, had admiring words for Mary. George Buchanan, a Scotsman transplanted to French soil and a tutor to upper-class young Frenchmen, wrote a Latin poem for Mary upon her return to Scotland in 1561 (later he was to become hostile to her because of her political and marital activities). Another interesting accolade was given to the Scottish princess by Antoine Fouquelin, before she was married to the Dauphin François. Fouquelin was a grammarian and rhetorician, and evidently he was impressed by Mary's proficiency in Latin; he therefore dedicated his *Rhétorique françoise* to her, with an opening salutation, "A Tresillustre Princesse Madame Marie, Royne d'Ecosse, Antoine Fouquelin son treshumble serviteur, Salut."

Fouquelin's *Rhétorique* was a rhetoric in the Ciceronian sense of the word, and the best example thereof in the sixteenth century. Fouquelin hoped, he said, to see in France men like Socrates and Plato, Aristotle and Zeno, Demosthenes and Cicero; therefore he put into French "the precepts of rhetoric faithfully amassed from ancient books in Greek and Latin." As for Mary Stuart and his reasons for dedicating his work to her, he catalogues her as a princess

divinely predestined, not only for the amplification and advancement of our language, but also for the illustration and honor of all knowledge. In which

---

25. *Ibid.*, VI, 68–69.
26. *Ibid.*, VI, 225. Du Bellay states this feeling in his "Ample Discours au Roy sur le faict de ses quatre estats," where he hopes that "l'Eglise"

> Gardera que le mal maintenant Escossois,
> En passant l'Ocean, ne devienne François.

connection you seemed to give a certain presage, when in the presence of the King, accompanied by the greater part of the Princesses and Noblemen of his court, you maintained in a fine Latin oration, and defended against the usual opinion, the fact that it was indeed appropriate for women to have knowledge of letters and the liberal arts. A propos of which I might tell of the admiration with which you were heard by each one, what judgment was made, and what aspirations were held for you by this whole noble company, if I could say it without suspicion of flattery.[27]

Evidently young Mary Stuart, with excellent presence and in creditable Latin, had given before the court a defense of the intellectual rights of her sex. To her beauty, then, Fouquelin would add a recognition of the quality of her mind.

III

As the years passed after Mary, Queen of Scots, left Calais for the risky passage across the foggy waters back to her native land, the French were shocked by the news that came out of Scotland. A young Frenchman in his early twenties was, as has been said, aboard her galley, which managed to evade the English vessels and reach the port of Leith north of Edinburgh. He was Pierre de Bourdeilles, sieur de Brantôme, who was to become famous in the second half of the sixteenth century as one of France's most prolific chroniclers. In the division of his writings called *Des Dames* he has a discourse, "Sur la Reyne d'Escosse," which traces the highlights of the career of Mary Stuart. It is well to look now at some of the things he saw and heard.

Since Brantôme's story was not written until more than three decades after his trip to the North Sea in Mary Stuart's galley, some of the incidents he recalls may be clouded by the passage of time—although he says he has used an anonymous history of Mary's martyrdom published

27. Antoine Fouquelin, *La Rhétorique françoise* (Paris, 1557), p. 3. There had been an earlier edition in 1555. All the excerpts quoted come from the Dedication. The longer passage reads as follows in the original:

diuinement predestinée, non seulement pour l'amplification & auancement de nôtre langue, mais aussi pour l'illustration & honneur de toute science. De quoy vous me semblates donner vn certain presage, alors qu'en la presence du Roy, accompaigné de la plus part des Princes & Seigneurs de sa court, vous soutenies par vne oraison bien latine, & defendies contre la commune opinion, qu'il estoit bien seant aus femmes de sçauoir les lettres & ars liberaus. Au quel endroit ie diroy en quelle admiration d'vn chacun vous auries esté ouye, quel jugement auroit esté fait, & quelle esperance auroit esté conceüe de vous, par toute cette si noble compaignie, si ie le pouuoi dire sans soubson de flatterie.

in Edinburgh in 1587 to supplement his memory. He calls his chronicle of her life only an *abrégé*. It begins with a rather touching statement: "Those who may ever wish to write about this illustrious Queen of Scotland have two ample phases of her career to treat, of which one is that of her life and the other that of her death." This "most beautiful of the world's princesses, our Queen" was the daughter of Marie de Lorraine; and when Mary Stuart was near the age of fifteen, "her beauty began to show its light in full midday and to efface the sun when it shone at its brightest." She knew Latin very well and loved poetry and poets, especially "M. de Ronsard, M. du Belay [*sic*], and M. de Maisonfleur, who did some beautiful poems and elegies for her, even about her departure from France, which I have seen her read both in France and Scotland, with tears in her eyes and sighs in her heart." [28] She had a very pleasant speaking voice, even in "her own language, which of itself is quite rural, barbarous, and unpleasant in sound." She played the lute and sang to it, shining forth as she did so brighter than "the sun of her Scotland," which at times was visible only five hours a day. Brantôme, it might be said in passing, reflects the typical Frenchman's prejudice against other languages and other climes, both of which in his opinion are likely to be *barbares*. At this juncture Brantôme includes some sixty-six lines of Mary's own composition, and it is probable that they are authentic creations of the Scottish Queen. They are far from brilliant, but Brantôme calls them the "regrets" of the "triste reyne," whose brightness of color was now growing pale.[29]

Brantôme next describes Mary's departure from Calais:

after six days of sojourn in Calais, having said piteous and most sorrowful goodbyes to all the large company which was there, from the most important to the least, she embarked (along with her uncles, M. d'Aumalle, the grand prior, and M. d'Elbeuf, and M. d'Amville, today M. le connestable, and a great number of us in the nobility who were with her) in the galley of M. de Meuillon, because it was the best and most handsome.

28. See Brantôme, pp. 403–406, for these excerpts; the translations are my own. Brantôme's original French may be confirmed in the Lalanne edition of his works. The opening statement above reads in Brantôme's phrasing: "Ceux qui voudront jamais escrire de ceste illustre reyne d'Escosse en ont deux très-amples subjects, l'un celuy de sa vie, et l'autre celuy de sa mort."

This M. de Maisonfleur is a surprising inclusion, along with Ronsard and Du Bellay, as one of Mary Stuart's favorite poets; he wrote some thirteen *cantiques*, but Mary is not mentioned in any of them. Brantôme thought that Mary herself had poetic gifts and had composed some verses that were "beaux et très-bien faicts."

29. *Ibid.*, pp. 407–413.

Brantôme was thus aboard and remembers that Mary kept repeating
sorrowfully, "adieu France." She slept on deck in order to be in sight of
France as long as possible; when the wind died she was able to look at
the French coast, which was dimly visible throughout the night. Finally,
according to Brantôme, she said: "Adieu la France! Cela est faict. Adieu
la France! je pense ne vous voir jamais plus." The seigneur de Chastellard, who was considerably infatuated with Mary and who was also on
the galley, said in regard to lighting the navigation light during the long
first night at sea: "There will be no need for this beacon nor for this
torch, to light up the way for us, since the beautiful eyes of our Queen
are sufficiently strong to illumine with their fine fires the whole of the
sea." There were two galleys and two cargo vessels in the convoy; after a
four-day passage, most fortunate in evading hostile English ships, it
reached the coast of Scotland in the midst of a fog—a bad omen. Mary
Stuart and her retinue then proceeded to Holyrood on bad horses and to
a reception of poor music, "psalms so badly sung and so poorly in tune."
The second and most lugubrious phase of Mary Stuart's career was
about to begin.[30]

Mary's new husband, Lord Darnley, whom she secretly married on 9
July 1565, was slain on 10 February 1567. Mary did not approve of the
slaying, says Brantôme, despite the accusations of George Buchanan.
She was imprisoned by her enemies at Lochleven in June 1567 and
escaped almost a year later. Brantôme is most sketchy concerning Mary
Stuart's futile military efforts against England, her strange marriage to
Bothwell, and other political and personal details that are still not fully
explained. Brantôme's theory is that Queen Elizabeth subsequently
imprisoned Mary Stuart in England because she did not like her and was
"jealous of her beauty." His description of Mary's last days and the
circumstances surrounding her death form the most sympathetic
(though probably biased) part of his story.[31]

According to Brantôme, Mary Stuart was informed by the emissaries
of Elizabeth that she was to be beheaded on 17 February 1587. This
announcement gave Mary little time, as she lay in prison at Fotheringay
Castle, to prepare for the ordeal—to write the formal Catholic confes-

30. *Ibid.*, pp. 415–419. The story of the seigneur de Chastellard is told by Brantôme at the end
of his narrative on Mary Stuart. Chastellard, the nephew of Bayard, was so infatuated with Mary
that he followed her to Scotland and hid in her bedroom not once but twice. For the second
intrusion he was decapitated in 1563.

31. *Ibid.*, pp. 420–424.

sion that she was not permitted to make to a priest, to compose letters to her friends and relatives, and to make appropriate presents to her servants and staff. She did manage to send letters to the King and Queen of France (France was now under the dominion of the insipid Henri III, the last of Catherine de Médicis' pallid sons), and letters and some family relics to her Guise relatives. She then told her staff goodbye and gave them some of her personal things as remembrances of her. A black velvet dress would have been assigned to one of her ladies in waiting, but Mary Stuart needed it to die in, with dignity. Brantôme has given a tender description of her last moments spent with the women who had been in service—"she who had been Queen of the kingdoms of France and of Scotland, of one by birth and of the other as a gift of fortune, after having triumphantly received without stint honors and grandeurs, there she was passed humiliatingly into the hands of an executioner." But, says Brantôme, she was "innocent nevertheless." [32]

With an ivory cross in hand she made ready to follow to the hall of the scaffold the members of the commission who were to lead her there; these *commissaires* were impressed by her beauty and calm. She asked that her own feminine attendants be allowed to accompany her to the scaffold, which was twelve feet square. Her chamberlain assisted her up the scaffold, but her Catholic chaplain was not permitted to go with her; whereupon Mary stated that she was dying because of her Romanist faith—and refused the proffered services of a Protestant minister. Without assistance she knelt and prayed in French and Spanish for her friends and family, for the Pope, and for the Queen of England. In a typical, gossipy aside, Brantôme states that the executioner snatched aside Mary's pourpoint, thereby revealing "her beautiful bosom"—and then apologized for the act. In the presence of some four or five hundred people, with a handkerchief over her eyes, she chanted in Latin as the executioner's axe descended. Her hair had been whitened by her sorrows, says Brantôme, but she retained her beauty until the moment of her death. Her body was put in a lead coffin and buried in profane ground, while the place of her execution was scoured to avoid its becoming a site of pilgrimage. [33]

Before the end of the sixteenth century a tragedy had already been written about the sad career of Mary, Queen of Scots, thus beginning

32. *Ibid.*, pp. 425–430.
33. *Ibid.*, pp. 431–441.

the long series of dramas based on her life and death. This tragedy, *L'Ecossaise* or *La Reine d'Ecosse* (both designations were used as a title), was composed by a young man in his twenties, Antoine de Montchrestien. It was first published with four others of Montchrestien's tragedies in 1601, but it had been written some years earlier. Montchrestien, a gifted but violent youth, had fled to England from France in 1602 because he had killed a man in a duel. He offered to James I, the son of Mary Stuart, a copy of *L'Ecossaise*; the monarch evidently was pleased with it, since he welcomed Montchrestien at his court and sought to obtain his pardon from the King of France.[34]

Montchrestien showed audacity in treating a subject that was still so fresh in the memories of many people in France. His tragedy, as drama, is almost static and made up of a series of separate discourses in which the primary protagonists, Mary Stuart and Queen Elizabeth, never confront each other. However, Montchrestien was a fine poet and apparently quite familiar with the legend that was already growing around Mary. *L'Ecossaise* presents a sympathetic treatment of Mary's last days, and is very similar in many details to Brantôme's account, which Montchrestien could have known in manuscript. It is well to look at some of the highlights of the play, which opens with a long speech by "La Reine d'Angleterre"; in it, though she is suspicious of Mary Stuart, she praises her beauty and especially the shining stars of her eyes, which may presage Elizabeth's own death:

> Tes yeux que tous les coeurs prennent à leurs appas,
> Sans en estre troublez, verront-ils mon trespas?
> Ces beaux Astres lui sans au ciel de ton visage,
> De ma funeste mort seront-ils le présage?[35]

The second act finds the *Choeur des Estats* (there are two choruses in the play) advising Elizabeth to punish Mary; Elizabeth demurs, saying that one can not destroy a queen as one would a commoner. However, in the third act Mary has intimations of her fate and laments it, recalling happier years in France, which she first saw at the age of seven (Montchrestien's error—it was really at the age of five). As Mary

---

34. Montchrestien, *Les Tragédies de Montchrestien. Nouvelle édition d'après l'édition de 1604 . . . par L. Petit de Julleville* (Paris, 1891), pp. xxii–xxiii.
35. *Ibid.*, p. 73.

continues her lamentation, Elizabeth's courier arrives to tell her that "her beautiful veiled head" will fall under the executioner's axe. In the fourth act Mary says a long goodbye (about four pages) to Scotland, to friends and relatives, and to France; it is reminiscent of Brantôme's account, particularly the "Adieu France":

> Adieu France iadis seiour de mon plaisir,
> Où mille et mille fois m'emporta le desir
> Depuis que ie quittay ta demeure agreable,
> Par toy ie fus heureuse, et par toy miserable. . . .[36]

Mary then asks her *demoiselles* to make certain that her body is not defiled by the executioner, and the *Choeur* states that God will welcome the deserving into His realm on high.

Since deeds of violence were not done on stage in French tragedy, the beheading of Mary is presumed to have occurred between the fourth and fifth acts. Maistre d'Hostel speaks of the scandal of Mary's death at the hands of "cette Barbare" (obviously Elizabeth), and a long description of her execution is given by a messenger who has just arrived. Mary was calm in her pale beauty, disdainful of death; everybody admired her beautiful eyes and the dignity of her bearing. She offered a prayer and told the executioner to strike, and her head bounced three or four times "dessus la place"—all of which is very similar to Brantôme's account. The *Choeur* concludes the play with praise of Mary's charms, which are now celestial—hair, face, mouth; and her eyes, now stars and suns, have an added fire:

> Beaux yeux de ce beau Ciel en clarté nompareils,
> Beaux Astres, mais plustost deux rayonnans Soleils,
> Aveuglans tout ensemble et bruslans de leurs flames,
> Autrefois vos regards doucement courroucez,
> Furent autant de traits rudement eslancez,
> Pour faire en leur desir mourir l'espoir des ames.[37]

The French in later centuries did not forget Mary. One of the most plaintive and provocative poems concerning her was written in the nineteenth century by the *chansonnier* Béranger. It is called "Les Adieux

36. *Ibid.*, p. 103.
37. *Ibid.*, p. 112.

de Marie Stuart," and its chorus is probably the most touching of all her farewells to France:

> Adieu, charmant pays de France,
>   Que je dois tant chérir!
> Berceau de mon heureuse enfance,
> Adieu! te quitter c'est mourir.

For Mary, Queen of Scots, to leave France was to die.[38]

---

38. P. J. de Béranger, *Oeuvres complètes* (Paris: Perrotin, 1850), I, 115.

VIII. Ronsard on the Marriage of Poetry, Music, and the Dance

Isidore Silver · *Professor Emeritus of Humanities, Washington University*

I. *The Illusory Convergence of National and Hellenic Musical Traditions*

In an article entitled "Sebillet, Du Bellay, Ronsard: L'Entrée de Henri II à Paris et la révolution poétique de 1550," V. L. Saulnier rightly defines the literary renovation accomplished by Ronsard and his colleagues as "cette révolution poétique qui, en milieu de siècle, constitue sans nul doute l'événement le plus imposant dans tout le cours de notre littérature renaissante." He adds that "ces fêtes [the royal entries] apparaissent comme une sorte de manifeste de nouvelles tendances, comme la consécration monumentale de ce qui fait l'esprit même de la Renaissance triomphante, principalement dans le retour à l'antique." [1]

N.B.: References unaccompanied by any letters (e.g., XIV, 172) or preceded by *L.* are to the critical edition of Ronsard by Paul Laumonier. Paris is the place of publication unless otherwise specified.

   Abbreviations: Huguet—Edmond Huguet, *Dictionnaire de la langue français du seizième siècle*; MPSS—Jean Jacquot, ed., *Musique et poésie au XVIe siècle* (1954); RHLF—*Revue d'histoire littéraire de la France*; RM—*Ronsard et la Musique*, numéro spécial de la *Revue Musicale*, [7], 1 May 1924; RPL—Paul Laumonier, *Ronsard poète lyrique* (2nd ed., 1923); S.—Isidore Silver, ed., *Les Œuvres de Pierre de Ronsard*. Texte de 1587, 8 vols. (Chicago, St. Louis, Paris, 1966–70).

   1. *Les Fêtes de la Renaissance*, I. Etudes réunies et présentées par Jean Jacquot (1956), pp. 31, 32. I do not believe there is any fundamental contradiction between this position and that of Laumonier:

> Rien de "soudain" ne s'est produit en 1549–50. La *Deffence* et les *Odes* ne sont pas le signal d'une révolution, mais le terme d'une évolution. L'histoire ne présente pas de ces sauts brusques, inattendus, inexplicables. La conquête de l'art poétique des Anciens a été entreprise avant Ronsard, et les poètes de la Brigade sont venus les derniers parmi les conquérants. Cela d'ailleurs n'enlève rien à leur mérite, car les plus grands inventeurs sont souvent ceux qui perfectionnent plutôt que ceux qui découvrent: les premiers artistes sont même rarement les princes de leur art (*RPL*, pp. 718–719).

Whether we call the work of the Pléiade a revolution or the final term of an evolution does not change the fact that the movement initiated by Peletier, Ronsard, and Du Bellay radically transformed the literary scene. The decade of 1541–50 is a genuine watershed in the history of French poetry. And particularly in respect of the significance for that poetry of the return to Greek antiquity, the term "revolution" seems plainly justified.

This tendency to return to antiquity, including an attempt to renew the musical tradition of ancient Greece, is very marked in Ronsard's preface to the *Odes* of 1550 and did much to determine the nature of the musical supplement that appeared with the *Amours* of 1552. Though he contributed more than any of his contemporaries toward the success of the poetic revolution of the sixteenth century, there was nevertheless something visionary and intrinsically unreal about his wish to revive the ancient Hellenic musical tradition. The results of this effort, however, were not so ephemeral as the suppression of the preface in 1553 might suggest. Ronsard's initiative may ultimately have contributed to the creation by Jean-Antoine de Baïf, with the collaboration of the composer Joachim Thibaut de Courville and other musicians, of the Académie de Poésie et de Musique whose *Lettres Patentes* were signed by Charles IX in November 1570.[2] "Tout indique en ces années [from 1550 onward] que l'estime, le respect deviennent communs entre deux groupes d'artistes qui ont le sentiment de renouer avec une tradition perdue depuis l'Antiquité grecque."[3]

On the other hand, Ronsard's undertaking was not quite so great an innovation as he at first seemed to think. We know that the alliance of poetry and music was by no means unknown in France, and more than one writer had been aware that ancient Greece had shown the way.[4] In the very preface in which Ronsard announced his hope of restoring the lyre to its former glory, he referred to Clément Marot's work, "à la poursuite de son Psautier" (I, 44), which had strengthened the intimate association of the two arts, though its inspiration was not Hellenic. In later years Ronsard twice acknowledged the priority of Saint-Gelais in uniting poetry and music.[5] Thus, Comte and Laumonier accurately concluded, at the end of their article on Ronsard and the musicians of

2. Edouard Fremy, *L'Académie des derniers Valois* (1887), p. 50. Undoubtedly the example of Italian musical humanism was more directly influential than Ronsard's preface to the odes or even the musical supplement to the *Amours* in the establishment of Baïf's Académie. See Augé-Chiquet, *La Vie . . . de . . . Baïf* (1909), pp. 431–432; Frances A. Yates, *The French Academies of the Sixteenth Century* (London, 1947), pp. 9–10, 15–16; D. P. Walker's articles in *The Music Review* of 1941–42; and his "The aims of Baïf's *Académie de Poésie et de Musique*," *Journal of Renaissance and Baroque Music*, 1 (1946), 91–100; B. A. Terry, "Baïf's Academy and the Critics," *Renaissance Papers 1967* (1968), pp. 1–10.

3. F. Lesure, "La chanson française au XVIe siècle," *Hist. de la mus.*, ed. Roland-Manuel (1960), p. 1060.

4. See Chap. IV of my *Ronsard and the Grecian Lyre and Flute*, in progress.

5. VIII, 157; XIII, 25–26.

the sixteenth century, that Ronsard, "loin d'innover et de rompre avec les habitudes nationales, est resté un poète de tradition, du moins au point de vue qui nous occupe. . . . il est resté le disciple et le continuateur des poètes français du moyen âge, du XVᵉ siècle et de la génération de Clément Marot."[6]

In a strictly musical sense Ronsard may indeed be said to have retreated from a position reached by forerunners, including Saint-Gelais, who had composed the music for their own verses.

Ronsard vient au lendemain du jour où la poésie et la musique, en France, intimement unies chez les troubadours, se sont émancipées pour de bon l'une de l'autre. A l'instant de ce congé réciproque et chacune croyant n'aller que vers l'avenir, c'est le passé qui les ramène un moment l'une à l'autre. Passé moins lointain, moins mort que ne le dit Ronsard, quand il se prétend disciple et rénovateur de Pindare, il n'est que le petit-fils et l'héritier d'Adam de La Hale ou de Guillaume de Machault sans être comme eux musicien autant que poète. Son appel à la musique est, au fond, un adieu.[7]

Valuable as this insight may be, it remains true that as Ronsard was saying "Vale" to the possibility of personally setting his poetry to music, he was uttering a sincere "Ave" to the concept of a Hellenic alliance of the two arts. There may be more than symbolism in the fact that Marc-Antoine de Muret was the first to write music to Ronsard's poetry:

It is little known that the musicians' answer to Ronsard's appeal took place inconspicuously, on July 5, 1552, by the publication—in an anthology of French *chansons*, the *Dixiesme livre* of the printer N. du Chemin—of the ode *Ma petite colombelle* [L., I, 246], set to four-part music by the Humanist Marc-Antoine de Muret, a friend of the poet.[8]

It does no violence to the imagination to suppose that the learned Muret, who was then teaching the Greek and Latin poets at the Collège de Boncourt and was soon to write both the erudite *Commentary* on the *Amours* for Cassandre and the four-part music for a sonnet of that sequence, shared Ronsard's enthusiastic but insubstantial vision of

6. C. Comte and P. Laumonier, "Ronsard et les musiciens du XVIᵉ siècle," *RHLF*, 7 (1900), 380–381.

7. Jean Chantavoine, quoted by André Cœuroy, *RM*, p. 181 [85].

8. F. Lesure, *Musicians and Poets of the French Renaissance*, trans. from the French by Elio Gianturco and H. Rosenwald (New York, 1955), pp. 59–60. Comte and Laumonier had known in 1900 of this publication by Muret (*RHLF*, vol. 7, p. 349).

reviving the ancient alliance of poetry and music, and undertook to assist in its realization.[9]

Four successive passages in the article by Comte and Laumonier seem to reveal their emerging recognition of the illusion that Ronsard and his musical collaborators were pursuing. Their study opens with this positive assertion: "Parmi les nombreux mérites de Ronsard, il en est un dont le poète se montre particulièrement jaloux: c'est d'*avoir restauré* l'antique alliance de la poésie et de la musique." Soon they add: "Ronsard pensait . . . que . . . l'imitation des Italiens était une façon de faire renaître en France l'art ancien; chanter ses vers au son du luth, *c'était ressusciter* le procédé des lyriques grecs." About thirty pages farther on we read a more discreet restatement of this idea: "Mais ce qui était vraiment nouveau, dans l'entreprise de Ronsard, c'était de *vouloir restaurer*, dans sa savante complexité, l'union si chère aux Grecs, de la musique et de la poésie. . . ." Finally, on the last page of their investigation, we find: "Il a cru, *ou a feint de croire*, qu'il importait en France les moeurs artistiques de la vieille Grèce. . . ."[10]

The gradual invasion of doubt that we witness here may represent to some degree what went on in the poet's mind from the time of the first rash assertions of the preface to the *Odes* of 1550 until its suppression three years later. Surely the essential reason for that suppression was Ronsard's growing appreciation of the fact that its arrogance of tone and language was calculated to alienate a public whose sympathies he wished rather to engage. But perhaps he also came to realize vaguely, though he may not consciously have admitted it to himself, that the Greek lyre and the music associated with it were irretrievably lost. That he continued to write as though the national and Hellenic traditions could be joined was hardly more than a poet's desire to sustain a vision to whose humanistic content he was deeply committed. It was a vision destined to have significant consequences. "Bien qu'il se soit trouvé maint humaniste avant la Pléiade pour louer l'accord entre la musique et la poésie, c'est à Ronsard qu'il revient d'avoir créé, par ses écrits et son exemple, une 'mystique' de l'union entre les deux arts, qui va marquer profondément l'avenir de leurs rapports."[11]

9. See Isidore Silver, *The Intellectual Evolution of Ronsard*, Vol. I, *The Formative Influences* (St. Louis, 1969), pp. 75–76.

10. Pp. 341, 343, 371, 381; my emphases.

11. Lesure, "La chanson française. . . ," p. 1058.

II. *"La Poesie & la Musique seurs"*

Ronsard's hopes for the alliance of the sister arts were particularly strong in 1549, when he must have been writing the preface to the *Odes*.[12] The "Hymne de France," to which I am indebted for the title of the present section (I, 32), was published in that year. Toward the end of 1549 he wrote "A sa lire," which celebrated the union of the two arts and the part he played in promoting the acceptance of that union in France:

> Adonc en France avec toi je chantai,
> Et jeune d'ans sus le Loir invantai
> De marier aus cordes les victoires,
> Et des grans Rois les honneurs & les gloires. . . .
>> (I, 164; cf. pp. 73, 126)

Earlier in the same year, in the ode "Au Roi" which opens the *Second livre des Odes*, he had already alluded to this "marriage":

> Et toi ma Françoise lire,
> Mieus que devant faut elire
> Un vers pour te marier . . . .
>> (I, 172)

In a note on *marier* Laumonier explains: "Traduction du mot pindarique ἐναρμόξαι, *Olymp.* III, 5. . . ." The reference is to verses in which Pindar says that he has discovered how to unite the voices of the singers to the Dorian rhythm.[13]

Throughout these early years (1549–54) one finds numerous additional passages in Ronsard relating to the alliance of poetry and music. In some he is not directly involved as an instrumentalist;[14] in others he describes his own "performance" as a poet-musician.[15]

If, as I believe, Ronsard's references to his lyre, lute, and guitar are generally metaphorical, we may reasonably infer that in his allusions to his own musical performances he merely adopted the convention established by Horace, which pretended that the poet sang his compositions to his own accompaniment on the lyre. It is in this sense, I think, that we must interpret the following verses written in 1563,[16] which seem so

---

12. The *privilège* is dated 10 January 1549 (1550, new style).
13. Cf. V, 260, and n. 1.
14. I, 215; II, 190; III, 127; IV, 41.
15. I, 130; II, 9, 119; V, 134.
16. For the date, see XII, 173, n. 4.

explicitly to affirm Ronsard's great versatility in uniting vocal and instrumental music:

> A la fin Apollon & ses sœurs volontiers
> En l'Antre Thespien m'aprindrent leurs mestiers,
> A bien faire des vers, à bien poulcer la Lyre,
> A scavoir fredonner, à scavoir dessus dire
> Les louanges des Roys, & en mille façons
> A scavoir alyer les cordes aux chansons. . . .
>   (XII, 176)

Laumonier's note on the last verse is once more opportune: "Expression d'Horace, *Carm.* IV, 9, 4." The line in question is: "Verba loquor socianda chordis."

Ronsard's *Art poëtique* is in some respects much more restrained than the preface to the *Odes* in its assertion in favor of the alliance of poetry and music. There is no reference to his intention of reviving the use of the Greek lyre, no insistence that the Greek lyre alone can give life to poetry. He simply says that "la Poësie sans les instrumens, ou sans la grace d'une seule ou plusieurs voix, n'est nullement aggreable, non plus que les instrumens sans estre animez de la melodie d'une plaisante voix" (XIV, 9). More than three centuries later Mallarmé expressed essentially the same thought in *La Musique et les Lettres* (1895), but with greater penetration and a more sophisticated sense of the intellectual and spiritual nature of the relationship of the two arts:

La musique sans les lettres se présente comme un très subtil nuage; elles, une monnaie si courante . . . son charme est vain, si le langage, par la retrempe et l'essor purifiant du chant, n'y confère un sens . . . la musique et les lettres sont la face alternative, ici élargie vers l'obscur, scintillante là avec certitude, du phénomène que j'appelai l'idée.[17]

In the fifth collective edition of 1578, at the end of the *Second livre des Hymnes*, Ronsard published two Sapphic odes (XVII, 396–399) that imitate as closely as the French language permits the metrical form of the strophe created by Sappho.[18] In the sixth collective edition of 1584 the two poems were transferred to the end of the *Cinquiesme livre des Odes* (pp. 399–400), followed only by Ronsard's *exegi monumentum*

---

17. Quoted by Louis Laloy, "Ronsard musicien," *RM*, p. 108 [12].
18. See XVII, 396, n. 1, and *RPL*, p. 701, for Laumonier's comments on the metrical characteristics of Ronsard's Sapphic odes.

entitled "A sa Muse" (*inc.* "Plus dur que fer . . ."). Neither in 1578 nor in 1584 were these Sapphic odes accompanied by any comment. In the seventh and final collective edition prepared by Ronsard for the press in 1585 and published in 1587 the position of the two Sapphic odes (t. II, 369–371) remains unchanged, but they are preceded by these remarks:

Les vers Sapphiques ne sont, ny ne furent, ny ne seront jamais agreables, s'ils ne sont chantez de voix vive, ou pour le moins accordez aux instruments, qui sont la vie & l'ame de la Poësie. Car Sapphon chantant ses vers ou accomodez à son Cystre, ou à quelque Rebec . . . leur donnoit plus de grace, que toutes les trompettes, fifres & tabourins n'en donnoient aux vers masles & hardis d'Alcee, son citoyen, & contemporain, faisant la guerre aux Tyrans. (XVIII, 227–228)

Thus, at the end of his life, Ronsard had not abandoned the vision, inspired by Hellenic practice, of the alliance of poetry and music. As Laumonier said of this little preface to the two Sapphic odes, "Elle montre les relations intimes qui existent entre la poésie et la musique. Les anciens l'avaient bien senti et R[onsard]. nous témoigne assez son sentiment à ce sujet." [19] But he no longer promises or recommends the revival of the Greek lyre. Nevertheless, his allusion to Sappho's "Cystre" [20] and to the grace it conferred on her poetry reveals that although his own Sapphics were apparently never set to music,[21] the nostalgia of that revival continued to live within him.

On at least one occasion, the marriage of Anne de Joyeuse, "premier mignon du Roy [Henri III]" with Marguerite de Vaudemont, 24 September 1581, the nostalgic vision was made "reality." Ronsard and Jean-Antoine de Baïf cooperated to arrange an appropriately sumptuous setting in verse and music for the nuptials: "Le Roy donna à Ronsard et à Baïf, poëtes, pour les vers qu'ils firent pour les mascarades, combats, tournois et autres magnificences des nopces, et pour la belle musique par eux ordonnée et chantée avec les instrumens, à chacun deux mil escus." [22]

19. Marginal note in Paul Laumonier's hand, p. 346, of his personal copy of the article he published in collaboration with Charles Comte, "Ronsard et les musiciens du XVIe siècle," *RHLF*, 7 (1900), 341–381. This copy is now in the Department of Rare Books and Special Collections of the Washington University Libraries in St. Louis.

20. Huguet, s. v. *cistre*, refers to *cithre*, "sorte de cithare."

21. Neither poem (*inc.* "Belle dont les yeux. . ." and "Ny l'âge ny sang. . . ") is found in the "Liste des incipit" of the *Bibliographie* by Thibault and Perceau.

22. G. Brunet, A. Champollion, *et al.*, eds., *Mémoires-Journaux de Pierre de l'Estoile* (1888), II, 23.

Frances A. Yates has published the program of these festivities:[23]
*Magnificences qui se doibvent faire aux nopces de Monsieur le Duc de
Joyeuse, en Septembre et Octobre, 1581*. Under the heading *Le lundi
XVIIIe dudit mois*[24] *des nopces,* we read: "Les accoustrements seront
blancz et dargent. Sera bon de faire reciter une epitalame a reprinses en
concert de musique [par des musiciens] habillez a lantique partye en
filles partye en garsons accompagnant Hymen, dieu des nopces." The
allusions to an epithalamium, to choruses of boys and girls escorting
Hymen, to musicians "habillez a lantique" strongly suggest that the
participants were attempting to resuscitate the "reality" of a wedding
ceremony in the manner of antiquity.[25] Ronsard might well have
thought that his classicizing initiatives were still effective on the highest
levels of French society as he wrote a description of this scene in his
"Epithalame de Monseigneur de Joyeuse" of 1581:[26]

> Je voy, ce semble, Hymen protecteur des humains,
> Le brodequin és pieds, le flambeau dans les mains,

23. "Poésie et musique dans les 'Magnificences' au mariage du duc de Joyeuse, Paris, 1581,"
MPSS, pp. 241–256. The quotation is from the *Appendice,* p. 258. See also Bodo L. O. Richter,
"*Venere pronuba*: The French Renaissance Epithalamia," in *From Marot to Montaigne: Essays on
French Renaissance Literature,* ed. Raymond C. La Charité, *Kentucky Romance Quarterly,* 19
(1972), Supp. No. 1, pp. 95–97.

24. The date of the engagement was 18 September.

25. "The musical humanists of the Renaissance desired to produce a purely 'classical' music with
as much ardour as the architects desired to erect purely 'classical' buildings. . . . But the musician
who wished to revive ancient music was trying to imitate an art of which practically no examples
survived, and of which the theory cannot, even now, be reconstructed with any degree of certainty"
(F. A. Yates, *The French Academies,* p. 46).

26. The same year witnessed the performance, 15 October, of Balthazar de Beaujoyeulx's *Ballet
comique de la royne, faict aux nopces de Monseigneur le Duc de Joyeuse & madamoyselle de
Vaudemont sa sœur.* Gustave Reese, *Music in the Renaissance* (New York, 1954), describes the
Ballet comique as the outcome of the efforts of the humanist poets and musicians to renew the
ancient alliance of poetry, music, and the dance:

> The environment in which the court ballet evolved was pervaded by the humanistic concepts of
> the Pléiade and the Académie. Baïf had formulated a principle of equal duration of steps and
> notes. The resulting *dance mesurée* was a fitting complement to *musique mesurée*; and Baïf and
> his followers believed that, with the union of their kind of dance, poetry, and music, they were
> reviving the tradition of the ancient drama. Poets like Jodelle, Ronsard, and Baïf supervised the
> court entertainments, and those traits of unity and relevancy of the parts emerged that found
> full expression in the *Ballet comique de la royne* of 1581 and make it the first genuine *ballet de
> cour* (p. 571).

It is doubtful, however, whether Ronsard and his friends would have been able to accept this
judgment and remain faithful to their own concept of the triple art of poetry, music, and dance.
They might have been inclined to reject certain ideas expressed in Beaujoyeulx's preface *Au lecteur*:
"Je me suis advisé qu'il ne seroit point indecent de . . . diversifier la musique de poesie, & entrelacer
la poesie de musique, & le plus souvent les confondre toutes deux ensemble: ainsi que l'antiquité ne
recitoit point ses vers sans musique, & Orphee ne sonnoit jamais sans vers. *J'ay toutesfois donné le
premier tiltre & honneur à la dance, & le second à la substance. . .*" (*Balet Comique de la Royne,*

Hymen conservateur des noms & des familles,
Separer en deux rangs les garçons & les filles,
Et les faire chanter à l'entour de ton lit,
Esclairez de son feu qui ta nopce embellit.
    J'oy desja *de leurs pas la cadance ordonnée,*
J'oy toute la maison ne sonner qu'Hymenée,
Et le cornet à l'huis faire un bruit, pour n'ouir
Les cris qui en pleurant la feront resjouir.[27]

(XVIII, 119–120; my emphasis)

III. *"Lire dorée que la dance oit"*

Ronsard's last epithalamium was an amplified echo of the first, indeed a description of its actualization so far as French cultural evolution during more than thirty years had made that possible. On 20 October 1548 he had composed for the marriage of the duc de Vendôme, suzerain of his family, the "Epithalame d'Antoine de Bourbon et Janne de Navarre":

Quand mon Prince épousa
Janne, divine race,
Que le Ciel composa
Au moule d'une Grace,
Douze vierges venues
Ces beaux vers luy ont dit,
En *dansant* toutes nues
A l'entour de son lit:
O Hymen, Hymenée:
Hymen, ô Hymenée.

(I, 9–10; my emphasis)

1582. A cura di Giacomo Alessandro Caula [Torino, 1962], fac. ed., sig. e. iii^v [my emphasis]). In his article on "Ronsard et les fêtes de Cour" (*RM*, p. 140 [44]), Henry Prunières expressed what might have been some of the scruples of the poets and musicians associated with Ronsard and Baïf, none of whom was invited to collaborate in the creation of the *Ballet comique*:

> Nous ignorons ce qu'en pensèrent les membres survivants de l'*Académie de Poésie et de Musique,* mais ils durent considérer le *Ballet Comique* comme une véritable profanation. Retenus par des scrupules d'artistes et d'humanistes, ils n'avaient pu réaliser cette rénovation du drame antique dont l'idée les hantait, cette union intime, complète de la poésie, de la musique et de la danse, ils devaient voir avec amertume surgir cette magnifique caricature de leurs plus chères aspirations. Ils ne pouvaient comprendre que Balthazarini en s'imaginant ressusciter le drame antique avait fait beaucoup mieux qu'un travail d'humaniste, qu'il avait, en tentant de réaliser les idées de Ronsard et de Baïf qu'il ne comprenait qu'imparfaitement, inventé un genre dramatique nouveau: le Ballet de Cour, appelé à une éclatante fortune en France, en Angleterre, en Italie et dans toute l'Europe.

27. The probable source of this and other passages in Ronsard's epithalamium is Catullus' "In nuptias Juliae et Manlii," itself deeply indebted to the epithalamia of Sappho; see Georges Lafaye, *Catulle et ses modèles* (1894), p. 72.

In a variant introduced in 1555 (and which one still reads in 1587) the
two verses preceding the refrain assumed this form:

> Toutes d'une *cadence*
> Luy chanterent ces vers. . . .
> (*S.*, III, 242; my emphasis)

Raymond Lebègue correctly stated in his article on "Ronsard et la
musique" that although Ronsard's effort to revive the "lyrisme musical
de Pindare" had not been sustained by the public or, with some exceptions, by the composers, he had had "le mérite d'oser donner à la France
l'équivalent de la poésie chantée du poète thébain." [28] But the effort was
incomplete if Ronsard's intended renewal of the musical art of Greece
was not to be compromised. He was aware that when he had praised his
country because

> La Poesie & la Musique seurs . . .
> Y ont aquis leurs louanges antiques
> (I, 32)

he had omitted an essential component of the lyric art of Hellas. For as
Henry Expert had said:

En quoi, par quoi la Grèce et Rome renaîtront-elles? . . . Il faut rendre la vie à
cet art qui, *à la beauté eurythmique des corps, l'orchestique*, à la beauté du
verbe humain, la poésie, unit la beauté musicale, qui, elle, par ses mélodies et ses
rythmes, est l'âme même de *cet art triple*, de cet art suprême qu'on appelle le
Lyrisme. [29]

From a very early time Ronsard knew that the union of the sister arts
of music and poetry in the absence of choreography would not suffice to
"restaurer intégralement le lyrisme de Pindare." [30] He had placed at the
end of the first book of odes the poem "A sa lire," which begins with a
magnificent transcription of the opening verses of Pindar's first Pythian:

> Lire dorée, où Phebus seulement,
> Et les neuf seurs ont part egalement,
> Le seul confort qui mes tristesses tue,
> *Que la dance oit*, & toute s'evertue
> De t'obeir, & *mesurer ses pas*

---

28. *MPSS*, p. 114.
29. "La musique française au temps de la Renaissance," *Rev. de la Ren.*, 4 (1903), 166 (my
emphasis).
30. *RPL*, pp. 87–88.

> Sous tes fredons mignardés par compas,
> Lors qu'en bruiant *tu merques la cadanse*
> D'un avantjeu, *le guide de la danse.*
>   (I, 162; my emphasis)

Pindar had provided the full substance of these verses: "Lyre d'or, apanage commun d'Apollon et des Muses aux tresses violettes, à ta voix, le pas[31] rythmé des choreutes ouvre la fête, et les chanteurs obéissent à tes signaux, lorsque, vibrante, tu fais résonner les premières notes des préludes qui guident les chœurs."[32] Here, as Aimé Puech points out, all the significant elements of Greek lyric poetry are clearly visible: the choral song, the dance, the musical accompaniment.

The association of the Muses with the dance, by themselves or under the guidance of Apollo Musagetes, became a recurring theme in Ronsard's poetry. In the ode "A Madame Marguerite," probably composed in the summer of 1550, he says of the Muses:

> Ces riches maisons sumptueuses,
> Ces grand' villes presumptueuses
> Par l'orgueil d'un mur s'elevant,
> Ne sont les lieux où elles dansent,
> Et leurs pas serrent & avancent,
> Le Cynthien[33] sonnant devant.
>   (III, 100)

In the *Contr'estrene, au Seigneur Robert de la Haye,* presented on 1 January 1552, the role of Apollo surrounded by the dancing Muses is apparently bestowed on the recipient of the poem:

> Nul mieux soubz les raiz de la nuict,
>   Quand la Lune en son plein reluit
>   Sus l'herbe avec elles ne dance,
>   Suyvantes le poulce divin
>   De ce grand Alcée Angevin[34]
>   Qui devant sonne la cadance.
>
> Toy lors couronné du lien
>   Que donne l'Arbre Delien,[35]

---

31. The text reads "pays," an obvious typographical error; the reading is correct in the 1922 edition.

32. Aimé Puech, ed. and trans., *Pindare*, tome II: *Pythiques* (3rd ed., 1955), p. 28.

33. "Apollon Musagète, dieu né et adoré sur le Cynthe, colline de Délos." Note by Laumonier.

34. Joachim du Bellay.

35. The laurel of Apollo.

> Ores tu prens plaisir d'elire
> Le premier ranc, ou le meillieu,
> Entre elles marchant comme un Dieu[36]
> Qui s'egaye dessoubz la lyre.
>   (III, 167)

When Ronsard wishes to pay Cassandre the highest compliment in his possession he writes that she, not the dancing Muses, is the source of his poetic inspiration:

> Je ne suis point, Muses, acoustumé
>   De voir la nuict vostre dance sacrée:
>   Je n'ay point beu dedans l'onde d'Ascrée,[37]
>   Fille du pied du cheval emplumé.[38]
>
> De tes beaulx raiz chastement allumé
>   Je fu poëte: & si ma voix recrée,
>   Et si ma lyre, ou si ma rime agrée,
>   Ton œil en soit, non Parnase, estimé.
>   (IV, 137)

The significance of the compliment may be evaluated when these verses are compared to a passage in "A Janot Parisien" in which Ronsard dedicated the *Folastries* (1553) to Jean-Antoine de Baïf:

> Livre que les sœurs Thespiennes,[39]
> Dessus les rives Pympléennes,
> Ravi, me firent concevoir,
> Quand jeune garson j'allay voir
> Le brisement[40] de leur cadance
> Et Apollon le guidedance.[41]
>   (V, 4–5)

Sometimes Calliope, rather than Apollo, leads her sister Muses in the dance:

> Ma nourrice Calliope
> Qui du Luc musicien
> Dessus la jumele crope

---

36. Cf. X, 84, ll. 5–6, in which Ronsard assigns the role of leader of the Muses to Jean du Thier, "Compagnon d'Apollon."
37. Hesiod.
38. Pegasus, a blow of whose hoof created the fountain Hippocrene.
39. The Muses.
40. The beat (?); wanting in Huguet, but see *brisure*.
41. Cf. VIII, 78, l. 108.

> D'Elicon guides la trope
> Du saint chœur Parnasien.
>
> Et vous ses Sœurs, qui, recrues
> D'avoir trop mené le bal,
> Toute nuit vous baignés nues
> Dessous les rives herbues
> De la fontaine au cheval. . . .
>   (VII, 75)

In the "Hymne de l'Hyver" (1563) the *art triple* is represented in a particularly animated balance of musical, vocal, and choreographic elements:

> Apollon fit venir les Muses en la dance,
> La belle Calliope alloit à la cadance
> Sur toutes la premiere, & desur le tropeau
> Paroissoit comme un Pin sur un taillis nouveau.
> Tantost elle chantoit, tantost d'une gambade
> Elle faisoit sauter sa ronde vertugade:
> Pan le dieu boucager de sa fluste sonna,[42]
> Le haut palais doré mugissant resonna
> Soubs la voix des hauboix, ce pendant que la coupe
> Alloit de main en main en rond parmy la troupe.
>   (XII, 84; cf. XV, 386)

The epic formula that follows without interval—

> Apres que le desir de manger fut donté,
> Et l'apetit de boyre en boyvant fut osté . . .

—brings to mind the passages in Homer that suggest the great antiquity of the union of the arts of music, song, and dance: "Lors donc qu'on a chassé la soif et l'appétit, les jeunes gens remplissent jusqu'au bord les cratères, puis à chacun, dans sa coupe, ils versent de quoi faire libation aux dieux. Et, tout le jour, en chœur, les fils des Achéens, pour apaiser le dieu, chantent le beau péan. . . ."[43] In Homer's description of the Shield

---

42. Cf. V, 240, ll. 153–156.

43. *Iliad*, I, 469–473 (Paul Mazon *et al.*, eds. and trans., *Homère: Iliade* [1949]). The paean was "a Greek choral lyric . . . probably of Cretan origin . . . addressed to Apollo. . . . The song was sometimes, but not always, accompanied by a dance" (Paul Harvey, *The Oxford Companion to Classical Literature* [Oxford, 1951], p. 302, col. 1). Ronsard knew that the paean could be danced:

> Ces trois nobles esprits oyans telle nouvelle,
> Danceront un Pean dessus l'herbe nouvelle. . . .
>   (XVIII, 42)

of Achilles Ronsard might have discovered the remote origins of the nuptial songs and dances that, by way of Sappho and Catullus, had found renewed life in his epithalamia for Antoine de Bourbon and Janne de Navarre, for Anne de Joyeuse and Marguerite de Vaudemont:

Il [Héphaestos] y figure aussi deux cités humaines—deux belles cités. Dans l'une, ce sont des noces, des festins. Des épousées, au sortir de leur chambre, sont menées par la ville à la clarté des torches, et, sur leurs pas, s'élève, innombrable, le chant d'hyménée. De jeunes danseurs tournent, et, au milieu d'eux, flûtes et cithares font entendre leurs accents. . . .[44]

Echoes of these passages, adapted to a different epic environment, are heard from time to time in the *Franciade*:

> En-cependant la jeunesse Troyenne
> Haut invoquant la Berecynthienne . . .
> Les uns frapoient les tabourins enflez,
> Les uns au son de la flute persée
> Fouloient la terre, autres fols de pensée
> Comme agitez de fureur sauteloient,
> Autres chargez de grands bouclers baloient
> Un branle armé, autres de voix aigües
> Faisoient sonner les forestz chevelues
> Et retentir les rochers d'alentour.
> Les crus-vieillards d'un grand & large tour
> Icy dansoient à testes couronnées,
> Là, la jeunesse aux plaisantes années
> De pieds, de mains & de voix respondoient
> Et leurs chansons aux vieillards accordoient.[45]
>
> (XVI, 49–50)

But Ronsard had not waited until 1572, when the *Franciade* appeared, to reveal that his knowledge of the intimate interdependence of the three sister arts was not derived solely from Pindar. Almost twenty years earlier he had written in the seventh "Folastrie":

> Assez vrayment on ne revere
> Les divines bourdes d'Homere,
> Qui dit, que l'on ne peut avoir

44. *Iliad*, XVIII, 490–495.

45. "Chantaient d'accord avec la musique de la danse. La variante [aux flutes accordoient] est plus claire." Note by Laumonier. For other passages in the *Franciade* that portray the union of the arts of music, song, and dance after the manner of Homer, see XVI, 90 and 142. Cf. in particular XVI, 194, ll. 473–480, and *Iliad*, XVIII, 593–604.

> Si grand plaisir que de se voir
> Entre ses amis à la table,
> Quand un menetrier delectable
> Paist l'oreille d'une chanson,
> Et quand l'outesoif échanson
> Fait aller en rond par la troupe
> De main en main la pleine coupe. . . .
>   Tu voulois dire, bon Homere,
> Que l'on doit faire bonne chere
> Tandis que l'âge, & la saison,
> Et la peu maistresse raison,
> Permetent à nostre jeunesse
> Les libertez de la liesse,
> Sans avoir soin du lendemain:
> Mais d'un hanap de main en main,
> D'une trepignante cadance,
> D'un roüer autour de la dance,
> De meutes de chiens par les boys,
> De lutz mariez à la voix . . .
> Exerçer la douce pratique
> De la vertu Sybaritique.
>   (V, 42–44)

Of the first *alinéa* Laumonier rightly says: "Ce début est inspiré directement de l'*Odyssée*, IX, 5 et suiv." But the second, with its references to the youth whirling in the dance, to lutes married to the voice, is another reminder that Homer's representation of the Shield of Achilles had early enriched Ronsard's conception of the triune Hellenic art of μουσική.[46]

---

46. See *Iliad*, XVIII, 494, 593–594. The allusion to the leash of dogs in both Ronsard and Homer (578) confirms our attribution of the source.

IX. Oronce Finé and English Textbooks for the Mathematical Sciences

S. K. Heninger, Jr. · *Professor of English, University of British Columbia*

In 1556 Robert Recorde published *The Castle of Knowledge*, a treatise on astronomy which continued the series of textbooks in the mathematical disciplines that he had begun with *The Grounde of Artes* in 1542. *The Castle of Knowledge* is a thorough and up-to-date exposition of the science of the spheres, a work that rendered the English mathematical practitioner as well-informed as his counterpart on the Continent. It is best known, perhaps, for Recorde's reference to Copernicus (p. 165), the first in English, made a scant thirteen years after publication of the *De revolutionibus orbium coelestium, libri VI*. However, *The Castle* should be better known to students of Elizabethan literature because it offers a comprehensive cosmology in clear and simple terms. Recorde drew upon the best of astronomical writings in his effort to educate the neophyte astronomers of England, and his references to contemporary authorities show that unquestionably he was *au courant*.[1]

The foremost authority for Recorde was a Frenchman, Oronce Finé, whom he very quickly acknowledges. Despite the currency of his subject matter, Recorde chose to cast his discourse in the old-fashioned form of questions and answers between a *discipulus* and a *magister*. As a beginning, the Scholar tells the Master that he wishes to increase his "knowledge of the worlde and the partes of it" (p. 2), and that in consequence he has been reading Proclus and Sacrobosco. He has also been reading "Orontius cosmographye"—and the exposition takes off from there. The *De sphaera* of Proclus and the even more popular *De sphaera* of Sacrobosco were standard textbooks used in the schools, and are known even to modern readers. "Orontius cosmographye," however, has slipped into oblivion and requires a gloss. It is the *De mundi sphaera, sive cosmographia, libri V* of Oronce Finé, or Orontius

---

1. In addition to the full panoply of classical authorities, Recorde refers, for example, to Joachim Ringhelberg (p. 9), Johann Stöffler (p. 98), Erasmus Reinholdt (pp. 138–141, 189, 270), Jacques Le Fèvre d'Etaples (p. 154), and Johann Schöner (p. 270).

Finaeus, to use the Latinized form of the name. This important cosmography was first printed as an autonomous volume in Paris in 1542, but had appeared as early as 1532 in the *Protomathesis*, an omnibus textbook for the mathematical sciences that Finé published shortly after assuming the chair of mathematics at the Collège de France. Recorde draws heavily upon Finé throughout *The Castle of Knowledge*, and therefore we should inquire into this eminent authority from across the Channel. To date, he has been little noted in the annals of the history of science.[2]

Finé was born in 1494 at Briançon in Dauphiné. Hence his soubriquet, Delphinatus. He was the son of a studious physician, who necessarily drew upon astrology in his ministration to patients. After the early death of Finé *père*, Oronce was educated in Paris, and by 1516 was giving tutorials in mathematics in the college of Navarre, one of the ancient establishments attached to the University. Quite naturally, he practiced the lucrative art of making astrological predictions, and by 1526 he had gained a reputation for his expertise. In that year Heinrich Cornelius Agrippa referred to him in a letter as "the noted mathematician and astrologer of Paris."[3] The culmination of his academic career came on 27 March 1530/31, when Francis I appointed him to a regius professorship of mathematics at the Collège de France in Paris. The newly founded Collège was intended to foster the humanities, which had been slighted at the University. At the same time that the regius professorship of mathematics was instituted, the King, under advice from Guillaume Budé, designated two other royal chairs, one in Hebrew and the other in Greek. Finé held his chair with distinction until his death in 1555. He was widely known and highly respected, the center of an active circle of mathematical practitioners—astrologers, cosmographers, navigators, geographers, cartographers. Among his friends he numbered the learned Jean Fernel, the prodigious Charles de Bouelles, and the notorious Antoine Mizauld, and for a time he was in close touch with John Dee. Most remarkably, perhaps, he was the author or editor

2. The fullest accounts of Finé, none of which is complete, are as follows: (1) *Biographie Universelle*; (2) Lucien Gallois, *De Orontio Finaeo, gallico geographo* (Paris, 1890); (3) Moritz Cantor, *Vorlesungen über Geschichte der Mathematik* (4 vols.; Leipzig, 1894–1908), II, 375–378; (4) Lynn Thorndike, *A History of Magic and Experimental Science* (8 vols.; Columbia University Press, 1923–58), V, 285–286; (5) Eva G. R. Taylor, *Tudor Geography 1485–1583* (London, 1930), pp. 86–87.

3. Cited by Thorndike, V, 285.

of a large number of textbooks in the mathematical sciences, so that Recorde could well have looked to him as a model in his own effort to educate English apprentices. Finé was a pedagogue with a flowing pen.

Finé edited several earlier works in astronomy, thereby giving them renewed viability. His first offering in print was an edition of the traditional *Arithmetica* by Joannes Martinus, published at Paris in 1519. In 1521 Finé reprinted with his own preface the *De motu octavae sphaerae, opus mathematica atque philosophia plenum* of Agostino Ricchi, originally published at Trino in 1513. In this treatise Ricchi argues against the existence of any heavenly spheres that do not contain visible bodies—i.e., the ninth or "cristalline" sphere, and the tenth sphere or "primum mobile." He limits the number of spheres to eight, and Finé follows suit.[4] Finé also edited the much more influential *Theoricae novae planetarum* of Georg Peurbach, a somewhat out-of-date but widely used textbook that had been in print since Regiomontanus published it in Nuremberg about 1474. Finé's edition appeared in 1525 (reprinted 1534), and in 1528 he published a paraphrase in French entitled *La théorique des cielz, mouvemens et termes practicques des sept planètes.* Finé's version of Peurbach became the standard version in French and reappeared in 1557, 1607, and 1619. A somewhat larger project was an edition of Gregor Reisch's *Margarita philosophica*, a sizable compendium of learning in the encyclopedia tradition. Although Reisch's text is organized according to the medieval schema of the seven liberal arts, it nonetheless provided a survey of knowledge at the turn of the sixteenth century. It was first printed at Fribourg-en-Brisgau in 1503, and rapidly went into successive printings. Finé's edition—the best available—first appeared in 1523 when Finé was still associated with the college of Navarre. It was reprinted in 1535, reprinted once again as late as 1583, and went into an Italian translation in 1599. Finé made notable contributions to the world of science through these editions.

During his twenties Finé edited the works of others, but at the age of thirty he began a large corpus of original writings. In 1526 he published the *Aequatorium planetarum* and in 1527 the *Quadrans astrolabicus*, two small manuals that furthered the use of measuring instruments then

---

4. Recorde refers to this thesis in *The Castle of Knowledge*. The *magister* admonishes his *discipulus*, "I thinke it best to tell you of no mo spheres, then are perceptible by sighte, for so manye are we certaine of" (p. 10).

rapidly developing. The first was reprinted in 1538 and the second in 1534. In 1536 he offered an extensive critique of Euclid, *In sex priores libros geometricorum elementorum Euclidis Megarensis demonstrationes*, which retained its authority through a third edition in 1551. In 1543 he published a practical handbook for using the ephemerides, *Les canons & documens très amples, touchant l'usaige & practique des comuns almanachs*. This handy little volume was reprinted in 1551, 1556, and 1557, and about 1558 was rendered into English by Humphrey Baker as *The Rules and Righte Ample Documentes, Touchinge the Use and Practise of the Common Almanackes* (STC 21449). In 1544, in a large folio entitled *Quadratura circuli, tandem inventa & clarissimè demonstrata*, Finé published his deliberations on the perennially fascinating problem of squaring the circle; and although Finé's solution was later refuted by Pedro Nuñez[5] and by Jean Buteo (i.e., Borrel),[6] his treatment of the problem set a new standard of preciseness in the venerable tradition that has accrued to this topic. Near the end of his career Finé demonstrated his continuing commitment to astrology with an advanced manual of definitions, theory, method, and tables entitled *De duodecim caeli domiciliis, & horis inaequalibus, libellus* (Paris, 1553). Finally, in 1556, the year after Finé's death, his son Jean published posthumously a compendium of applied geometry, *De re & praxi geometria, libri tres*, which was translated into French by Pierre Forcadel in 1570, and which was reprinted in both Latin and French as late as 1586. In addition to the treatises mentioned here, there are numerous others, some in early printed editions and many still in manuscript.

Furthermore, Finé enjoyed considerable repute as a mapmaker. His *Nova totius Galliae descriptio* appeared in 1525, his double cordiform *Nova, et integra universi orbis descriptio* in 1531, and a single cordiform map of the world in 1536.[7] As Miss Taylor comments, "He did for France what Gemma did for the Low Countries, and Mercator at a later date for Western Europe at large, he prepared maps and texts synthesizing the vast mass of conflicting material which the discoverers brought home more quickly than the public could digest it."[8] Finé's

---

5. *De erratis Orontii Finaei . . . liber unus* (Coimbra, 1546). See Thorndike, V, 292–293.
6. "Confutatio quadraturae circuli ab Orontio Finaeo factae" in *Opera geometrica* (Lyons, 1554). Buteo had been a pupil of Finé, and likewise used the soubriquet Delphinatus.
7. These are reproduced in facsimile at the end of Gallois, *De Orontio Finaeo*.
8. *Tudor Geography*, p. 86.

maps also graced editions of the late classical Pomponius Mela and the contemporary Henri Glarean. We can understand John Dee's attraction to Finé when Dee was teaching mathematics in Paris in 1550.

By far the most important work of Finé, however, was the *Protomathesis* (Paris, 1532), a massive folio expounding the theory and practice of the mathematical sciences. It was published shortly after Finé assumed his chair as regius professor of mathematics at the Collège de France, and it established without question his credentials for that exalted position. The title page proudly announces his new honor: *liberalium disciplinarum professor regius*. The *Protomathesis* is dedicated to Francis I, and contains the first printing of several of Finé's best-known treatises. It comprises four books of arithmetic, two books of geometry, five books of cosmography, and four books on dialling (i.e., the construction and use of sundials and similar instruments). It followed the tradition for such omnibus textbooks for the sciences established by the mathematical compendia of Jacques Le Fèvre d'Etaples,[9] Giorgio Valla,[10] and Pedro Sanchez Cirvelo.[11] It was a worthy successor of these early monuments of humanistic science, and in fact rendered them obsolete. It was a triumph in the newly rediscovered discipline of mathematics.

Although the *Protomathesis* was never reissued in its entirety,[12] its various parts were reprinted in separate volumes so that it was continuously available for several decades. The four books of arithmetic appeared separately and slightly revised as *Arithmetica practica, libris quatuor absoluta* in 1535, in 1542, in 1544, and in 1555. The second of the two books of geometry appeared separately as *Liber de geometria practica* in 1544 at Strasbourg. The four books on dialling appeared posthumously in a separate volume entitled *De solaribus horologiis, et quadrantibus, libri quatuor* in 1560.

9. *In hoc opere contenta. Arithmetica [Jordani Nemorarii] decem libris demonstrata. Musica libris demonstrata quattuor. Epitome in libros arithmeticos divi Severini Boetii. Rithmimachiae ludus* (Paris, 1496); and *In hoc libro contenta. Epitome compendiosaque introductio in libros Arithmeticos divi Severini Boetii. . . . Introductio in geometriam [Caroli Bovilli]. . . . Insuper astronomicon* (Paris, 1503).

10. *De expetendis, et fugiendis rebus opus* (2 vols.; Venice, 1501), which among much else contains three books of arithmetic, five books of music, six books of geometry, and four books of astrology (including astronomy).

11. *Cursus quattuor mathematicarum artium liberalium* (Alcalá, 1516), which covers the quadrivial sciences.

12. At a surprisingly late date Cosimo Bartoli translated it into Italian and published it as *Opere di Orontio Fineo* in Venice, 1587. This translation was republished (surely as a curiosity?) in Venice as late as 1670.

The most popular portion of the *Protomathesis*, however, was the five books of cosmography. It was recognized as an authority in the field rivaled only by Peter Apian's *Cosmographicus liber* (Landshut, 1524, and several later editions). With the title *De mundi sphaera, sive cosmographia, libri V*, it was reprinted in a folio format in 1542, and again in abbreviated form as an octavo in 1542. A version revised by Finé was printed in quarto in 1551 with a preface addressed to Edward VI, King of England. This text was reprinted in 1555. Moreover, a French translation by Finé himself with the title *La sphère du monde* was printed in 1551 and again in 1552. It was probably the best-known textbook of cosmography in England at the beginning of Elizabeth's reign.

Recorde, as we have noted, rates "Orontius cosmographye" as a text of fundamental importance, ranking it with such revered standbys as Proclus and Sacrobosco. Throughout *The Castle of Knowledge* he refers to it repeatedly,[13] always with great deference. At the beginning of the fourth part, for example, the Scholar complains that there are too many tracts on the sphere to read them all, but "the beste wryters of them for my studye, were Proclus, Ioannes de Sacrobosco, and Orontius the Frencheman" (p. 98). The organization of Recorde's material, in fact, follows the arrangement of material in Finé's cosmography, starting with Finé's definition of the universe: "Orontius defineth the worlde to be the perfect and entiere composition of all thinges: a divine worke, infinite and wonderfull, adorned with all kindes and formes of bodies, that nature coulde make" (p. 3). Aristotle and Cleomedes and the Sibyl are then quoted, but only in confirmation of the French authority. It may not be too much to say that Recorde saw himself as the English Orontius, and that he wrote his textbooks and patterned his career in the image of Finé.

A younger Englishman soon followed Recorde and provided another superlative textbook of astronomy and geography. In 1559 William Cuningham, then a twenty-eight-year-old physician of Norwich, published a very handsome folio entitled *The Cosmographical Glasse*. Cuningham's treatise is also in the form of a dialogue—between Spoudaeus, the "serious" man who plays the role of student, and Philonicus, the "lover of victory" who plays the role of teacher. Like

13. E.g., pp. 2–3, 98, 100, 188, 252.

Recorde, Cuningham relies heavily upon classical and medieval authorities, but he, too, is knowledgeable in the writings of his contemporaries.[14] And quite early he recommends Finé as an authority in the mathematical disciplines. Cuningham begins with the usual praise of cosmography, the "moste excellent of all other naturall science" (p. 4), and easily moves to the assertion that arithmetic and geometry are a necessary basis for this art. When Spoudaeus rather smugly announces that he has already studied Recorde's textbooks in these disciplines, Philonicus urges him to read further and suggests several authors: "Orontius Arithmeticke, Scheubelius Algeber, Euclides Elementaries, and Theodosius of spherike Demonstrations" (p. 5). From here Cuningham launches a definition of cosmography, and soon he is well into his subject. Cuningham again cites Finé when he lists those who have defined the terms "sphere" (p. 14), when he gives his own "table of declination of th'Ecliptike" (p. 31),[15] and when he proves the sphericity of the earth (p. 49). And there is tacit dependence upon Finé for several diagrams—e.g., the drawing on page 10 of *The Cosmographical Glasse* that shows the dichotomy between "the heavenly Region" and the "Elementarye" region is obviously copied from the *Protomathesis* (sig. O2ᵛ), and the drawing on page 42 that shows the concentric arrangement of the four elements is clearly from the same source (sig. O3ʳ).

Another strong link between Cuningham and Finé appears on the title page of *The Cosmographical Glasse*. The printer, John Day, cut a special full-page woodblock as a title page for this important book, and just above the space where the title is set in type he prominently displayed the aphorism, *Virescit vulnere veritas*. These words are a modification of the motto that Finé had adopted as a personal credo. At the end of his *Protomathesis*, Finé published a *totius operis conclusio* addressed to the reader and culminating in the dictum, *Virescit vulnere virtus* ("Virtue grows stronger from being wounded," sig. Dd6ᵛ). The printers, Gerard Morrhé and Jean Pierre, repeated the motto on the facing page at the bottom of the register, as well as on each half-title page throughout the volume, and later printers of Finé's works, such as Simon de Colines and Michèle Vascosan, regularly flaunted the same

---

14. For example, he refers to Johann Scheubel (pp. 5, 17), Palingenius (p. 26), Regiomontanus (pp. 28, 85), Georg Peurbach (p. 28), Erasmus Reinholdt (pp. 30, 49, 68), Henri Glarean (pp. 55, 59, 83), Cyprianus von Leowitz (p. 104), Peter Apian (p. 106), and Gemma Frisius (p. [163]). He also refers to Recorde (pp. 4, 30, 51).

15. Cf. *Protomathesis*, sig. P3ᵛ.

motto.[16] The point of this *impresa* perhaps goes back to the troublous year 1517, when many academicians opposed an edict of Francis I that affected the universities. The King acted quickly to suppress the seditious movement and imprisoned many of the most refractory, including Finé. It is uncertain exactly how long a time Finé spent in prison, but he did not regain his unmitigated freedom until 1524. His motto may well refer to these years of persecution. In any case, it was recognized as a slogan for academic freedom, and *Virescit vulnere virtus* appears also on the title page of the *Protomathesis* in a position corresponding to that of *Virescit vulnere veritas* on the title page of *The Cosmographical Glasse*.

On several other occasions, John Day used the handsome title page that he had cut for Cuningham's book, most notably perhaps for the translation of Euclid by Henry Billingsley that he printed in 1570. This printing of *The Elements of Geometrie* represents a high point in mathematical textbook preparation in England. It is a thick folio painstakingly printed in a variety of types, splendidly decorated with historiated initials and incidental ornaments, and profusely illustrated on almost every page with geometrical diagrams. It is introduced with a learned preface by John Dee, then at the height of his remarkable career, and augmented by the so-called sixteenth book on the five regular solids written by Flussas (i.e., François de Foix, comte de Candale). Billingsley made every effort to provide a definitive edition of this basic text in geometry. Wherever appropriate, he offered multiple demonstrations of the theorems, calling upon a wide range of classical, medieval, and contemporary authorities. Although Finé is not cited nearly so often as several others, he is referred to in at least one marginal gloss. In addition to Euclid's demonstration of how to construct a hexagon inside a circle, Billingsley gives "an other way to do the same after Orontius" (fol. 123ʳ), followed by yet "an other way . . . after Pelitarius" (i.e., Jacques Peletier).

At this time astrology was a mathematical science as legitimate as geometry or arithmetic or astronomy, and Finé's writings on the subject were accorded appropriate respect. As we have seen, Humphrey Baker translated Finé's *Canons & documens* into English about 1558, and this was the first published work of the man whose arithmetic, *The Well-*

---

16. Every work of Finé that I have examined displays this motto in a prominent place—on the title page, after the prefatory matter, or at the end.

spryng of Sciences (London, 1568), became the only serious competitor of Recorde's *Grounde of Artes*. It is impossible to trace the influence of Finé on the writers of almanacks and ephemerides in English, but one notable example has come to my attention, and we may assume that it is not unique. In 1555 Thomas Gemini, who catered to mathematical practitioners, printed *A Prognostication of Right Good Effect* compiled by Leonard Digges.[17] This was a perennial almanack—that is, it was not confined to one year and it made no specific predictions. Instead, it gave general rules for forecasting the weather and certain natural catastrophes such as droughts and the plague. One extended section is given over to judging the weather according to the aspects of the planets (sigs. B3ᵛ–C1ᵛ), and this section is no more than a translation from Finé's *Canons & documens*.[18] Although Digges makes no acknowledgment of his debt to Finé, many of his readers may have recognized the source of his highly technical information.

At the time of assuming his regius professorship in 1530/31, Finé published a verse epistle in the vernacular extolling the worthiness of mathematics. This slight publication, addressed to Francis I and bearing the lengthy title, *Epistre exhortative, touchant la perfection et commodité des ars liberaulx mathématiques* (Paris, 1532), was reprinted at the end of *La sphère du monde* (Paris, 1551 and 1552), Finé's translation of his own *De mundi sphaera, sive cosmographia, libri V*. It carried great weight in making mathematics a respectable discipline, the "ground of arts" that Recorde took it to be:

> Il est donc cler les mathematiques
> Tres nobles sont perfettes, authentiques,
> Et le miroer de toute certitude.[19]

Coupled with the dedicatory epistle of this volume addressed to Henri II, King of France,[20] this *Epistre* conditioned the reverence for the mathematical sciences that Recorde exhibits in his preface to *The Castle of Knowledge*, and perhaps also the professional attitudes that John Dee expresses in the well-known "Mathematicall praeface," which he prefixed to Henry Billingsley's translation of Euclid.

17. There had been an earlier edition of 1553, as Digges indicates in the dedicatory epistle to Sir Edward Fines, but no copy has survived.

18. Cf. Finé, *Rules and Righte Ample Documentes, Touchinge the Use and Practise of the Common Almanackes*, trans. Baker, sigs. E4ᵛ–E8ᵛ.

19. *La sphère du monde* (Paris, 1551), sig. P2ᵛ.

20. *Ibid.*, sigs. aa2ʳ–aa3ᵛ.

Despite the high repute of Finé in Paris—and in London—during the middle decades of the sixteenth century, his influence quickly waned. New hypotheses and new discoveries, which came with increasing frequency, soon rendered his textbooks obsolete. By the end of the century, Finé was largely forgotten. His writings were out of print (except in Italian translation), and his circle of acquaintances—which had reached into Spain, Germany, the Low Countries, and England— had long ago been shattered. When Thomas Hylles published *The Arte of Vulgar Arithmeticke* (London, 1600), he provided a list of "Arithmeticians, Mathematians, and Philosophers . . . [who] have contributed to this present worke" (sig. C4^v). Although Hylles cites thirty-six authorities, Finé is not among them. And when Thomas Blundeville published his astronomical treatise, *The Theoriques of the Seven Planets* (London, 1602), he cites the authors whom he has consulted: "I have collected . . . [the theoriques of the planets] partly out of *Ptolomey,* and partly out of *Purbachius,* and of his Commentator *Reinholdus,* also out of *Copernicus,* but most out of *Mestelyn* [i.e., Michael Maestlin], whom I have cheefely followed" (sig. A3^r). Finé, the regius professor who represented the best of humanistic science at midcentury, has been left on the shelf to gather dust.

There is one aspect of Finé's career that we have not mentioned. It appears last in order to complete his image as the well-rounded Renaissance man. In addition to his achievements in the sciences, Finé was recognized as an artist of considerable competence. Although we have no drawings other than those that went into book production, these show his interest in perspective and in design. He was a draughtsman of no mean skill.

Finé prepared the diagrams and ornaments for many of his own textbooks, and he applied his talents in the illustration of several books by friends. As early as 1526 he drew the elaborate title page border of Jean Fernel's *Monalosphaerium, partibus constans quatuor* printed by Simon de Colines. This is a treatise on the sphere that features an improved astrolabe. He also prepared the woodcuts and ornaments for Charles de Bouelles' *Livre singulier & utile, touchant l'art et practique de géometrie* (Paris, 1542), printed as well by Simon de Colines. This is a useful manual of geometry in the vernacular, and Finé's drawings are notable for their simple elegance. Bouelles' gratitude to Finé is expressed

VIRESCIT VVLNERE VIRTVS

ORONTII
FINEI DEL-
PHINATIS, LIBE-
RALIVM DISCIPLI-
NARVM PROFESSO-
RIS REGII,
PROTOMATHESIS:
Opus uarium, ac scitu non minus utile
quàm iucundum, nunc primùm in
lucem foeliciter emissum.
Cuius index uniuersa-
lis, in uersa pagina
continetur.

PARISIIS ANNO
1532.

Cum gratia & priuilegio Christianissimi
Francorum Regis, ad Decennium.

Hanc Author proprio pingebat marte figuram.

Plate 1: Oronce Finé, *Protomathesis* (Paris, 1532), title page.

in his dedicatory epistle, and clearly the textbook was considered a joint project between author, illustrator, and printer.

Finé's masterpiece of book illustration, though, is the *Protomathesis*, the volume that he prepared with the greatest care. For this tribute to Francis I in celebration of the honors the King had bestowed upon him, Finé designed a magnificent woodcut title page of heroic proportions (Plate 1). It is an architectural fantasy reminiscent of a triumphal arch, featuring the mythological motif of Hercules slaying the hydra. At the top amid much lavish decoration a pair of dolphins alludes to Dauphiné, the author's birthplace; and his motto, *Virescit vulnere virtus*, provides the capstone for the structure. So proud was Finé of the result that at the bottom he inserted the pointed inscription, "The author drew this design by his own skill." [21]

Finé also prepared the numerous diagrams, illustrations, and ornaments that make this one of the handsomest folios printed in sixteenth-century Paris, and again he claims credit. At the bottom of the table of contents on the verso of the title page, after the list of headings for each book, there appears the notice: "All of which are illuminated with appropriate figures drawn by the author himself." [22] A particularly successful example of Finé's art-work is a decorative headpiece that appears at the top of the first page of the treatise on arithmetic and recurs repeatedly in the volume (Plate 2). At its center is a rudimentary armillary sphere with five rings to mark the climatic zones and an inclined ring to mark the circle of the zodiac. The sphere is flanked by a quadrant and a planisphere, then a pair of half-distended compasses each followed by a square, and finally two tablets, the one on the left displaying geometrical figures and the one on the right an arrangement of whole numbers. These diverse items are held together in a unified design by tasselled ribbons and stylized festoons, and a divine hand stretches forth from each upper corner to lend it support. The initials "O. F.," of course, stand for Orontius Finaeus. The quality of this ornament is indicative of the quality of profuse decoration throughout the book.

Probably the most artistic of the approximately 210 figures in the

21. *Hanc Author proprio pingebat marte figuram.*
22. *Quae quidem omnia decentibus figuris, ab ipsomet Authore depictis, . . . sunt illustra* (sig. AA1ᵛ).

⸙ORONTII FINEI⸰

DELPHINATIS. DE ARITHMETICA
PRACTICA. LIBRI IIII.

⸭⸰

⸰ LIBER PRIMVS, DE INTEGRIS : HOC ⸰
est, eiusdem speciei, siue denominationis numeris.

De fructu, & dignitate ipsius Arithmeticæ : Procemium.

NTER LIBERALES MATHEMATICAS QVAE
solæ disciplinę uocantur, Arithmeticam primum lo-
cum sibi uendicasse: nemo sanæ mentis ignorat. Est *Dignitas Arithme-*
enim Arithmetica omniū aliarū disciplinarū mater, *ticæ.*
& nutrix antiquissima: numerorum qualitates, uim,
& naturam, ac id genus alia demonstrans, quæ abso-
lutum uidentur respicere numerū. Cuius principia
tanta excellunt simplicitate, ut nullius artis uideatur
indigere suffragio. sed cūctis opituletur artibus. Ad
cuius puritatem illud etiam plurimū facit : quoniam
nulla diuinitati adeo conexa est disciplina, quantum Arithmetica. Nam unitas o-
mnium numerorū radix & origo, in se, á se, ac circum seipsam unica uel impartibi-
lis permanet: ex cuius tamen coaceruatione, omnis consurgit & generatur, omnisq̄
tandē in eam resoluitur numerus. Quemadmodū cuncta quæ seu discreta, siue cō-
posita inspectentur uniuerso, á 'ummo rerum conditore in definitum digesta, reda-
ctaue sunt, & demum resoluenda numerū. Quot autē utilitates cognita, quótue *Fructus Arithme-*
labyrinthos ignota præbeat Arithmetica : conspicere facilè est. Numerorū etenim *ticæ.*
ratione sublata, tollitur & musicarū modulationū intelligentia: geometricorū, cœ-
lestiúmue arcanorū subtilis aufertur ingressio : tollitur & uniuersa philosophia, siue quæ diuina, seu quæ cōtemplatur humana: imperfecta relinquitur legum admi
nistratio, utpote quæ iustitiam quibusuis pro dignitate dispēsans, arithmetico semper uidetur indigere suffragio. Ex humanæ præterea uitæ, quàm sit amplexanda,
cognoscitur usu: nā ad suppputationes, ad rerū sumptus, permutationes, diuisiones,
ad cōuentiones, cæteraq̄ eiuscemodi discutiēda, rationem sola præstat Arithmetica. Merito igitur Plato, primum numeros mandat pueros esse docēdos: sine quibus *Plato.*
nec priuatas, nec publicas res, satis cōmodè administrari posse cōfessus est, omnia in
ipsorum numerorū (ueluti Pythagoras) cum dispositione, tū facta harmonia, mor- *Pythagoras.*
talia uersari demonstrans. Mathematicas itaq̄ disciplinas, cunctis bonarū artium
& literarū studiosis, pro uiribus impertiri, uel saltē aperire desiderantes: operæpre-
tiū duximus, ea in primis ex Arithmeica tradere, quæ ad succedentiū operum, imò
& vniuersalem mathematicarum intelligentiā, non utilia tantumodo, sed adprimè
requisita sunt. Et quoniam ordo, cum singulis, tum mathematicis uidetur admo- *Ordo tractandorū.*
dum cōuenire disciplinis: nostram Arithmeticam in quatuor libros, & librū quē-
libet in sua capita distinguemus. Primo autem libro, expeditam integrorū, hoc est,
.A. eiusdem

Plate 2: *Protomathesis*, sig. A1ʳ.

Tetraſtichon Authoris.
Florida diuinæ quiſquis ſecreta matheſis
Scire cupis, facili mente fruare decet:
Nam licet aſſiduo poſſis ſuperare labore,
Mens generoſa tamen plurima ſola capit.
FINIS.

Plate 3: *Protomathesis*, sig. O1ᵛ.

Protomathesis is Plate 3. It is a full-page drawing of Urania, the Muse of Astronomy, instructing Finé, who holds an astrolabe in his right hand and a textbook in his left. On the ground beside him are a quadrant and an horologium. Over their heads is a fully articulated armillary sphere, with each of its parts carefully labeled. The initials of the artist are barely visible in the rings that support the sphere at each side. This drawing is used twice in the volume—after the prefatory material (sig. AA8ᵛ) and before the treatise of cosmography (sig. O1ᵛ)—though in each instance with a different tetrastichon of the author and inscription around the border.

Perhaps we should leave Finé fixed for all time in this attitude of studious attention to his Muse, surrounded by the accoutrements that complement the advice in the margin: "Drive frail thoughts from your troubled mind, so that you may strive to reach the upper regions by serious study." As the prefaces of Robert Recorde and William Cuningham indicate, they thought they were doing just that.

X. On Interpreting Don Quixote's Character

Richard L. Predmore · *Professor of Romance Languages, Duke University*

It is a curious fact that twentieth-century *Quixote* criticism still offers unbelievably divergent views of Don Quixote's character.[1] One might have thought that the increasing attention which the subject has received from intelligent and learned critics for more than three and a half centuries would have led at last to a fairly general consensus, but such does not seem to be the case. Seen in simplified retrospect, the recorded appraisals of Don Quixote's character have evolved gradually from the almost uniformly unfavorable ones of the seventeenth century to the highly favorable ones of the nineteenth and early twentieth centuries. But twentieth-century criticism is characterized by the coexistence of clearly antithetical attitudes toward the Manchegan Knight: the highly sympathetic and the harshly critical. No doubt a number of circumstances help to account for this disagreement, but surely one of the most important has to do with the way readers view Don Quixote's madness. The purpose of this study is to expound a view of the Knight's madness that might lead to a fairer understanding of his character. But first it will be useful to illustrate the extreme views suggested above.

One extreme is the idealistic vision of Don Quixote. Although its beginning may be found in the eighteenth century, it did not emerge in substantial form until the Age of Romanticism. Thereafter it blossomed. By the second half of the nineteenth century, Turgenev was comparing Don Quixote to Christ;[2] by the first years of the twentieth century the deification was complete. As witnesses to it one may cite José Enrique Rodó's "Christ on Horseback,"[3] Rubén Darío's *Litany of Our Lord Don Quixote*,[4] and Miguel de Unamuno's lifelong cult of "our Lord Don Quixote," whose story should be, Unamuno said, "the

---

1. This is a substantially revised version of the twentieth annual Cervantes Lecture delivered at Fordham University on 3 May 1972. It will ultimately appear in a volume of Cervantes Lectures.
   2. See *Hamlet and Don Quixote*, trans. R. Nichols (Edinburgh, 1930), p. 29.
   3. See "El Cristo a la jineta," in *El mirador de Próspero* (Montevideo, 1965), I, 84–86.
   4. See "Letanía de Nuestro Señor Don Quijote," in any edition of Darío's *Cantos de vida y esperanza*.

national Bible of the patriotic religion of Spain."[5] It would be easy to mention other exaltations of the Knight's character, but no other quite rises to the apotheosis just alluded to.

It was natural, I suppose, that a reaction should set in against such extravagant reverence for Cervantes' mad hero, but some well-known scholars have pushed this reaction to the opposite extreme. Professor Helmut Hatzfeld, who has contributed much to certain aspects of Cervantine studies, may be presented as an outstanding exponent of the anti-idealistic extreme. In 1948 he published an article titled "Don Quixote Ascetic?"[6] wherein he seemed to undertake what Amado Alonso was to call "his systematic denigration of Don Quixote."[7] According to Professor Hatzfeld, Don Quixote was hypocritical, boastful, irascible, egoistic, proud, gluttonous, concupiscent, frivolously curious, complaining, and very cowardly (*cobardísimo*). It is not altogether surprising that Amado Alonso repudiated this characterization, asserting that Don Quixote was an exemplary knight and Christian. On this side of the ledger, too, it would be easy to cite other clear examples; let me present one that introduces ideas of particular interest to the thesis of this essay.

In 1969 the British Hispanist P. E. Russell published an article called "'Don Quixote' as a Funny Book."[8] If Professor Russell's sole purpose were to demonstrate that *Don Quixote* used to be regarded as a funny book and should still be so regarded, I would not have chosen his article as an example of the unsympathetic view of Don Quixote's character; but it is everywhere apparent that he disapproves of those interpretations of the Manchegan Knight that try to make of him "something other than a merely laughable figure" (p. 324). Here are some of the key points presented in Russell's article: Don Quixote is principally a funny book (p. 312); readers should take into account the Knight's madness, which is inseparable from the fun (p. 313); seventeenth-century opinion considered madness funny (pp. 320–321); Cervantes accepted this view (p. 321); such seventeenth-century Spanish writers as Avellaneda, Quevedo, and Gracián accepted Don Quixote as a madman, as did such English writers as Robert Burton, Edmund Gayton, and Samuel Butler

---

5. "Sobre la lectura e interpretación del 'Quijote,'" *Obras completas* (Madrid, 1966), I, 1231.
6. See *Nueva Revista de Filología Hispánica*, 2 (1948), 57–70.
7. *Ibid.*, p. 336.
8. *Modern Language Review*, 64 (1969), 312–326.

(pp. 315–316); most of these men disliked or strongly disapproved of Don Quixote (*ibid.*). Russell briefly entertains the possibility that Cervantes may have thought of him as something more than a merely laughable figure but rejects the possibility, concluding that "Cervantes, right up to the end of Part II, seems to go out of his way to insist on the ridiculous figure Don Quijote cuts" (p. 324).

Russell's account of the seventeenth-century reaction to Don Quixote is probably accurate. Other studies are in substantial agreement with it. Professor Edward M. Wilson, for example, examines in somewhat more detail than Russell how Cervantes' writings were used by Edmund Gayton, Francis Beaumont, and Samuel Butler, who, Wilson believes, all regarded *Don Quixote* as a burlesque novel. An important difference between the views of Russell and those of Wilson is that Wilson does not appear to think that seventeenth-century attitudes toward Don Quixote do full justice to Cervantes' characterization of him. Wilson's attitude comes out in passages like the following:

As we read the novel Cervantes himself shews us that both these statements [about the first crude hints given of the characters of Don Quixote and Sancho] are too simple; but the seventeenth-century reader can hardly be blamed if, like Gayton, he saw in this great novel, only the tale of a madman squired by an idiot. For that is what its author said it was.[9]

A sharp difference between seventeenth-century readers and those of the twentieth century is that the former could look upon insanity as comical whereas the latter cannot. Crucial questions are: Was Cervantes content to create a merely comical figure, and can his presentation of madness be contained within seventeenth-century understandings of it? By way of reproaching Cervantine critics for not paying more attention to Don Quixote's madness, Russell calls attention to the serious interest that certain modern authorities on insanity take in Cervantes' portrayal of it. It is clear, however, that he does not agree with their views. Quotations from some will show why. Here is the first:

Cervantes has deep compassion for this foolish and insane knight who becomes a martyr to his idealism and a symbol of the highest strivings of man. . . . When Cervantes succeeds in making the reader identify with Don Quixote he is

9. "Cervantes and English Literature of the Seventeenth Century," *Bulletin Hispanique*, 50 (1948), 34. Some other studies supporting Russell's view of seventeenth-century reactions to Don Quixote are Maurice Bardon, *"Don Quichotte" en France au XVIIe et au XVIIIe siècle* (Paris, 1931); Edwin B. Knowles, "Cervantes and English Literature," in *Cervantes Across the Centuries*, ed. Angel Flores and M. J. Benardete (New York, 1947), pp. 267–293; Alberto Navarro, *El*

illustrating the principle that the mentality of the psychotic includes the essential qualities of normal thinking.[10]

Another authority, speaking of both Cervantes and Shakespeare, writes: "Doubtless, both testify more to a tragic experience of madness appearing in the fifteenth century, than to a critical and moral experience of Unreason developing in their own epoch."[11] Russell is right to call attention to the widespread critical neglect of Don Quixote's madness, but is he right to assume that it can be fully understood by seventeenth-century notions? Before expounding my own views, let me present very briefly one last study of Don Quixote. This one takes his madness with utmost seriousness.

In his article "El *Ingenioso* Hidalgo" (1957), Professor Otis Green uses the psychological theories of the sixteenth-century writer Huarte de San Juan to explain Don Quixote's madness. He writes the article to show

that well-read contemporaries of Cervantes, even if they did not know Huarte's extremely popular book (1575), would have followed with clear understanding the course of Alonso Quijano's transition from a country gentleman of *choleric temper* to an *imaginative* and *visionary* monomaniac, and would have interpreted this transformation, as Cervantes had conceived it, in the light of their knowledge of Greek-Arabic physiological and psychological theories regarding the balance and imbalance of the bodily humors.[12]

Green's demonstration of the correspondences between Cervantes' portrayal of Don Quixote and Huarte's humoural theories is convincing enough to persuade the reader that Cervantes knew and used those theories but not to persuade him that they are adequate to account for the complexity of Cervantes' depiction of madness. A few examples will suggest why they are not.

In a discussion of the effects of Don Quixote's excessive reading of the books of chivalry, we come across this sentence: "With the increase of cerebral dryness through lack of sleep the *hot-dry* passion of *boldness*

Quijote español del siglo XVII (Madrid, 1964); P. E. Russell, "English Seventeenth-Century Interpretations of Spanish Literature," *Atlante*, 1 (1953), 65–77.

10. Franz G. Alexander and Sheldon T. Selesnick, *The History of Psychiatry* (New York, 1966), p. 101.

11. Michel Foucault, *Madness and Civilization, a History of Insanity in the Age of Reason*, trans. Richard Howard (New York, 1965), p. 31.

12. *Hispanic Review*, 25 (1957), 176. Professor Green has treated these matters in at least two other publications: "Realidad, voluntad y gracia en Cervantes," *Ibérida: Revista de Filología*, 3 (1961), 113–128; and *Spain and the Western Tradition* (Madison, 1966), IV, 60–73.

becomes increasingly powerful: 'ocasiones y peligros donde, acabándolos, cobrase eterno nombre y fama'" (chances and dangers, by the overcoming of which he might win eternal honor and renown).[13] This fragment of a sentence from Chapter One of *Don Quixote* appears to be quoted as proof of the boldness that was beginning to develop in the Knight. Actually the phrase merely expresses one part of the book-inspired ideal of chivalry which Don Quixote's mad fancy took as the pattern for his new life. Don Quixote's new ideal, repeatedly expressed, was threefold: to right wrongs, to serve a great lady, and to seek good fame. For him, to be a knight meant to honor these ideals—which is to say, they governed his conduct. I mention this because there are scholars who use quotations about Don Quixote's quest for good fame to prove something about his character or temperament; that he was vainglorious or that cerebral dryness had produced the hot-dry passion of boldness.

Huarte's theories, as used by Green, leave unexplained such important aspects of Don Quixote's behavior as the artful stratagems contrived by his madness to defend his chivalric illusions. Much of what the Knight does is presented as physiologically determined. Consider, for example, the flow and ebb of choler: "But it is no less true that Don Quixote is *ingenioso* because he is *colérico*, that the flow and ebb of *cólera* determine the alternation of his spates of *disparates* with those 'lucid intervals' in which the Knight recognizes a science for what it is, or discourses on the problems of State" (p. 193). But Don Quixote's behavior often fails to conform to that kind of physiological determinism. A good illustration can be found in his answer to the charges of the "grave Ecclesiastic," in which he shows himself to be simultaneously angry, crazy, and yet very lucid (pp. 674–675). Perhaps the greatest weakness of the humoural theories as explanations of Don Quixote's character is that they tend to convert his physiological type into his destiny: "Don Quijote's adventures could have happened only to a *colérico* . . . " (p. 177); he is "constitutionally pre-psychotic" (p. 185). In short, humoural theories leave madness largely unrelated to the role of the human spirit in man's struggle to survive in a frustrating world.

In a footnote, Green mentions a few examples of how Sancho seems to break out of the type assigned to him. Green's comment is: "Cer-

13. Green, "El *Ingenioso* Hidalgo," p. 177, n. 4.

vantes does what he can to preserve verisimilitude" (p. 178, n. 7). I am
not at all sure what this comment means. What I think it ought to mean
is that sixteenth-century psychological theories are not adequate to explain the full complexity of Cervantes' characters, and such inadequacy
suggests to me that it may be necessary to turn to modern theories to
account fully for the works of genius of past ages. I am aware that some
scholars turn pale at the very thought of using Freud, let us say, to
explain Hamlet. Whether or not efforts to do so have proved successful,
I would argue that there is no *a priori* reason for rejecting the possibility.
Great writers practiced psychology long before it was ever formulated
in any modern sense. To assume that Cervantes could not portray
madness more fully and more subtly than can be justified by the theories
of his day is to deny to a man of genius the fruits of his own observation.
I believe we can enlarge our understanding of Don Quixote's mad
character by approaching it from the point of view of modern psychology, which tends to look upon insanity as an adaptation aimed
at survival.

In December of 1954 and January of 1955, the famous psychoanalyst
Dr. Robert Lindner published in *Harper's Magazine* a two-part article
called "The Jet-Propelled Couch." It purports to be the case history of
Kirk Allen, a young research physicist whose half-mad life seems to me
in several essential ways quite similar to Don Quixote's. The similarities
are not perfect, but they are very suggestive. By presenting them here, I
hope to sketch a contemporary view of Don Quixote's madness without
venturing beyond my depth into the technical description of psychotic
behavior. It will be well to begin with a quick look at the origins of Kirk
Allen's psychosis.

Kirk was the only child of an elderly father, stationed for years on a
small Pacific island, and of a young mother who neglected him. According to Dr. Lindner's findings, the peculiar troubles of his insular childhood drove Kirk to seek refuge and fulfillment in the realm of books.
Among the books he read, he was fascinated particularly by certain
novels of interplanetary adventure. These he read and reread until the
adventures related therein grew as familiar to him as the events of his
own life. Gradually the world in which they took place became to him
so real that he was able to believe he visited it and participated in its life.
In short, he went insane.

We do not know all of the conditions and motives of Don Quixote's surrender to books, but we may surmise that one of the most powerful was the endless boredom of idle village life in the rusting twilight of Spain's heroic age. This much of a clue Cervantes provides: "The reader must know, then, that this gentleman, in the times when he had nothing to do—as was the case for most of the year—gave himself up to the reading of books of knight errantry; which he loved and enjoyed so much that he almost entirely forgot his hunting, and even the care of his estate." [14] The time he devoted to reading was clearly excessive, for "from little sleep and much reading, his brain dried up and he lost his wits" (p. 32). Like Kirk Allen, Don Quixote constructed a world of fantasy with the materials of fiction. Like Kirk Allen, he recreated himself in the image of his fictional heroes. Perhaps we should note this dissimilarity: Don Quixote tried to find his new abode in the world of his contemporaries; Kirk Allen lived his new life on distant planets.

Three times Kirk Allen came across his own name in his reading. The third time it was as the name of the hero of the space adventures already mentioned. Dr. Lindner believes that this fortuitous correspondence of names was all that was needed "to create the bridge across which Kirk traveled from painful reality to all-satisfying fantasy." [15] The country gentleman of Cervantes' tale did not find his own name in the romances of chivalry, but he did believe himself descended from the fifteenth-century knight Gutierre Quijada, and in the romances of chivalry he did discover an "ancient custom of knights errant, who changed their names when they pleased or as the occasion required" (p. 577). Feeling need for a name in keeping with the kind of man he aspired to be and authorized by the ancient custom of knighthood, the gentleman set himself to invent one. Eight days he spent on this all-important business, and the name he coined is the one by which he is universally known: Don Quixote. But this is not all. From the inception of his madness till the day of his death, he was ever prone to create or accept titles in harmony with his newly eventful life: the Knight of the Sad Countenance, the Knight of the Lions, the Shepherd Quixotiz, Alonso Quijano the Good. Perhaps it is fair to say that Cervantes confirms Dr. Lindner's understanding of the role names may play in man's struggle to be reconciled to his life.

14. *The Adventures of Don Quixote*, trans. J. M. Cohen (Baltimore, 1950), p. 31. All quotations from *Don Quixote* are from this translation.
15. "The Jet-Propelled Couch," *Harper's Magazine* (Jan. 1955), p. 78.

Kirk Allen lived two lives and by two kinds of time. When he chose to spend sufficient time on this planet, he was regarded by his associates as a competent scientist and a reasonably normal person. Only when he spent too much of his time on the planets of his fantasy did his sanity become suspect. As a normal member of society he was governed by the clock that governs us all; as the fabulous hero of an interplanetary empire he could live a year in a period we would measure in minutes.

The texture of Don Quixote's life was woven with the same two strands of madness and sanity. All who knew him well thought him "mad in patches, full of lucid streaks" (p. 583). Cervantes expressed the universal judgment thus:

Could anyone hear this last discourse of Don Quixote's and not take him for a person of singular intelligence and excellent intentions? For as has often been said in the course of this great history, he went astray only in the matter of chivalry, but in the rest of his talk showed a clear and unbiased understanding, so that his acts discredited his judgment and his judgment his acts at every step. (p. 740)

Don Quixote differed from Kirk Allen in that he lived his fantasy in the inadequate environment of the everyday world. Obviously this made it difficult for him to escape the tyranny of the clock that ruled his contemporaries. Only in dreams was this sometimes possible for him. Example: in Chapter 22 of Part Two we read that he had himself lowered into the depths of the Cave of Montesinos. While there he met some famous knights of old and even saw his lady Dulcinea. On emerging from the cave, he told his companions about his experiences below. On the basis of the scant hour they knew he had spent below, they questioned his report. His answer: "That cannot be right, for night fell there and morning rose, and three more nights and mornings; so that, by my reckoning, I must have stayed three days in those remote and secret regions" (p. 620).

As he studied his patient, Dr. Lindner realized that Kirk's madness was precisely what sustained his life. He also realized that Kirk was dimly aware of this truth and would therefore defend his fantasy with all his strength. Like Dr. Lindner, Cervantes knew that madness could be a condition of survival. Like Kirk Allen, Don Quixote sensed the mortal danger that lurked beyond the confines of his private world. This is shown by the stratagems he employed to defend his illusion.

Before Don Quixote set out upon the roads of Spain to restore the age of chivalry, he had certain preparations to make. One was to invent fitting names for himself, his horse, and his lady fair. Another was to polish and repair his rusty ancestral armor. Inspection having revealed that his helmet lacked a visor,

he ingeniously made good this deficiency by fashioning out of pieces of pasteboard a kind of half-visor which, fitted to the helmet, gave the appearance of a complete head-piece. However, to see if it was strong enough to stand up to the risk of a sword-cut, he took out his sword and gave it two strokes, the first of which demolished in a moment what had taken him a week to make. He was not too pleased at the ease with which he had destroyed it, and to safeguard himself against this danger, reconstructed the visor, putting some strips of iron inside. . . . (p. 33)

Unwilling to let a defective helmet stand between him and his purpose, he decided not to test it again. This is only one of a number of examples of how he bolstered his illusion with nothing but the force of his will.

Don Quixote often found the everyday world quite hostile to his fantasy. Fortunately for him, a ready-made defense was available in the fiction that shaped his fantasy. When the Peerless Knight of fiction suffered a temporary setback, it was often because evil enchanters had taken cards in the game. Don Quixote knew this, and the knowledge served him on many occasions. When the outcome of his adventures was other than expected or desired, his customary explanation was enchantment. Wizards and evil enchanters changed giants into windmills and armies into sheep in order to defraud him of his laurels justly won. And even when he triumphed, they were ready to turn bitter the cup of victory by reducing the stature of his foes. How much Don Quixote needed these wicked enchanters is revealed in words he spoke as he was being hauled home in a cage on an oxcart toward the end of Part One: "I most certainly know that I am enchanted, and that is sufficient to ease my conscience, which would be greatly burdened if I thought that I was not under a spell, and yet remained in this cage like an idler and a coward, defrauding the many distressed and needy of the succour I could give them" (p. 434). Enchanters, for all their malice, helped Don Quixote to see himself as an authentic knight. But as his story progressed, they began to baffle him. At the end of the unsuccessful adventure of the enchanted boat, he could only exclaim: "Two powerful enchanters must have met in opposition in this adventure, the one frustrating the other's designs. One provided me with the boat, and the other threw me out. God help us, but this whole world is tricks and devices, one against the other. I can do no more" (p. 661). Finally, by transforming Dulcinea into an ugly peasant wench, as he believed, enchanters threatened to extinguish the light of his life. When asked who wrought Dulcinea's sad transformation, Don Quixote replied:

> That accursed race, born into the world to obscure and obliterate the exploits of the good, and to light up and exalt the deeds of the wicked. Persecuted I have been by enchanters. Enchanters persecute me, and enchanters will persecute me till they sink me and my high chivalries into the profound abyss of oblivion. They damage and wound me where they see I feel it most. For to rob a knight errant of his lady is to rob him of the eyes with which he sees, of the sun by which he is lighted, and of the prop by which he is sustained. (p. 680)

Don Quixote spoke these melancholy words toward the middle of the second half of his story. From that point on he was less inclined to turn to enchantment to wipe away the bitterness of defeat or the clouds of bewilderment. And he was sometimes forced to defend his fantasy with less knightly expedients. At the conclusion of the adventure of Clavileño, after Sancho had described his vision in the sky, "Don Quixote went up to Sancho and whispered in his ear: 'Sancho, if you want me to believe what you saw in the sky, I wish you to accept my account of what I saw in the Cave of Montesinos. I say no more'" (p. 735). These are only a few of the stratagems employed by our knight to defend the crumbling walls of his illusion. If he defended them grimly, it was because he sensed what was at stake.

For many years Kirk Allen's madness was a private one nourished in and by the isolation he had known since early childhood. Only after he had gone to work at X Reservation did he become aware that he might be regarded as insane, but so convinced was he of his own sanity that this awareness caused him no concern. When he came under the constant observation and care of Dr. Lindner, however, he could not fail to realize that his private world was threatened. For more than a year he succeeded in defending it, and his success might have endured if Dr. Lindner had not been inspired to try on him the technique of participating in his psychosis. With this technique the therapist deliberately engages in the same psychotic behavior as the patient, thus compelling the patient to see himself as others see him. By this technique Kirk was gradually pried loose from his madness and with no apparent ill effects.

As previously remarked, Don Quixote sought fulfillment of his fantasy in the workaday world. His early efforts to conduct himself as a knight in this inadequate setting brought him hard knocks, moments of confusion and care, but no sustained attack on his fantasy. Little by little he became aware that most people did not accept his chivalric vision of the world and that some of them were inclined to try to talk him out of it. This awareness brought him no pleasure, of course, but by itself and for a time it did not weaken his faith in his vocation. The strength of this faith at the time of his third and last sally from home is manifest in these words addressed to his niece and housekeeper:

For myself I have more arms than learning, and my inclination is to Arms, for I was born under the influence of the planet Mars. So I am almost compelled to follow that road, and must pursue it despite the whole world; and it will be vain for you to weary yourselves in persuading me to go counter to the heavens' wishes, Fortune's decrees, reason's demands and, more than that, against my heart's desires. (p. 506)

These words appear early in Part Two. As we shall see, they represent a confidence soon to wane.

Part Two of Don Quixote's story differs from Part One in many ways. In Part One Don Quixote wandered over the region of La Mancha living his adventures as he found them. In Part Two he often fell into adventures that other people had created either to restore his sanity or to alleviate their boredom. Since these adventures were artfully contrived in the chivalric manner, he was initially inclined to take them as new support for his fantasy. Their long-range effect was to destroy his fantasy, contribute to the recovery of his sanity, and hasten the hour of his death.[16] They played in his life a role analogous to Dr. Lindner's intrusion into the illusory world of Kirk Allen.

Early in Part Two Don Quixote encountered the Knight of the Mirrors, who challenged him to single combat. The motive of the challenge was the relative beauty of the knights' ladies; the conditions of the battle were that the vanquished should be at the disposal of the victor and confess that the victor's lady was fairer than his own. The Knight of the Mirrors was no knight at all but Sampson Carrasco, a student from Don Quixote's village who thought to restore his neighbor

---

16. Using Don Quixote as an example, Michel Foucault makes the point that dissipated madness may lead to death: "Madness dissipated can be only the same thing as the imminence of the end; 'and even one of the signs by which they realized that the sick man was dying, was that he had returned so easily from madness to reason'" (op. cit., p. 32).

to sanity by defeating him in battle and requiring him on his honor to return home for the space of a year. Against all probability, Don Quixote won the battle. Understandably, this gave his morale a lift. Nevertheless, his victory did not fall entirely clear of the growing tangle of uncertainty. When our knight had unlaced the helmet of his fallen foe, whose face did he discover but that of his fellow villager Sampson Carrasco! Don Quixote attributed this transformation to envious enchanters; but this explanation did not fully satisfy Sancho Panza, and the doubts he voiced may have lingered in his master's mind. As for Carrasco, we know by the words he addressed to his squire that he will seek a return engagement with his neighbor: "it would be folly to suppose that I shall go back home till I have thrashed Don Quixote. And it will not be the desire to restore him to his senses that will drive me after him, but the desire for revenge; for the pain in my ribs will not allow me to entertain a more charitable purpose" (p. 561). At this point the reader may wonder, like the squire, "which is the madder, the man who's mad because he can't help it, or the man who's mad by choice?" (*ibid*).

Toward the middle of Part Two we read that one afternoon Don Quixote and Sancho met a real duke and duchess and were welcomed to their castle. Having read Part One of Don Quixote's story, the duke and the duchess were prepared to receive him as the famous knight he believed himself to be. But, despite their ceremonial manner and gracious words, they showed themselves more eager to entertain their idle hours than disposed to show him genuine respect. For their amusement he was subjected to indignities and solicited with counterfeit adventures. Twenty-six chapters are needed to recount all that went on in and around the ducal palace. For our purpose it will suffice to say that Don Quixote endured the indignities with dignity, accepted the adventures in good faith, and at last took his leave of the duke and duchess with immense relief. The relief he experienced on finding himself again in open country is revealed in the heartfelt words he addressed to his squire:

Liberty, Sancho, is one of the most precious gifts Heaven has bestowed upon man. No treasures the earth contains or the sea conceals can be compared to it. . . . I say this, Sancho, because you have witnessed the luxury and abundance that we have enjoyed in this castle which we are now leaving. Yet in the midst of those highly-spiced banquets and snow-cooled drinks I seemed to be confined within the straits of hunger, since I did not enjoy them with the same liberty as if they had been my own; for obligations to return benefits and favours received are bonds that curb a free spirit. (p. 837)

Don Quixote's escape from the uncomfortable feignings of sane but frivolous people was short-lived. In Barcelona he was entertained by another rich person equally inclined to have fun at his expense. And then on the beach of Barcelona he met and fought the Knight of the White Moon. The motive and conditions of their battle were the same as those of his combat with the Knight of the Mirrors. The outcome was different. Don Quixote came to earth with a grievous fall and opened his eyes to see his conqueror's lance at his visor. Unwilling to acknowledge that his conqueror's lady was more beautiful than his own, he proclaimed as though from within a tomb: "Dulcinea del Toboso is the most beautiful woman in the world, and I am the most unfortunate knight on earth; nor is it just that my weakness should discredit that truth. Drive your lance home, knight, and rid me of life, since you have robbed me of honour" (p. 890). This time our knight did not call his defeat the work of hostile enchanters. Accepting full responsibility for his defeat, he could yet make one last knightly gesture: to offer his life for his love. Sampson Carrasco, alias the Knight of the White Moon, spared his life but in fulfillment of the conditions of their duel exacted a promise that for a period of a year or more he would stay at home and give up the practice of chivalry. Don Quixote's code allowed him no escape from this exaction, and so his occupation was gone.

Too battered and sick to undertake the homeward journey, "Don Quixote stayed six days in bed, melancholy, sorrowful, brooding and in a bad way, turning over and over in his mind the misfortune of his defeat" (pp. 892–893). When Don Quixote was able to travel, he and Sancho left Barcelona. As they passed the place of his defeat, he said: "Here stood Troy. Here my ill-luck, and not my cowardice, despoiled me of the glory I had won. Here fortune practised her shifts and changes upon me. Here my exploits were eclipsed. Here, in short, my happiness fell, never to rise again" (p. 896). From this point to the day of his death, Don Quixote was unable to get a firm grip on his life. As he himself said, "I am not fit to give crumbs to the cat, my wits are so shaken and shattered" (p. 898). And always he was troubled in mind, and "his thoughts, like flies round honey, set upon him and stung him" (p. 900).

On the way home Don Quixote had yet to be trampled at night by a herd of swine and carried off to the palace of the duke and duchess for one more bogus adventure. But at last, travel-weary, despairing of the disenchantment of Dulcinea, and bound by his honor to the life that had driven him mad, he reached home. His death was at hand. "Whether that event was brought on by melancholy occasioned by the contemplation of his defeat or whether it was by divine ordination, a fever seized him and kept him to his bed for six days . . . " (p. 934). Both his doctor and his other friends believed "that melancholy and despondency were bringing him to his end" (p. 935). Toward the end of this last illness, he woke from a long sleep blessing God for His boundless mercies. Asked by his niece what mercies he meant, he replied: "The mercies, niece, are those which God has shown me at this moment, mercies to which, as I have said, my sins are no impediment. My judgment is now clear and free from the misty shadows of ignorance with which my ill-starred and continuous reading of those detestable books of chivalry had obscured it" (p. 935). Aware that he was dying, he asked to confess and make his will. Tearful Sancho urged him to get well and begin a new life as a shepherd. "Let us go gently, gentlemen," said Don Quixote, "for there are no birds this year in last year's nests. I was mad, but I am sane now. I was Don Quixote de la Mancha, but to-day, as I have said, I am Alonso Quixano the Good. May my sincere repentance restore your former esteem for me" (p. 938). At last, in a calm and Christian manner and amid the compassionate tears of his friends, he died.

Throughout his treatment of Kirk Allen, Dr. Lindner was ever conscious of the possibility that to cure his patient might be to kill him. He was particularly chary of employing any of the more drastic methods of psychiatric therapy such as shock treatment. With infinite patience and the gentle method we have recalled, he returned his charge safely to sanity. As we look back over Don Quixote's slow and painful return to sanity, we may believe that his cure was essentially similar to Kirk's. But there are at least these differences: Kirk was a younger man, Don Quixote about fifty; Kirk's psychosis was invaded by a cautious doctor, Don Quixote's by persons ignorant of the harm they might do; Kirk suffered no physical punishment nor violent shock, Don Quixote was overwhelmed by both. Perhaps we may say that the similarity accounts for Don Quixote's return to sanity, the differences for his death.

Early in this essay I asked whether Cervantes had been content to create in Don Quixote a merely comical figure. After demonstrating that he was such a figure to seventeenth-century readers, Professor Russell poses the same question. He examines the possibility that Cervantes may have had more in mind, but notice the self-retracting effect of his words: "It is true that there are a few, very few, passages which, taken in isolation, might seem to suggest that Cervantes conceived, at least momentarily, that it might be possible for his readers, or some of them, to see the knight as something other than a merely laughable figure." [17] I think it can be shown that there are many passages that reveal something more than a burlesque intention. I have used some, but by no means all, of those passages in the comparisons I have drawn between Kirk Allen's psychosis and that of Don Quixote. I do not claim that my comparisons establish perfect correspondence between the two; I do claim that by the light of these comparisons Don Quixote's madness strikes us not simply as a device for provoking laughter but also as a coherent and meaningful expression of human experience, which is one reason why it has the power to move those modern readers who accord it the attention it deserves.

17. "'Don Quixote' as a Funny Book," p. 324.

XI. The Religious Conversion of Profane Poetry

Bruce W. Wardropper · *Professor of Romance Languages, Duke University*

" . . . but one puritan amongst them, and
he sings psalms to hornpipes."
(*The Winter's Tale*, IV.iii)

" . . . but they do no more adhere and keep
place together than the Hundredth Psalm to
the tune of Green Sleeves."
(*The Merry Wives of Windsor*, II.i)

George Herbert wrote only religious poetry. But his ear was attuned to secular love poetry. In Herbert's line "Busie enquiring heart, what wouldst thou know?" T. S. Eliot detects an echo of John Donne's famous *alba* "Busie old foole, unruly Sunne." [1] More conclusive is the evidence provided by the poem called "A Parodie," which is not a travesty but a religious conversion of a love poem variously attributed to Donne and to William Herbert, Earl of Pembroke. [2] The opening lines of the original and the imitation will serve to illustrate the phenomenon of reverse parody, the purloining of another's verse in the hope not of burlesquing it but of enhancing it in a spiritual sense.

[Original Version]	[Conversion]
Soules joy, now I am gone,	Souls joy, when thou art gone,
And you alone,	And I alone,
(Which cannot be,	Which cannot be,
Since I must leave my selfe with thee,	Because thou dost abide with me,
And carry thee with me)	And I depend on thee;
Yet when unto our eyes	Yet when thou dost suppresse
Absence denyes	The cheerfulnesse
Each others sight,	Of thy abode,
And makes to us a constant night,	And in my powers not stirre abroad,
When others change to light. . . .	But leave me to my load. . . .

1. *George Herbert* (London, 1962), p. 30.
2. For a summary of the authorship debate, see *The Works of George Herbert*, ed. F. E. Hutchinson (Oxford, 1941), p. 541. Both texts are cited from this edition, pp. 183, 541.

As Eliot has detected and Louis Martz observes, "Sacred parody of love-poetry plays an essential part in much of Herbert's best work";[3] but such explicit rewriting is unusual in his corpus. Even in this example Herbert abandons line-by-line imitation after the third line, thereafter following only the rhythmic pattern of his model. His purpose in thus adapting profane poetry, as Rosemond Tuve has shown, is far more than to make a "protest against love poems."[4] It is to glorify even more the glorious lyric poetry of his age by turning it into devout song in praise of God. Such adaptations are better not called parodies, for the object of parody is to demean.[5] I shall use instead the term *contrafacta*, which in recent years has been applied to continental manifestations of the phenomenon.[6]

Although in *The Poetry of Meditation* Martz incidentally discusses the phenomenon with his customary insight, scholars concerned with English literature have largely overlooked it. This neglect is perhaps not surprising among seventeenth-century scholars: there are rather few examples as clear as Herbert's. But in earlier periods it was somewhat less uncommon.

The first record of an Englishman's anticipating Martin Luther, the Wesleys, and General Booth in stealing "the devil's tunes"[7] takes us back to the time of Alfred the Great. William of Malmesbury tells us that Saint Aldhelm (d. 709) used to trap non-churchgoers by blocking

---

3. *The Poetry of Meditation: A Study in English Religious Literature of the Seventeenth Century* (New Haven, 1954), p. 186.

4. *A Reading of George Herbert* (Chicago, 1952), p. 185.

5. In their article "Parody" in the *Encyclopedia of Poetry and Poetics*, ed. Alex Preminger *et al.* (Princeton, 1965), Robert P. Falk and William Beare do not consider the possibility of an uplifting kind of parody. Eccentrically, John Crosbie—"Amoral 'a lo divino' Poetry in the Golden Age," *MLR*, 66 (1971), 599–607—maintains that religious "parodies" were written not to propagate devotion but to display ingenuity. If this view is accepted, they are indeed little more than conventional parodies.

6. Kurt Hennig used a Germanic form of the Latin term in his doctoral dissertation, *Die geistliche Kontrafaktur im Jahrhunderte der Reformation* (Halle a. S., 1909). Based on this usage and the Spanish formula *contrahecho a lo divino*, I launched the term *contrafactum* in my *Historia de la poesía lírica a lo divino en la cristiandad occidental* (Madrid, 1958); see esp. pp. 5–6. The term has since come into general use.

7. The adoption of secular tunes for religious ends parallels the appropriation of secular poetry by divinizers. There are several medieval instances. The MS of "Sumer is icumen in," usually dated 1230–40 (but 1340 according to Manfred F. Bukofzer), contains a religious Latin text—"Perspice christicola"—intended to be sung to the same melody. See Bukofzer, *"Sumer is icumen in": A Revision* (Berkeley, 1944). The tune of the drinking song "Bring us in good ale, good ale" was recommended by fifteenth-century Franciscans for the Christmas carol "Nowell, Nowell, Nowell, / This is the Salutation / Of the Angel Gabriel." See J. M. Gibbon, *Melody and the Lyric from Chaucer to the Cavaliers* (London, 1930), p. 17.

the traffic on a bridge while singing popular songs; when a good-sized crowd was assembled, he surreptitiously introduced Scriptural words into the frivolous songs, thus bringing the truants back to their senses.[8] Elsewhere, William notes that Thomas of Bayeux, Archbishop of York (d. 1100), regularly converted every profane song he heard into a hymn of praise.[9] The Old English "The Way of Christ's Love" ("Lytel wot yt ony man") is almost certainly a religious imitation of "The Way of Woman's Love," and not the other way round.[10] But it was the development of the Middle English religious carol that produced an abundance of *contrafacta*. Franciscan friars wrote Latin and (by the middle of the fourteenth century) vernacular religious words to popular, profane carols. "By the xv century . . . these religious adaptations had become so popular with the non-literate laity that their original intention of religious propaganda was lost sight of, and they became as natively popular as the first secular songs which they had been intended to replace."[11]

Among the Protestants of the sixteenth century, metrical versions of the Psalms came into vogue to oust the Romish plainsong. The Huguenots in France provided the impetus. Clément Marot appropriated the tunes of popular airs for his translations of the Psalms, some of which are clearly reflected in Sidney's English versions.[12] Long before Sidney, the young Edward VI's music master, Christopher Tye, had adapted the Acts of the Apostles to the ballad meter of "Chevy Chase."[13] The popular ballad about Henry VIII—

> The hunt is up,
> The hunt is up,
> And it is wellnigh day;
> And Harry, our King,

---

8. "Populum eo tempore semibarbarium, parum divinis sermonibus intentum, statim cantatis missis, domos cursitare solitum. Ideo sanctum virum, super pontem qui rura et urbem continuat, abeuntibus se apposuisse obicem, quasi artem cantitando professim. Eo plusquam semel facto, plebis favorem et concursum emeritum. Hoc commento sensim inter ludicra verbis scripturarum insertis; cives ad sanitatem reduxisse: qui ei severe et cum excommunicatione agendum putasset profecto profecisset nichil" (*Apud* G. B. Chambers, *Folksong—Plainsong: A Study in Origins and Musical Relationships* [London, 1956], p. 114).

9. G. L. Brook, *The Harley Lyrics: The Middle English Lyrics of MS. Harley 2253* (Manchester, 1948), p. 16.

10. *Ibid.* See also pp. 87–88.

11. R. H. Robbins, "The Earliest Carols and the Franciscans," *MLN*, 53 (1938), 239.

12. Gibbon, pp. 71–72.

13. *Ibid.*, p. 38.

> Is gone hunting
> To bring his deer to bay.

—was quickly, and ineptly, transformed into:

> With hunt is up,
> With hunt is up,
> It is now perfect day;
>
> Jesus, our King,
> Is gone hunting—
> Who likes to speed, they may.[14]

H. E. Rollins lists a large number of "moralized" ballads, including such popular favorites as "Greensleeves."[15] In Scotland, John, James, and Robert Wedderburn introduced *contrafacta* into their *Gude and Godlie Ballatis* (1567):

Welcum, Fortoun, welcum againe,	Welcum, Lord, Christ, welcum againe,
The day and hour I may weill blis,	My joy, my comfort, and my bliss,
Thow hes exilit all my paine,	That culd me saif from hellis paine,
Quhilk to my hart greit plesour is.	Bot onlie thow nane was, nor is.[16]

In England whole poetic anthologies, like *The Court of Venus*, were converted to religion—*The Court of Venus* under the title of *The Court of Virtue*.[17]

In spite of this array of apparent precedents to Herbert's "A Parodie," it is still surprising to note how sporadically and seldom *contrafacta* put in an appearance in Renaissance Britain, compared with their abundance on the continent of Europe. It is in fact the recusants, many of whom had perforce traveled abroad, who seem to have cultivated

---

14. Gibbon publishes both secular and sacred versions of the ballad, pp. 31, 39. Jean Jacquot notes that another religious version of this ballad by John Thorne has as its theme "la chasse que le Christ donne à un gibier qui est l'âme qu'il veut sauver" (*Musique et poésie au XVIe siècle*, ed. Jacquot [Paris, 1954], p. 272).

15. "An Analytical Index to the Ballad-Entries in the Registers of the Company of Stationers of London," *SP*, 21 (1924), 1–324. See items numbered 819, 1051, 1175, 1193, 1627, 1693, 1994, 2033, 2035, 2331–35, 2612, 2840, 2921. On the "moralized Greensleeves," see Germaine Bontoux, *La Chanson en Angleterre au temps d'Élisabeth* (Oxford, 1936), p. 166.

16. A. F. Mitchell, ed., *A Compendious Book of Godly and Spiritual Songs Commonly Known as "The Gude and Godlie Ballatis"* (London and Edinburgh, 1897), pp. 171–172, 222. Not every scholar accepts the attribution of this collection to the Wedderburns.

17. Russell A. Fraser, ed., *The Court of Venus* (Durham, N.C., 1955), pp. 56 ff. See also his edition of John Hall, *The Court of Virtue* (London, 1961).

contrafacta most assiduously. If Raleigh could deflate Marlowe's idyllic "The Passionate Shepherd to His Love" in his "Nymph's Reply"[18] and Donne could "metaphysicalize" it in "The Baite," Richard Verstegan had no compunction in divinizing it in "Our Lady's Lullaby" (1601):

> Live stil with mee, and bee my love,
> And death wil mee refraine,
> Unlesse thow let mee dy with thee,
> To live with the[e] againe.
> Sing lullaby my litle boy,
> Sing lullaby my lives joy.[19]

It was Father Robert Southwell, however, who most strenuously endeavored to bring into English poetry a technique that by this time had been fully developed on the Continent. Pierre Janelle has shown how Southwell adapted to a divine sense one of Petrarch's sonnets (*Rime*, No. 134) in the poem entitled "What Joy to Live?"

> Pace non trovo e non ho da far guerra;
> E temo e spero, et ardo e sono un ghiaccio;
> E volo sopra 'l cielo, e giaccio in terra;
> E nulla stringo, e tutto 'l mondo abbraccio.
>
> I wage no warre yet peace I none enjoy,
> I hope, I feare, I frye, in freesing cold.
> I mount in mirth still prostrate in annoy,
> I all the world embrace yet nothing holde.[20]

Petrarch's entire poetic work, as we shall see, had been recast and reinterpreted in a divine sense by several Italian writers of the sixteenth century. It seems unlikely that Southwell was unacquainted with their adaptations. He preferred, of course, to rewrite English poems. Unlike Herbert, Southwell does not merely use opening lines as a springboard but stays close to his original throughout the adaptation. A tour de force

---

18. The attribution to Raleigh of "The Nymph's Reply to the Shepherd" in *England's Helicon* is contested.

19. Louise Imogen Guiney, ed., *Recusant Poets* (London, 1939), p. 212.

20. *Robert Southwell the Writer: A Study in Religious Inspiration* (London, 1935), pp. 215–216. The Petrarch sonnet is cited from Francesco Petrarca, *Le rime*, ed. Giosuè Carducci and Severino Ferrari, *Nuova tiratura* (Florence, 1949), p. 212 (Poem No. CXXXIV). Southwell's version is taken from *The Poems of Robert Southwell, S.J.*, ed. James H. McDonald and Nancy Pollard Brown (Oxford, 1967), p. 53. Contrary to Janelle's opinion, the editors suggest (p. 145) that Southwell may have imitated an English translation by Thomas Watson.

comparable to the efforts of the Italian divinizers of Petrarch is his remarkably sustained *contrafactum* of Sir Edward Dyer's long poem "A Fancy," which he calls "A Phancie Turned to a Sinners Complaint." In the *contrafactum* genre, the moral tone is often improved at the expense of the poetry. Southwell succeeds in surpassing his model.

DYER	SOUTHWELL
Hee that his mirth hath loste,	Hee that his mirth hath lost,
Whose comfort is dismaid,	Whose comfort is to rue,
Whose hope is vaine, whose faith is scornd,	Whose hope is fallen, whose faith is cras'de,
Whose trust is all betraid;	Whose trust is found untrue:
If hee have held them deare,	If he have held them deere,
And cannot cease to moane,	And cannot cease to mone;
Come, let him take a place by mee:	Come, let him take his place by me,
He shall not rue alone.	He shall not rue alone.[21]

Southwell's extra and prompt emphasis on repentance, on ruing, gives a tautness to these first two stanzas that is absent from Dyer's love elegy.[22] "Southwell's campaign to convert the poetry of profane love into poetry of divine love had, it seems, a strong impact upon the seventeenth century."[23] But it did not produce a spate of true *contrafacta*. Such fidelity to the secular original is indeed rare in the British Isles. For the purpose of comparison it will now be necessary to look at the continental background of Southwell's achievement.

The Biblical Song of Songs was recognized by the Spanish Friar Luis de León as the first spiritual *contrafactum*, an eclogue with a divine meaning.[24] The early Church, after many hesitations and reservations, approved the use of pagan letters and learning as models for the new Christian literature in Latin.[25] Saint Augustine, recalling that Jehovah

---

21. Both texts are cited from the McDonald-Brown edition, pp. 36, 135.

22. The term "love elegy" seems to me correct. Martz comments: "Dyer's poem is not, strictly speaking, a love-poem: it seems to be a lament on his fall from Elizabeth's favor. But it uses the imagery and themes of a lover's complaint" (*op. cit.*, p. 189).

23. *Ibid.*, p. 184.

24. "Este libro, en su primer origen, se escribió en metro, y es todo él una égloga pastoril, donde con palabras y lenguaje de pastores hablan Salomón y su Esposa, y algunas veces sus compañeros, como si todos fuesen gente de aldea" (introduction to his translation of "El Cantar de los Cantares," in *Obras completas castellanas*, Biblioteca de Autores Cristianos, III [Madrid, 1959], p. 63).

25. R. R. Bolgar, *The Classical Heritage and Its Beneficiaries* (Cambridge, 1954).

had encouraged the Hebrews to "spoil the Egyptians" before leaving the land of bondage, urged Christian writers similarly to despoil Cicero and Vergil.[26] As early as the fourth century, Saint Ephraem is reported to have rewritten the pagan songs of Harmonius in a Christian sense.

The initial impetus to absorb into sacred writing the excellencies of pagan style never entirely disappeared. From Saint Ephraem to the present day, in all of Christendom, religious writers have coveted, appropriated, and divinized secular poetry. But there have been historical moments when this activity has been particularly prevalent. The period in which *contrafacta* were most rife was the one that embraces the late fifteenth, the sixteenth, and the early seventeenth centuries. One of the problems facing the literary historian is, then, to account for the rise, the flourishing, and the decline of divinizations at that time. To understand this historical problem we must see what had happened to the religious sensibility of the Middle Ages.

Early in medieval times there were *contrafacta*. It is quite possible that Gonzalo de Berceo's thirteenth-century "Eya velar" was a Christian rendering of a military watch-song.[27] However that may be, we possess from the same century a number of indubitable *contrafacta*, the work of Gautier de Coinci and other poets of northern France.[28] These early French examples are, within their genre, excellent. *Pastourelles, chansons de toile*, and other secular songs were converted, often by changing only a few details, into penitential hymns, songs of praise, or vituperations against the World, the Flesh, and the Devil.

Although the Middle Ages could produce good *contrafacta*, they were rare compared with those of the great period; and the energy of the early divinizers seems quickly to have been spent. What abound before the fifteenth century are not so much literary divinizations as divinizing tendencies in literature. For example, the tune of the one *canso* by William of Aquitaine whose music has been preserved was so hymnlike that it was without difficulty incorporated into the Provençal mystery play, the *Jeu de Sainte-Agnès*.[29] And the courtly poetry of the troubadours, first in the Limousin and later in Catalonia, shows a

---

26. *De doctrina christiana*, ed. H. J. Vogels (Bonn, 1930), pp. 46–47.

27. This opinion is expressed by Dámaso Alonso in *Poesía española: ensayo de métodos y límites estilísticos* (Madrid, 1950), p. 240, n. 16.

28. For some examples, see Alfred Jeanroy, "Imitations pieuses de chansons profanes," *Romania*, 18 (1889), 477–486.

29. Jean Beck, *La Musique des troubadours* (Paris, 1928), p. 23.

progressive trend toward divine subjects until in the fourteenth century the golden violet awarded by the Sobregaya Companhia dels Set Trobadors de Tholosa is presented only to poets submitting religious works. The only lady who might then be the object of the troubadours' homage was the Virgin Mary. To her or to God were addressed the *tornadas* (or *envois*) of their songs. In this way the *gaya ciencia* ended by becoming the handmaiden of religion. But these religious troubadours continued to use, with slight adjustments, the language of courtly love. *Midons, ma dame* became, characteristically, *Notre Dame*.[30] The Blessed Ramon Lull wrote poems of courtesy to his saintly lady.[31] And in Gallaeco-Portuguese verses King Alfonso the Wise of Castile declared himself the suitor of Mary. Henry Suso was known as the *Minnesinger* of *Gottesminne*. But even apart from the troubadour tradition the despoiling of the Egyptians continued. Popular French refrains of the thirteenth century were counterfeited in ecclesiastical Latin. A *pastourelle* acquires a divine meaning by the insertion of Latin words between the French verses:

> L'autr'ier matin el mois de mai,
> *regis divini munere,*
> que par un matin me levai,
> *mundum proponens fugere. . . .*[32]

The parallelistic love songs of thirteenth-century Galicia were written to celebrate ecclesiastical feasts. And there is abundant documentation of the widespread medieval custom of performing secular dances in church. The trend was from the profane to the religious.

Meanwhile, poets were "moralizing" Ovid and turning Alexander the Great into a "parfit" Christian knight. Saint Francis and his followers were thinking of themselves as minstrels of the Lord, *joculatores Dei*. Saint Bernard, especially in his commentary on the Song of Songs, was already pleading—against Abelard—for a less subtly intellectual, more personal and affective kind of devotion.

All of these pieces of evidence add up to the fact that, while there was remarkably little personal poetry of devotion in the early Middle Ages, a frame of reference was being fashioned into which the abundance of

---

30. Amédée Pagès, *Auzias March et ses prédécesseurs: essai sur la poésie amoureuse et philosophique en Catalogne aux XIVe et XVe siècles* (Paris, 1912), pp. 124–129.

31. *Ibid.*, p. 126.

32. Cited in F. J. E. Raby, *A History of Secular Latin Poetry in the Middle Ages* (Oxford, 1934), II, 334.

Renaissance *contrafacta* would soon neatly fit. Even the technical side of poetry was awaiting the pleasure of the counterparodists. The Provençal troubadours had created the most complex and disciplined metrical system of all time. The poetical competitions of various Romance lands, in which the challenger was required to refute an amorous thesis in the meter and rhymes chosen by his opponent, prepared a tradition of close adherence to externals while a dissenting thought was being expressed. And the recent discovery of the Spanish *jarchas* (some antedating William of Aquitaine) reminds us that, even before the invention of Provençal metrics, Hebrew and Arabic poets on Spanish soil were practicing the adaptation of popular Romance refrains to wholly inappropriate *muwasshahas* (as, for example, a popular *alba* to a panegyric). The rise of *contrafacta* in great numbers was at least technically feasible in the early 1400s.

The beginnings were humble enough. In the fifteenth century the fashion of divine counterfeiting developed in the Netherlands. In Germany, Heinrich von Loufenberg and other poets gave songs like "Innsbruck, ich muss dich lassen" new, moral words like "O Welt, ich muss dich lassen."[33] In Italy, with the setting of *laudi* to popular tunes and with the spiritual versions of frivolous Florentine carnival songs, *contrafacta* were rapidly accepted by the people.[34] "Viva, viva, la ragione," sang the *uomini salvatici*; "Vivi, vivi, in contrizione," replied the faithful.[35] In Spain the first undoubted *contrafactum* was the lullaby that ended the Nativity play by Gómez Manrique around the middle of the fifteenth century. A secular lullaby beginning "Callad, fijo mio / chiquito" provided the model. The divine version goes:

> Callad vos, Señor,
> nuestro Redentor,
> que vuestro dolor
> durara poquito.[36]

The lullaby is a minor lyric genre, but it lends itself admirably to sacred treatment. The Virgin is easily imagined singing to her divine child

33. Philipp Wackernagel, *Das deutsche Kirchenlied von der ältesten Zeit bis zu Anfang des XVII. Jahrhunderts* (Leipzig, 1870), III, 952–953 (Song No. 1140).

34. Federico Ghisi, " 'L'Aria di maggio' et le travestissement spirituel de la poésie musicale profane en Italie," in Jacquot, *Musique et poésie*, pp. 265–273.

35. Federico Ghisi, *Canti carnascialeschi nelle fonti musicali del XV e XVI secolo* (Florence-Rome, 1937), p. 101.

36. R. Foulché-Delbosc, ed., *Cancionero castellano del siglo XV*, NBAE, XXII (Madrid, 1915), II, 56.

much the same sort of soporific song as any less prominent mother or nurse. Following Gómez Manrique's lead, the first poet from Madrid, Juan Álvarez Gato, wrote a number of *contrafacta*. By the 1490s a veritable school of Franciscan poets had come into existence in Spain. One of them, Friar Ambrosio Montesino, took a popular refrain— "You're just a little girl, and already you're in love; what will you be up to when you grow up?"—and composed from it a *villancico* to the Child Jesus:

> Eres niño y has amor:
> ¿qué farás cuando mayor? [37]

By the end of the fifteenth century a tradition of *contrafacta* had been firmly established in several European countries.

In sixteenth- and seventeenth-century Spain the activity of the divinizing poets gathered momentum. Most of their *contrafacta* were based on simple popular songs. But occasionally more ambitious transpositions were attempted: stanzas from Jorge Manrique's famous elegy on the death of his father, or from the works of difficult poets like Góngora or Quevedo.[38] Sebastián de Córdoba undertook the enormous task of turning the entire poetic work of Boscán and Garcilaso into religious poetry.[39]

In Italy religious versions of the carnival songs continued to appear in the sixteenth century. But more indicative of the divinizers' new spirit of enterprise was the series, already mentioned, of sacred Petrarchs: by Malipiero, Umbruno da Civitella, Salvatorino, and Sagliano, among others.[40]

In France it was the Huguenots who first thought of making the ribald *vaudeville* songs godly. The *vaudeville* is itself a new song set to

---

37. Dámaso Alonso, ed., *Poesía de la Edad Media y poesía de tipo tradicional* (Buenos Aires, 1942), p. 279.

38. The ambition of some counterparodists went so far as to give a divine meaning to extensive prose fiction. In 1582, for example, Friar Bartolomé Ponce rewrote in a divine sense all seven books of the pastoral romance *La Diana*, published by his friend Jorge de Montemayor about 1559.

39. *Obras de Boscán y Garcilaso trasladadas a materias cristianas y religiosas* (Úbeda, 1575). The *contrafacta* of the Garcilaso canon alone has been published in modern times: Sebastián de Córdoba, *Garcilaso a lo divino*, ed. Glen R. Gale (Madrid, 1971).

40. Girolamo Malipiero, *Il Petrarca spirituale* (1536); Feliciano Umbruno da Civitella, *Dialogo del dolce morire di Gesù Christo sopra le sei Visioni de M. Francesco Petrarca* (1544); Gian Giacomo Salvatorino, *Thesoro di Sacra Scrittura sopra rime del Petrarcha* (1547); Pietro Vincenzo Sagliano, *Esposizione spirituale sopra il Petrarca* (1590). Other spiritual interpretations of Petrarch are known—and others, conjectured—to exist.

an old air. As a genre, it became dignified and respectable largely because the Protestants based their *chansons spirituelles* on it.[41] Polyphonic music was regarded by the sixteenth-century Reformers as effeminate and voluptuous, and for this reason less suited to devotional purposes than the music to which the robust if unseemly *vaudevilles* were set. Marguerite de Navarre converted "Sur le pont d'Avignon" into "Sur l'arbre de la Croix."[42] One of Marot's lighter pieces, "Adieu amours, adieu gentil corsage," was transformed by an unknown poet into "Adieu la chair, adieu mondain servage."[43] The Protestant hymnals contain many of these revamped secular poems. The Huguenots' success in this venture was such that French Catholics quickly followed suit.

As for Germany, the best-known author of *contrafacta* was Martin Luther. Following the example set by earlier German divinizers, Luther systematically created on the basis of worldly songs a vast corpus of devotional hymns. The famous "Ein' feste Burg ist unser Gott," for example, is a reworking of a marching song. But Luther was not alone; throughout the sixteenth century German poets, both Lutheran and Catholic, forged a great chain of religious *contrafacta*.[44]

I have been unable, in the space at my disposal, to do more than note a few highlights in the international vogue of *contrafacta* during the centuries when they thrived. My account of their decline must be even sketchier. The bare facts are these. In the seventeenth century, Spanish *contrafacta* were gradually relegated to the theater[45] and to chapbooks. Right through the eighteenth century, obscure, badly printed pamphlets continued to make available to the masses atrocious divinizations of popular songs. By the beginning of the nineteenth century the practice disappeared underground into the oral tradition, where it survives

---

41. One wonders whether the notoriously lascivious sixteenth-century Spanish dances called the *zarabanda* and the *chacona* became majestic court dances, the saraband and the chaconne of Bach, as a result of their having been dignified through the divinization of the lyrics that accompanied them. See Wardropper, *Historia. . .* , pp. 205–232.

42. *Les Marguerites de la Marguerite des princesses*, ed. Félix Frank (Paris, 1873), III, 105.

43. See Mitchell, *A Compendious Book*, pp. cx–cxi.

44. For further information on German *contrafacta* in the sixteenth and seventeenth centuries, see Wolfgang Stammler, *Von der Mystik zum Barock, 1400–1600* (Stuttgart, 1950), pp. 158–159.

45. *Contrafacta* appear in the texts of the Spanish allegorical Eucharistic plays known as *autos sacramentales* as well as in hagiographic and historical dramas. It is important to realize that dramatists may also divinize their own secular plays. Calderón, for example, rewrote his famous *La vida es sueño* (ca. 1635) as an *auto sacramental* with the same title (ca. 1673).

today. Divinized versions of the old Spanish ballad "Por el rastro de la sangre" were discovered not many years ago by collectors of folk songs in Nicaragua.[46] Since the time of Lope de Vega *contrafacta* have never recovered literary prestige in Spain or Spanish America.

In seventeenth-century France, Father Joseph Surin, the mad exorciser of the devils of Loudun, wrote some vulgar and incompetent *contrafacta*. One of his worst—set to the tune of a drinking song, "J'ai rencontré un Allemand"—is called "Les Saints enivrés d'amour."[47] It is worth remembering that this particular form of "bad taste" was enjoying quite a vogue in the "tasteful" age of Boileau. In the following centuries French examples became rare.

It is the strange, new, revivalist sects of England and Scotland—the Methodists, the Glassites, the Salvation Army—that release occasional floods of *contrafacta* in the modern period. Some of the best specimens come from the mountain folk of the Appalachians. The Scottish song "Will you go, Lassie, go / To the braes o' Balquhidder?" was made over by them into the hymn "Sinners go, will you go / To the highlands of heaven?"[48] But few of these more recent counterparodists have attained the disciplined imitative skill of the Wedderburns or of Southwell. The *contrafactum*, in the English-speaking world as elsewhere, is now at its nadir.

How, then, are we to account for the remarkable continental popularity of spiritualized poetry from 1450 to 1625? Part of the explanation lies in the fact that popular art—ballads, folk songs, proverbs—piqued the curiosity of the cultivated men of the Renaissance, who adopted it and adapted it for the very different needs of courts and ducal palaces.[49] Neoplatonism, moreover, was blunting the sharper medieval distinction between divine and human love. Finally, the *Ars Nova* in music, bringing about a greater complexity of composition, encouraged *contrafacta* in a negative way. By the end of the fifteenth century, popular songs were the only monodic music available, so that, if a congrega-

46. Ernesto Mejía Sánchez, *Romances y corridos nicaragüenses* (Mexico City, 1946), pp. 78–79 and 80–81, where two divinized versions of the old ballad are transcribed.

47. Aldous Huxley, *The Devils of Loudun* (New York, 1952), p. 299.

48. George Pullen Jackson, ed., *Spiritual Folk-Songs of Early America* (New York, 1937), p. 19.

49. A classical example is the appearance of vast numbers of folk songs in the so-called *Cancionero musical de Palacio* in the reign of Ferdinand and Isabella. See *La música en la corte de los Reyes Católicos*, IV–1, IV–2: *Cancionero musical de Palacio*, ed. José Romeu Figueres (Barcelona, 1965).

tional hymn rather than a polyphonic mass or motet was desired, one virtually had to appropriate a popular tune. The temptation to assimilate some of the words along with the music was hard to resist. But neither the Renaissance fondness for folk art nor the musical history of the time can explain the devotional atmosphere that fostered the writing and singing of *contrafacta*.

It is to the *devotio moderna* that we must look for the key.[50] This spiritual movement, emanating from the Brethren of the Common Life at Deventer in Holland, urged fifteenth-century believers to pay less attention to dogmatic theology, and to seek instead an intimate personal relationship with Christ, analogous to the relationship between human friends. The masterpiece of the *devotio moderna* was Thomas à Kempis' *Imitation of Christ*, composed around 1420. This work encouraged the individual Christian to use Christ's life on earth as a model for his daily living. The deity to whom the modern acts of devotion were directed was Christ, the humanized God, rather than the other, less human, persons of the Trinity. But while Thomas recommends complete detachment from the world, the uncloistered disciples of the *devotio moderna* had perforce to come to terms with the world. As Ortega y Gasset writes, the *devotio moderna* was an "intrahuman religion" that inspired the fifteenth-century European to "live out of God, but face-to-face with the world" ("vivir desde Dios, pero cara al mundo").[51] It was a religion of sensibility. Tears replaced dogma. Visible personal devotion, which played only a small part in medieval Christianity, dominated the fifteenth-century scene. A blessed simplicity was cultivated. The Christian Renaissance, the *devotio moderna*, implied that the devout man had been "born again." In this personal religion, cleverness and originality had no place. The cult of blessed simplicity denied all respect to art. The clearest example of this tendency, which overflowed into the sixteenth century, is found in Saint Teresa, with her scorn for the cultivated style, writing as incorrectly as she spoke.[52] And Saint Ignatius of Loyola, teaching his followers through his *Spiritual Exercises* to visualize the human circumstance of

50. Albert Hyma, *The Christian Renaissance: A History of the "Devotio Moderna"* (New York, 1925).

51. "En torno a Galileo," in *Obras completas* [sic] (3rd ed., 1947; rpt., Madrid, 1955), V, 156.

52. Ramón Menéndez Pidal, *La lengua de Cristóbal Colón*, Colección Austral, 280 (Buenos Aires, 1942), pp. 80–82, 129–153.

Christ, made men see divine things as if they were human: men's imaginative powers were thus developed without, at first, their finding expression in art.[53] In Germany the culmination of this affective religion is found in Martin Luther, who destroyed secular literature in the name of religion. As Erasmus put it, "Wherever Lutherism [sic] is dominant, the study of literature is extinguished."[54] The *devotio moderna* produced immense reverberations in both factions of the schismatic Christianity of the Renaissance.

In this spiritual environment *contrafacta* arose and thrived naturally. In their inartistic art they provided a means of direct, unmediated devotion for the childlike mind of the man who had been born again. Blessed simplicity is the keynote of the early Spanish *contrafacta*. The lyric genres most imitated in a divine sense are minor ones: children's games, dancing airs, *serranillas*, *seguidillas*, *chanzonetas*, *ensaladillas*, *nanas*—simple poetic kinds whose very existence is ignored by most historians of literature. But of all these lyric genres the most popular, among the common people and the divinizers, was the *villancico*. Waiting for church festivals to begin, the faithful sang secular *villancicos* to while away the time. It was inevitable that for such occasions devout writers should have deflected this impulse to sing away from the popular words to ones more appropriate to the ecclesiastical event. It was in this way that the secular *villancico* began its evolution into the Christmas carol of Spain, the *villancico de Navidad*. Its development thus parallels that of the English Christmas carol.[55]

If simplicity is one of the elements of the *devotio moderna* present in the *contrafacta*, another is transformed worldliness: "living out of God, but face-to-face with the world." The original secular songs, besides being well known, were usually to some degree appropriately chosen. When nuns in Italian convents, aroused from their slumbers to sing matins, walked through drafty cloisters to the cold, dark chapel, it was

53. By the end of the sixteenth century St. Ignatius' effect on sophisticated religious poetry was of course considerable. In addition to Martz's explanation of his impact on English poetry of meditation, see—for the application of the composition-of-place principle—Leo Spitzer, "Lope de Vega's 'Al triunfo de Judit,'" *MLN*, 69 (1954), 1–11, and Elias L. Rivers, "'Soneto a Cristo Crucificado,' Line 12," *BHS*, 35 (1958), 36–37.

54. Cited by Johan Huizinga, *Erasmus of Rotterdam*, trans. F. Hopman (London, 1952), p. 178.

55. Sister Mary Paulina St. Amour, *A Study of the Villancico up to Lope de Vega* (Washington, D.C., 1940). Antonio Sánchez Romeralo, *El villancico: estudios sobre la lírica popular en los siglos XV y XVI* (Madrid, 1969), passes over the historical problem.

natural that they should cheer themselves by singing a Christianized version of the old *pastourelle* "Levaimi un bel mattino." [56] In *contrafacta* the known is used to make religious experience familiar and friendly, to reduce the divine to a scale encompassable by the childlike mind. When the believer concentrates on the humanity of the Godhead, the numinous barrier of religious awe is removed.

The *devotio moderna* explains much about popular piety in the sixteenth century. But there was a minority, an intellectual élite, that resisted its blandishments. Humanists, neo-scholastics, and learned poets asserted the value of complexity, finesse, and creativity. Secular poetry, despite the anathematizing of it by strict moralists, reached new heights of sophistication with Tasso, Garcilaso, Ronsard, and Sidney. Mannered style invaded literature of all kinds. Accordingly, the composers of *contrafacta* had to adjust themselves to these maneuverings of the cultured world. The counterparodists made a valiant attempt to absorb into their essentially simple craft these complex thoughts, images, genres, modes, and styles. Previously, the writers of *contrafacta* had been content to give a singable form to moral dilemmas or to impose human dimensions on the facts of Christ's life. Now, starting from the known, they would seek—by rewriting sophisticated poetry—to use analogy in order to grope for the unknown, expounding or elucidating the most incomprehensible of Christian mysteries. When theology crept into the *contrafactum*, it met its nemesis. Friar Bernardo de Cárdenas writes an impossible sonnet representing Don Quixote as the defender of the purity of the Immaculate Conception. [57]

It is true that some divinizers of cultivated poetry, like Sebastián de Córdoba or Malipiero, had a certain modest success. But the majority were as inept as the mad poet in the anonymous Spanish interlude of *The Lunatic Asylum* (*El hospital de los podridos*). Rewriting Garcilaso's *Égloga tercera* in a religious sense, he grapples with the lines

> Cerca del Tajo, en soledad amena,
> de verdes sauces hay una espesura.

He can think of no substitute for "sauces" ("willows") except "santos," and has to explain that his rendering—"Near the Tagus, in pleasant

---

56. Ghisi, " 'L'Aria di maggio'. . . ," p. 268.
57. Justo de Sancha, ed. *Romancero y cancionero sagrados*, BAE, XXXV (Madrid, 1855), p. 54, no. 92.

solitude, / there is a thicket of green saints"—refers to those saints whose day is celebrated in the green season of spring.[58] Imitation of the mannered style also caused some spectacular gaffes. In an unfortunate poem to Saint Clare, López de Úbeda introduces the words "clear," "clarified," "clarity," and similar cognates into every line, *annominatio* run wild.[59] Few of these efforts to reduce complex art to devotion succeeded. Father Southwell's triumph was not often matched, either in England or on the Continent. It was surpassed only by that of a great saint who was also a great poet, John of the Cross.

Saint John of the Cross's devotional and mystical poetry is surprisingly dependent on *contrafacta*. The key to this dependence is provided by the saint himself. In a note which precedes the prose commentary to his masterpiece, the "Llama de amor viva," he reveals indirectly that he has been reading Sebastián de Córdoba's *Obras de Boscán y Garcilaso trasladadas a materias cristianas y religiosas*. To illustrate his own metrics, he cites three lines which he attributes to Boscán. They are in fact from Garcilaso's *Canción segunda*. But more important than this error—a venial one since the works of the two poets were always published together and referred to as "un Boscán"—is the fact that he quotes not the original but Córdoba's adaptation.[60] Hence, we know that Saint John read some of his poetic models in *contrafactum* form.

Another detail relates Saint John to the *contrafactum* movement. One of his more famous "minor poems" begins:

> Que bien sé yo la fonte que mana y corre,
> aunque es de noche.

Apart from the refrain—"aunque es de noche"—the work is written in learned and Italianate hendecasyllables. But Dámaso Alonso has shown that the poet created his first hendecasyllable by rearranging the typically irregular lines of a folk song, a song about the spring bathing rites of the early Middle Ages.[61] The archaic word "fonte"

---

58. Emilio Cotarelo y Mori, ed., *Colección de entremeses, loas, bailes, jácaras y mojigangas desde fines del siglo XVI á mediados del XVIII*, NBAE, XVII (Madrid, 1911), I, 95.

59. Justo de Sancha, *op. cit.*, p. 309, no. 743.

60. Jean Baruzi, *Saint-Jean de la Croix et le problème de l'expérience mystique* (Paris, 1924), pp. 108–112.

61. *La poesía de San Juan de la Cruz (desde esta ladera)* (Madrid, 1946), pp. 117–128; see also pp. 310–311. The poems cited, translated into English verse by Roy Campbell, may be found in St. John of the Cross, *Poems* (Harmondsworth, Eng., 1960). A more accurate prose translation by Elias L. Rivers is in his *Renaissance and Baroque Poetry of Spain* (New York, 1966).

(modern "fuente") provided the clue. The popular song must have had three lines:

> Que bien sé yo la fonte
> que mana y corre,
> aunque es de noche.

The assonance (ó–e) presumably froze "fonte" in its archaic form. The saint's poem is thus a gloss on a secular song, an erotic song of great antiquity.

Even more impressive evidence of Saint John's attraction to *contrafacta* is found in another "minor poem," which hovers strangely over the boundary between the profane and the sacred, between the pastoral and the parable.

> Un pastorcico solo está penado,
> ajeno de placer y de contento,
> y en su pastora puesto el pensamiento,
> y el pecho del amor muy lastimado.
>
> No llora por haberle amor llagado,
> que no le pena verse así afligido,
> aunque en el corazón está herido;
> mas llora por pensar que está olvidado.
>
> Que sólo de pensar que está olvidado
> de su bella pastora, con gran pena,
> se deja maltratar en tierra ajena,
> el pecho del amor muy lastimado.
>
> Y dice el pastorcico: ¡Ay desdichado
> de aquel que de mi amor ha hecho ausencia,
> y no quiere gozar de mi presencia,
> y el pecho por su amor muy lastimado!
>
> Y a cabo de un gran rato se ha encumbrado
> sobre un árbol, do abrió sus brazos bellos,
> y muerto se ha quedado, asido de ellos,
> el pecho del amor muy lastimado.[62]

It is not until the reader reaches the last strophe, in which the shepherd dies with outstretched arms on the tree, that he fully realizes[63] that the poem is a religious meditation on the crucifixion. The final detail forces

---

62. Dámaso Alonso, *La poesía de San Juan de la Cruz*, pp. 308–309.
63. The reader is first alerted to the divine sense of the poem by the masculine references in the penultimate stanza.

the reader to return to the earlier strophes with a fresh perspective. The foreign land, for example, is now seen to be not a different country but the world of man, to which the divine resident of heaven has descended. It is a moving and beautiful poem, in which God's self-sacrifice is subjected to the commonplaces of the pastoral convention. Much of its effectiveness comes from its deceptively secular appearance.

Now, it was comparatively recently, in 1949, that a manuscript containing a similar poem was discovered:

> Vn pastorcillo solo está penado,
> ageno de plazer y de contento,
> y en su pastora firme el pensamiento,
> y el pecho del amor muy lastimado.
>
> No llora por pensar que está oluidado,
> que ningún miedo tiene del oluido,
> mas porque el corazón tiene rendido
> y el pecho del amor muy lastimado.
>
> Mas dize el pastorcillo: —¡Desdichado!,
> ¿qué haré cuando venga el mal de avsençia,
> pues tengo el corazón en la presençia
> y el pecho del amor muy lastimado?
>
> Ymagínase ya estar apartado
> de su vella pastora en tierra agena,
> y quédase tendido en el arena,
> y el pecho del amor muy lastimado.[64]

This anonymous work turns out to have been the secular original upon which Saint John of the Cross constructed his poem. It is a rather good example of a miniature eclogue, a kind of poetry that is generally *la banalité même*. Saint John has effected minimal changes in the original text in order to endow it with a Christian meaning. In enhancing the poem's significance, he has at the same time increased its poetic effectiveness, producing one of his great—though so-called "minor"—works of art.

Such complete successes in the close rewriting of profane texts occur infrequently. In this brief excursion into the realm of *contrafacta* we

---

64. José Manuel Blecua, "Los antecedentes del poema del 'Pastorcico,' de San Juan de la Cruz," *RFE*, 33 (1949), 378–380 (rpt. in *Sobre poesía de la Edad de Oro: ensayos y notas eruditas* [Madrid, 1970], pp. 96–99).

have seen only one other case of a close adaptation that improved upon the original. This was Southwell's transposition of Dyer's "A Fancy." It is consoling to think that Southwell, the persecuted English recusant, was in such good poetic and religious company as that of John of the Cross, the ascetic Spanish saint.

John Leon Lievsay: A Bibliography

Books

Stefano Guazzo and the English Renaissance 1575–1675 (Chapel Hill, Univ. of North Carolina Press, 1961). Pp. xvi, 344.

The Elizabethan Image of Italy, Folger Booklets on Tudor and Stuart Civilization (Ithaca, Cornell Univ. Press, 1964). Pp. iv, 60.

The Englishman's Italian Books 1550–1700 (Philadelphia, Univ. of Pennsylvania Press, 1969). Pp. xii, 104.

Venetian Phoenix: Paolo Sarpi and Some of His English Friends (1606–1700) (Lawrence, Univ. Press of Kansas, 1973). Pp. x, 262.

Edited and Compiled Works

(with Clark Emery and Henry Thoma), *Practice in Reading and Writing* (Boston, Houghton Mifflin, 1942). Pp. xvi, 436.

(with R. B. Davis), *Studies in Honor of John C. Hodges and Alwin Thaler*, special number of *Tennessee Studies in Literature* (Knoxville, Univ. of Tennessee Press, 1961). Pp. vi, 209

(with R. B. Davis and Alwin Thaler), *Tennessee Studies in Literature*, vol. 7 (Knoxville, Univ. of Tennessee Press, 1962). Pp. vi, 136.

Medieval and Renaissance Studies, II. Proceedings of the Southeastern Institute of Medieval and Renaissance Studies (Durham, N.C., Duke Univ. Press, 1968). Pp. x, 174.

The Sixteenth Century: Skelton Through Hooker. Goldentree Bibliography (New York, Appleton-Century-Crofts, 1968). Pp. xii, 132. (Second printing pub. by AHM Publishing Corp., Northbrook, Ill.)

Medieval and Renaissance Studies, IV. Proceedings of the Southeastern Institute of Medieval and Renaissance Studies (Durham, N. C., Duke Univ. Press, 1970). Pp. viii, 183.

Daniel Tuvill: Essays Politic and Moral and Essays Moral and Theological. Folger Documents of Tudor and Stuart Civilization, No. 20 (Charlottesville, Univ. Press of Virginia, 1971). Pp. xx, 231.

Chapters or Sections of Books

"Some Renaissance Views of Diogenes the Cynic," in James G. McManaway, Giles E. Dawson, and Edwin E. Willoughby, editors, *Joseph Quincy Adams Memorial Studies* (Washington, Folger Shakespeare Library, 1948). Pp. 447–455.

"Studies in the Relations between England and Italy," in Louis B. Wright, editor, *Tudor and Stuart History* (Washington, Folger Shakespeare Library, 1959). Pp. 15–19.

"A Later Level of the Italian Renaissance," in Louis B. Wright, editor, *Society and History in the Renaissance* (Washington, Folger Shakespeare Library, 1960). Pp. 49–56.

"Italian *Favole Boscarecce* and Jacobean Stage Pastoralism," in Richard Hosley, editor, *Essays on Shakespeare and Elizabethan Drama in Honor of Hardin Craig* (Columbia, Univ. of Missouri Press, 1962). Pp. 317–326.

"Emblem," "Pattern Poetry," and (with O. B. Hardison, Jr.) "Renaissance Poetry," in Alex Preminger, Frank J. Warnke, and O. B. Hardison, Jr., editors, *Encyclopedia of Poetry and Poetics* (Princeton, Princeton Univ. Press, 1965). Pp. 217, 607–608, 695–699.

"Paolo Sarpi's Appraisal of James I," in Heinz Bluhm, editor, *Essays in History and Literature Presented . . . to Stanley Pargellis* (Chicago, The Newberry Library, 1965). Pp. 109–117.

"The Council of Trent and Tudor England," in O. B. Hardison, Jr., editor, *Medieval and Renaissance Studies, I.* Proceedings of the Southeastern Institute of Medieval and Renaissance Studies (Chapel Hill, Univ. of North Carolina Press, 1966). Pp. 15–39.

"The Writing of Ecclesiastical History in the Renaissance," in J. A. Ward, editor, *Renaissance Studies in Honor of Carroll Camden, Rice University Studies*, 60 (1974), 123–129.

Articles

"Spenser and Guazzo: A Comparative Study of Renaissance Attitudes," *University of Washington Abstracts of Dissertations*, 3 (1938), 323–329.

"Shakespeare's 'Golden World,' " *Shakespeare Association Bulletin*, 13 (1938), 77–81.

"Robert Greene, Master of Arts, and 'Mayster Steeven Guazzo,' " *Studies in Philology*, 36 (1939), 577–596.

"Stefano Guazzo and the *Emblemata* of Andrea Alciati," *Philological Quarterly*, 18 (1939), 204–210.

"A Suggested New Source for Sebastian Mey's *Fabulario*," *Romanic Review*, 30 (1939), 231–234.

"Notes on *The Art of Conversation* (1738)," *Italica*, 17 (1940), 58–63.

"Greene's Panther," *Philological Quarterly*, 20 (1941), 296–303.

"Braggadochio: Spenser's Legacy to the Character Writers," *Modern Language Quarterly*, 2 (1941), 475–485.

"Trends in Tudor and Stuart Courtesy Literature," *Huntington Library Quarterly*, 5 (1942), 184–188.

"Newgate Penitents: Further Aspects of Elizabethan Pamphlet Sensationalism," *Huntington Library Quarterly*, 7 (1943), 47–69.

"An Immediate Source for *Faerie Queene*, Bk. V, Proem," *Modern Language Notes*, 59 (1944), 469–472.

"Spenser in Low Company?" *Shakespeare Association Bulletin*, 19 (1944), 186–189.

"Tuvill's Advancement of Bacon's Learning," *Huntington Library Quarterly*, 9 (1945), 11–31.

" 'Silver-tongued Smith,' Paragon of Elizabethan Preachers," *Huntington Library Quarterly*, 11 (1947), 13–36.

——— and John C. Hodges, "English in Tennessee Colleges," *The Tennessee Teacher* (1948), 13–14, 19.

" 'D. T., Gent.,' Spenser, and the Defense of Women," *Journal of English and Germanic Philology*, 47 (1948), 382–386.

"Daniel Tuvill's 'Resolves,' " *Studies in Philology*, 46 (1949), 196–203.

"Hacía una nueva generación," *Entre Nosotros*, 11 (1949), 3–4.

"Bacon Versified," *Huntington Library Quarterly*, 14 (1951), 223–238.

"Seventeenth-Century Italian Books in the Library," *Newberry Library Bulletin*, 3 (1953), 88–92.

——— and Richard B. Davis, "A Cavalier Library—1643," Univ. of Virginia *Studies in Bibliography*, 6 (1954), 141–160.

"Glimpses of Perugia Through Fulbright Eyes," *Phi Kappa Phi Journal*, 35 (1955), 38–46.

"Stefano Guazzo and His Circle," *Romanic Review*, 47 (1956), 3–12.

"Robert Burton's *De Consolatione*," *South Atlantic Quarterly*, 55 (1956), 329–336.

"A Word about Barnaby Rich," *Journal of English and Germanic Philology*, 55 (1956), 381–392.

"Tennessee College English Teachers' Conference," *The CEA Critic*, 18 (November 1956), 5, 8.

"William Barley, Elizabethan Printer and Bookseller," Univ. of Virginia *Studies in Bibliography*, 8 (1956), 218–225.

"Order and Decorum in *A Mirror for Magistrates*," *Tennessee Studies in Literature*, 2 (1957), 87–93.

"A Packet of Old Letters: Vicenzo Armanni in England," *Tennessee Studies in Literature*, 4 (1959), 83–90.

"Milton Among the Nightingales," in George Walton Williams and Peter G. Phialas, editors, *Renaissance Papers 1958, 1959, 1960*, Southeastern Renaissance Conference (Durham, N. C., 1961), pp. 36–45.

"Continental Antecedents of Elizabethan Drama," *Tennessee Studies in Literature*, 7 (1962), 87–97.

"Some Research Opportunities in Anglo-Italian Renaissance Drama," *Renaissance Drama Supplement*, 7 (1964), 10–12.

"Politic and Moral Maxims in Tassoni's *Annali*," in George Walton Williams
and Peter G. Phialas, editors, *Renaissance Papers 1967*, Southeastern Renaissance Conference (Durham, N. C., 1968), pp. 11–17.

Index

Included in the index are the names of all persons and written works occurring in this volume, with the exception of authors, editors, and titles of critical works published after 1700 and referred to only in the footnotes. Titles of known authorship are indexed under their authors' names.

Index prepared by
J. Samuel Hammond
Music Librarian,
Perkins Library, Duke University